Y0-BXI-123

BY THE SAME AUTHOR

Explosion
Escape from Canada!
Korea: Canada's Forgotten War
Cross of Valour
The Little Princes
Overtime, Overdue: The Bill Barilko Story

PILOTS

Canadian Stories from the Cockpit

JOHN MELADY

Copyright © 1989 by John Melady

All rights reserved. The use of any part of this publication reproduced,
transmitted in any form or by any means, electronic, mechanical,
photocopying, recording, or otherwise, or stored in a retrieval system,
without the prior consent of the publisher is an infringement of the
copyright law.

Canadian Cataloguing in Publication Data

Melady, John
  Pilots

Bibliography: p.
Includes index.
ISBN 0-7710-5863-2

1. Air pilots – Canada – Biography. 2. Aeronautics
– Canada – Flights. 3. Aeronautics – Canada –
History. I. Title.

TL539.M45 1989 629.13′092′2 C89-094734-1

Measurements of distance and speed have been given in imperial units
throughout this book in accordance with usage in the aviation industry.
''Knots'' is an aeronautical term used to measure distance and speed; one
knot is equivalent to one mile.

Design by Graham Ross

Printed and bound in Canada by T.H. Best Printing Co. Ltd.

McClelland & Stewart Inc.
The Canadian Publishers
481 University Avenue
Toronto, Ontario M5G 2E9

For
THEO AND CATHERINE
With thanks for your
help and encouragement

Contents

Preface

Since the dawn of time, human beings have wanted to fly. Perhaps that is why those who do are looked upon with some degree of envy, and even awe. There are, however, certain pilots who have been accorded special status within the flying fraternity itself. This book is about those individuals: about their exploits, their courage, and their fears.

The adventures recounted here happened to real people, in circumstances that were as diverse as the personalities of the individuals involved. Whether they took place in the high Arctic, over the North Atlantic, south of Sri Lanka, or above the Canadian prairies is of no particular import. They were, and are, examples of human perseverance and initiative that transcend both time and place. Many are triumphs of the human spirit in the face of adversity.

When I began researching this book, I set out to interview as many pilots as I could, given certain self-imposed financial and geographical restraints. As well, my contractual deadline was always a factor that I could not ignore. For these reasons, the men and women whose stories make up this book were selected not only because they had something to say, but because they were representative of others with similar experiences. This was particularly true in the sections dealing with the two world wars and Korea. In those conflicts, where heroism was commonplace, only the stories of a few were selected. There were far too many to include in one volume.

Researching the book enabled me to meet, fly with, and talk to a wide cross-section of pilots, civilian and military, male and

female, from every era of this twentieth-century vocation. At the
end of my quest, I was not surprised to find that, no matter what
their background, or where or when they flew, the pilots interviewed shared a spirit of adventure and a desire to push limits,
to test themselves, to test the machines they operated. As a group,
they displayed exceptional leadership skills and self-confidence.
They were people of action, participants rather than observers,
and they enjoyed being in charge. But most of all, they loved to
fly.

   These are their stories.

John Melady
Trenton, Ontario
June 1989

Acknowledgements

As with most projects of this sort, this book would not have been published had it not been for the help, advice, and encouragement of a number of individuals. In addition to those mentioned in the text, I would like to express my appreciation to the following: Christine Banville, Bill and Lana Barnicke, Mel Boulton, Colonel John Boyle, Lillian Bradley, Roger Burgess-Webb, Mary and Glenn Butters, Brigadier-General Scott Clements, Doreen Cummine, Tim Folkmann, Gordon Glasheen, Leon Golebiewski, Dave Green, Lois Haines, Joe Hoffman, René Jalbert, Tim Jordan of 409 Squadron at CFB Baden, Russ Kelley, Dave Legge, Greg Loughton, George Marshall, Dennis McCloskey, Mike McDonald, Kevin and Marie McKenna, Bill McKenzie, Jack McLaughlin, Ann Melvin, Marlene Miles, Father Wally Mucha, Dr. Bob Patrick, Allan Payton, Art Prince, Colonel Hugh Rose, Bob Ross, Yuri Rubinsky, Janet Silva-White, Reg Smith, Steve Snider, Ted Snider, Allan Snowie, Steve and Shawnee Spencer, Monte Stout, Gary and Lynn VanderHerberg, Dela Wilkins, and Joe and Marilyn Williams.

In addition to those men and women mentioned above, several others deserve a special word of thanks: Paul Tesseyman and Earl Hewison for helping me weave my way through the military bureaucracy; Captain Hart Proksch for his assistance during my research in Europe; June Boudreau for helping me to locate certain individuals I wanted to interview; Doug Gibson for his support of the project from the outset; Esther Parry for keyboarding yet another of my manuscripts; Lynn Schellenberg, my editor, for her kindness, understanding, and assistance in putting the whole thing together; and, as always, my wife, Mary, who had to live through all the stages of research and writing, yet never complained. My thanks to all.

1

First Flight

By mid-morning the news was out. It raced through the village, to houses along nearby sideroads, to lonely homesteads on distant hills. The weather was favourable. There was little wind and no hint of snow, and the ice on the salt-water lake was solid from shore to shore.

At noon, school was let out for the day. By two o'clock most stores had closed and almost everyone in the town had gathered at the lake. Several youngsters brought skates, and in no time a pick-up hockey game was under way. But the crowds of curious had not come to skate, nor had they come to watch hockey. They had come to see something far more exciting; something none of them had ever seen before. They had come to watch a man fly.

The date was February 23, 1909. The place was Baddeck, a dot on the map of Nova Scotia, about 200 miles north-east of Halifax. The lake was called Bras d'Or. Since 1890, this unlikely setting had been the place where the great inventor Alexander Graham Bell maintained a summer home called Beinn Bhreagh (''Beautiful Mountain'' in Gaelic). He had settled in Baddeck because, as he often boasted, its beautiful lakes and hills reminded him of his beloved Scotland, where he was born.

In the three decades since his invention of the telephone at Brantford, Ontario, Bell had become rich and had moved to Washington, D.C., but his keen, scientific mind was rarely at rest. He had long predicted that the day a human being would fly was as inevitable as tomorrow's dawn. It is small wonder, then, that with the excitement of the first flights by Wilbur and Orville Wright in 1903, Bell too would turn his inventive genius to the development of the flying machine. Much of that development was done at Baddeck.

The village was quiet, far from the bustle of any city, a backwater as inviting as it was invigorating: a place to think, to dream, to create. And on that winter day in 1909 one of Dr. Bell's most cherished creations was ready to be tested – tested publicly for all the world to see.

Though the Wrights were the first men to fly, their successes and their failures had been hidden from inquisitive outsiders. However, Alexander Graham Bell was never secretive; he did not just tolerate public scrutiny, he welcomed it. Many said he even cultivated it.

But what were the events leading up to that momentous day when 147 people gathered to gape at what they hoped would be the first powered flight in Canada?

Bell and his associates had been in Baddeck for months, designing and building a succession of kites. Each such contraption was constructed so that its aerodynamic properties could be examined, modified, improved upon, and tested, over and over again. Several were launched from the highest hills in the area. Some were set aloft in the breezes by the lake. A few were placed on floats and dragged across Bras d'Or behind the fastest motor launches available. But none was completely successful.

One evening in the fall of 1907, the inventor and his wife, Mabel, and two young engineering graduates from the University of Toronto, F.W. ("Casey") Baldwin and John McCurdy, were together at the Bells' Cape Breton home discussing the experiments currently under way. Because she had recently inherited a substantial fortune, Mabel Bell had been looking for an appealing investment opportunity. That evening, during a lull in the conversation, Mrs. Bell made a suggestion. Years later, John McCurdy recalled the incident.

"It was on a windy miserable night in September 1907, and we were all in the big living room of Beinn Bhreagh warming our backs against the fireplace and talking over our kite flights of that day. Mrs. Bell came in with some hot coffee, watched the conversation for a few moments and said: 'Now Alex, you have some pretty smart young engineers here. And they're just as interested in flight as you are. Why don't we form an organization.' "[1]

In no time, the Aerial Experiment Association was in place, funded with $35,000 from Mrs. Bell. The founding members included the inventor and his wife, John McCurdy, and Casey Baldwin. It was Bell's idea to also include two young Americans, Glenn Curtiss from Hammondsport, New York, and Lieutenant Thomas Selfridge, seconded from the United States Army. Curtiss ran a successful motorcycle factory, while the lieutenant was an acknowledged expert in the dynamics of flight. The contributions of both men were to prove invaluable to the Association's sole ambition: to get a man into the air.

Soon after the founding of the Association, the group travelled to Hammondsport to continue its work. The move was made because the engines required for flight testing were all manufactured in the Curtiss motorcycle plant. Obviously, it was more convenient to do the necessary modifications on the spot than to have to transport everything to and from Baddeck. Anyway, the winters were warmer in New York State than on Cape Breton.

Work proceeded apace. By the beginning of 1908 several model aircraft had been built, and by the end of February the models had become full-sized flying machines. They all were flimsy, awkward, and terribly ungainly – but each was better than the one before it. Finally, on March 12, a bamboo and silk runner-equipped monstrosity called the *Red Wing* was fitted with a Curtiss motorcycle engine and hauled out onto a nearby lake, and Casey Baldwin climbed aboard. The motor was started, and the *Red Wing* actually flew. It only went the length of a football field, and never much higher than the height of a man, but it flew!

When the motor quit, the young engineer landed the craft and listened to the cheers of his mates, factory hands, and scores of spectators who had come to watch the show. In making this flight, Baldwin had just become not only Canada's first pilot, but the first man anywhere in the world to fly before the public.

Later that spring, members of the Association made several flights, in different aircraft. Though Alexander Graham Bell himself never flew, he continued to encourage his young protégés. By the beginning of the summer, they were flying ever-greater distances for longer periods of time. On July 4, 1908, the American Independence Day, a little craft called the *June Bug* soared aloft in front of more than one thousand spectators. Unfortunately, Dr. Bell was not there to watch, but one of his daughters was. Later she wrote to her father and told him about the day. Her letter illustrates just how enthralled spectators were with what they had witnessed.

"In spite of all that I have read and heard," she wrote, "and all the photographs I had seen, the actual sight of a man flying through the air was thrilling to a degree I cannot express. We all lost our heads and shouted and I cried and everybody cheered and clapped, and engines tooted. I don't think any of us knew quite what we were doing. One lady was so absorbed as not to hear a train coming and was struck by the engine and had two ribs broken."[2]

The flying continued through the summer, and soon every member of the Association had flown, some of them several times. By October, McCurdy and Baldwin were anxious to return to Canada, and they convinced Bell that the move would be wise. Subsequently, two of the Association's planes were crated and shipped to Baddeck. One of these, the *Silver Dart*, was designed by McCurdy and equipped with a new Curtiss water-cooled V-8 engine, the first of its type to be used in an aircraft. McCurdy knew the power plant would work.

As the first snows swept Cape Breton, the engineers in the Bell shops at Baddeck went on with their work, but kept an eye on the ice build-up on Bras d'Or. It was on the lake, they reasoned, that the *Silver Dart* should be flown. Once solid, the ice surface would be smooth, large enough to permit takeoffs in virtually any direction, yet close enough to the shore that any last-minute adjustments would be easy.

As the crowds watched and waited, excitement grew. Few seemed to mind the cold; certainly no one dreamed of going home to get warm. All who were gathered at the lake's edge sensed that what they were about to see would be special.

Finally someone noticed a horse and sleigh beside the Bell shops. Several men rolled the *Silver Dart* out, hitched it behind the sleigh, and began the journey to the lake. Slowly, ever so slowly, the fragile craft bumped across the rutted snow by the shore, eased over the washboard ridges close to the bank, and reached smoother ice a stone's throw from land. Then the horse and sleigh moved away and Bell workmen on skates took over.

The skaters pushed the little plane across the ice as John McCurdy, bundled up in a heavy coat, high boots, toque, and mitts, walked alongside. Cheers rang out and the youngsters in the crowd swept forward in a shouting, thrilled, and milling mob. Barking dogs scampered along on the fringes of the procession.

Within minutes, the handlers had the *Silver Dart* where they wanted it for takeoff. McCurdy made a few final adjustments to the engine and settled onto the pilot's perch, and the propeller was spun. The little motorcycle engine sputtered into life, the men holding the plane let go, and the *Silver Dart* shot forward. In a few seconds it was off the ground.

The crowd erupted: cheers, whistles, screams, laughter. People jumped up and down, hugged each other, raced across the ice, threw hockey sticks and caps into the air, and yelled themselves hoarse as the steady throb of the tiny engine lifted the *Dart* thirty feet in the air.

McCurdy put on a good show. He accelerated to almost forty miles per hour, held his course, then turned and glided gracefully back to a gentle stop in front of the crowd. He had flown almost three-quarters of a mile.

The crowd surged around him, happy beyond words. For a time McCurdy sat in the plane, as if hoping the moment would never end. Finally, he stepped to the ice where the spectators thronged to welcome their new hero, pumping his hand and slapping him on the back.

Dr. Bell pushed through the crowd with his congratulations, but dissuaded the delighted flyer from attempting a second flight that day. Bell knew there would be many other opportunities to duplicate what had just been done. "I wouldn't want it to be spoiled," he said to McCurdy. "You can fly again tomorrow, but that's all for today." The inventor then turned to the crowd, caught their attention, and gave a little speech that would ring down through the years. "What we have seen just now," he said prophetically, "may well prove to be one of the really important pages of history."[3]

In the ensuing weeks, McCurdy flew again and again. But, as with the space shots of a later era, the novelty eventually wore off, and the crowds of the lakeshore drifted away. The Aerial Experiment Association was disbanded on March 31, 1909. McCurdy, the first man to fly in Canada, never lost his enthusiasm for the thrill of flying. But even he couldn't transfer that enthusiasm to certain members of the military establishment who watched a flying demonstration the following summer.

In late July 1909, Baldwin and McCurdy crated the *Silver Dart*
and took the flying machine with them to the big Canadian Army
training grounds at Petawawa, Ontario, one hundred miles north-
west of Ottawa. There, on August 2, on the sandy soil of a sports
field, they prepared to put on a flying demonstration for the
military. If the performance was a success, they hoped to convince
senior army officers that the airplane could be of value to them.
Until that time, the military had looked upon flying as little more
than a passing fad.

McCurdy made five flights that day, the first four highly successful. But on the fifth, the young engineers' dream died. At the
end of that flight, which had been almost a mile in length,
McCurdy made a sweeping turn, lined himself up over the field,
and touched down. The *Dart* lurched ahead, but the nosewheel
buried itself in the sand. The machine tipped forward, tore itself
apart, and threw its pilot out on the ground. McCurdy broke his
nose and was somewhat shaken up, but was otherwise none the
worse for wear. Nonetheless, the military were not won over.
The officers decided that the four successful flights were only
practices; the fifth was the one that counted, and because it was
a failure, so was the flying machine. They agreed that it would
have no military use.

Not long afterward, the disgusted McCurdy left to fly in the
United States. He flew for the crowds in several places and performed at least two notable feats. He became the first person to
send and receive a wireless message in the air, and he was the
first man in history to fly over the ocean – in this case, from
Florida to Cuba. The ocean flight brought him adoring fans and
the kind of attention media usually reserve for film stars, gang-
sters, and child prodigies. While they regarded him as a hero,
they were amazed he was so ordinary. Shortly before the departure for Cuba, a Florida reporter interviewed McCurdy, and then
described him:

> There is nothing odd or freakish about McCurdy; he is just
> a normal person of rather exceptional attainments, whose
> most distinguishing characteristic is his modesty when dis-
> cussing himself.
>   While not a total abstainer, Mr. McCurdy drinks sparingly
> of alcoholic beverages, though he smokes moderately, either

pipe, cigar or cigarette. He follows no special diet, either when preparing for an unusual flight or otherwise, neither does he have any set rules for sleeping.[4]

By the standards of the time, the crossing to Cuba was lengthy and risky, perhaps even foolhardy. Indeed, it was barely completed. Just as he approached the Cuban shore, McCurdy noticed oil leaking from the engine. A moment later the motor quit and he was forced to bring his plane down on the sea, about a mile and a half short of his goal. But the journey was nevertheless judged a great success.

McCurdy was taken to Havana, cheered in the streets, and fêted at a banquet hosted by the Cuban president, José Miguel Gomez. It was at this dinner that the triumphant Canadian was called to the podium and presented with an ornate envelope said to contain $10,000 from the president and the people of Cuba. McCurdy accepted the gift, thanked his gracious hosts, and retired to his room to rest before returning to Florida. Before going to bed, he opened the president's gift. In the envelope were a few scraps of newspaper, but no money.

Soon after, the *Silver Dart's* pilot came home.

2

Wood, Piano Wire, and Glue

Between 1909, when John McCurdy first flew, and 1914, when World War I broke out, flying in Canada was sporadic at best. (In those days, pilot's licences were issued by the Aero Club of America, an outfit affiliated with the Fédération Aéronautique Internationale of Paris. McCurdy had licence number 18.) Early in the fall of 1910, a young man named William Wallace Gibson designed, built, and flew one of his own creations on a farm near Victoria, British Columbia. The following year he flew another above the prairie at Calgary. Unfortunately, the second plane hit a badger hole on landing and tore itself to bits. A few days later Gibson went into another line of work.

Much the same thing happened to two Vancouver brothers, William and Winston Templeton, and their cousin William McMullen. These three constructed a biplane in the McMullen basement and attempted to fly it at Vancouver's Minoru Race Track. A few short flights were actually made, but on the last, the makeshift craft hit a race-track fence and fell apart. Undeterred, Winston and the two Williams collected the pieces and put them in a nearby storage shed. When the shed later burned to the ground, the hapless three threw in the towel. Not surprisingly, few remember them today.

In Winnipeg, novice aviator William Straith built at least three planes. He could only taxi the first two because they wouldn't fly. The third flew directly into several hydro wires. Straith was patched together at Winnipeg General Hospital. Nothing could be done for his plane.

One of the real flying pioneers in Canada also flew in the West.

He was Frank Ellis, a native of Nottingham, England, who, at age nineteen, came to Canada and settled near Stanmore, Alberta. Young Ellis had always been interested in planes and indeed had been building models of them for as long as he could remember. It was while working for the Hudson's Bay Company in Calgary that he teamed up with Tom Blakely, a kindred spirit who just happened to have a pile of junk stored in an Alberta chicken barn. The junk was the bits and pieces of a Curtiss biplane that Blakely had bought for $200, stored, and half forgotten.

In due course, Blakely and Ellis pooled their resources, scraped the chicken manure off the Curtiss, and began to assemble it. They bought, borrowed, and made the missing parts and finally found themselves with a complete airplane built of wood, piano wire, and lots of glue. The gas tank held enough fuel for a fifteen-minute flight. The three wheels on the craft had rubber tires, secondhand tubes, and scores of patches. A length of flat iron that dug into the ground passed for the brake. Yet the two were proud of their creation and eventually flew it several times. In his book, *Canada's Flying Heritage*, Frank Ellis described what flying was like in those days.

> First, the thrill of acceleration – the feeling that there's power enough behind you to thrust your machine up into the blue and out the other side of it. Then you are concentrating: watching the ground to catch your speed – for there was then no other method – listening continuously to the rhythm of the engine, hoping not to detect a warning cough, your tension mounting as the ground goes by at a faster clip. She's lifting, you think – yes! – no! – yes, she's up! And so you are concentrating for your very life as the ground falls away and you try to remember simultaneously everything you've ever learned about what to do in the air – that's high enough – don't push your luck! – level off.
>
> You look down now at the prairie below, suddenly aware of the height you have gained, and how flimsy your perch. Then a gentle forward pressure on the controls, and you're coming down, easing your foot off the throttle – down – down, take it easy – the ground gets closer – closer – you level off, touch, and bounce a bit too much perhaps, touch and bounce again, a wing comes up for a split second of

panic, then the wheels are on the ground together, the front one settles too, and you cut the throttle completely, by pulling the ignition switch, and roll to a standstill. It's all over!

There is no experience in the world like the surge of relief that comes over you. It's the way you might feel on an ordinary day perhaps, busy with your familiar daily routine, if everything started to slow down till it stopped – even the water dripping from the tap suspended in the air. All of a sudden the flow of life goes back to normal, and you feel a relief and a terrific exhilaration.[1]

While Ellis and others were practising their flying on isolated tracts of land, often far from the public eye, other individuals looked for opportunities to fly for crowds of the curious at autumn exhibitions, country fairs, and occasional air meets. Generally these young aviators, as they were then called, flew for little or no pay, in makeshift aircraft, from fields that were too small, too rough, and too close to buildings and trees. Often they performed in high winds, in low cloud, and under threat of being sued. More often than not, the promoter of the air meet had advertised the event for weeks in advance of the show. The crowds would show up, and the young pilots were ordered aloft no matter what the weather. There were accidents, of course, but in retrospect it is surprising that more of the flyers were not killed.

The first person to die in an air crash in Canada was a dark-haired, handsome young daredevil named Johnny M. Bryant. Late in the afternoon of August 6, 1913, he took off in a converted float plane from just outside the inner harbour in Victoria, British Columbia. He had flown twice earlier in the day, both times without incident, although gusty breezes were blowing in from the sea.

Watching her husband's departure that day was Alys Bryant, a pilot in her own right and the first woman to fly a plane in Canada. She had made her mark in history just a week earlier in Vancouver. Johnny had flown there as well.

On that fateful afternoon in Victoria, Johnny managed to get his float plane airborne for the day's third flight. He flew over the outer harbour and then swung back toward the city. In downtown Victoria, people stopped to marvel at the flying machine as it passed overhead. Many waved to Bryant while kids shouted, pointed excitedly, and ran in the direction the plane was moving.

Then, for some reason, perhaps to thrill his watchers below, Johnny Bryant dipped the nose of the plane, increased his speed, and dived toward the city. Suddenly, without any warning, the right wing snapped away from the fuselage. The aircraft spun crazily to one side and plummeted straight toward the horrified spectators.

Remarkably, no one on the ground was hurt, but the young flyer died instantly. He was not the only flyer Canada was to lose that day. After the stunned crowd had drifted away, Alys Bryant vowed she would never fly again.

But others did, and others died. After Thomas Selfridge became, in 1908, the first person in history to die in an air crash in the United States, the number of such fatalities increased steadily. The following year, three people died. In 1910 there were 29 deaths, and two years later the number soared to 122. It was not surprising, therefore, that personal physicians often accompanied the more well-to-do stunt pilots. One man who brought his doctor along was Count Jacques de Lesseps, perhaps the best-known pilot of his day. The dashing son of the man who built the Suez Canal, young de Lesseps was eager to fly from the moment he saw his first plane. He admired others of his generation who took to the air, and in 1910 he became the second person in history (Louis Bleriot was the first) to fly across the English Channel. In June and July of the same year, de Lesseps visited Canada.

For eight days, first in Montreal, then in Toronto, he and other pilots thrilled thousands with their stunt flying at the largest air exhibitions yet staged in Canada.

There were crashes and near-crashes, aerobatics, screaming dives over the crowds, and, wonder of wonders, a short period of time when those present watched three flying machines in the sky at one time! Never had such a marvel been seen in this country before. This was even more of a thrill than watching, at the same show, American Ralph Johnstone set a Canadian altitude record of 2,000 feet. Perhaps, though, the most dramatic event of the Toronto meet was a spectacular crash involving another American named Jack Stratton, who was to walk away from his plane.

During the first two or three days at Toronto, weather conditions made flying difficult. Several flights were aborted on the ground, one or two ended after just five or six minutes, and only a scant few ran their full duration. Stratton's flight was one of those that terminated early – and abruptly.

His plane barely wobbled off the ground in the face of a stiff crosswind, yet once in the air Stratton seemed to manage reasonably well. Then, five minutes into his flight, one of the control wires on the plane broke. Stratton immediately killed the motor, aligned the craft with the flying field, and began gliding back to earth. As the spectators watched, the little machine swooped lower and lower, its rigging whistling in the rushing wind. Then there came a point when everyone knew he would never make it.

Stratton was almost to the perimeter of the field when a stand of pine trees blocked his way. He missed some of them. The ones he hit ripped his plane apart. First one wing was sliced off, then the other. The motor tore away from the frame and half-buried itself in the turf below.

Stratton was thrown from his seat, but somehow wrapped himself around a tree limb and held on. He was still there when his rescuers arrived. One of them looked up at Stratton's perch and shouted: "Jack's a real bird man; he can fly, and he can light in a tree and stay there!"[2] No one knows if the stricken pilot, wounded only in his pride, appreciated the humour.

There were other bizarre accidents connected with early flying. Billy Stark was a well-known pilot in British Columbia. One day, during a flying exhibition in Vancouver, he took off and demonstrated his skills for hundreds of people gathered in Hastings Park. While he was airborne, some cows grazing in the park wandered into the area where he had hoped to land. When he did come down, he avoided hitting the cattle, but piled his plane into a perimeter fence. Stark came out of the crack-up unscathed, perhaps faring better than two men who had attempted to grab the plane and slow it down. One hurt his hand in the process, while the other was bumped by the aircraft and thrown to the ground. That unfortunate fellow may have been the first person in history to be run over by an airplane.

Not all the drama was lived-out on the West Coast. In 1912, American Charles Walsh was performing at the Nova Scotia Exhibition grounds in Halifax when he lost control of his aircraft. It crashed and was utterly demolished, but Walsh landed on the roof of a cattle barn and survived.

Eight days later, in another plane, the same pilot was in trouble again. Walsh encountered turbulence on takeoff and narrowly missed the same barn, but flew to safety under telegraph wires strung near it. He made an emergency landing in a field a short distance away.

A day later he took off again and avoided the barn. This time he crashed into a fence, but was able to walk away from his ruined aircraft. Unfortunately, Walsh's luck ran out a couple of weeks later when his plane went down at Trenton, New Jersey. His broken body was found in the wreckage.

Men such as Thomas Selfridge, Johnny Bryant, and Charles Walsh were not just pioneer pilots; their lives were the price of aviation advancement. And even though that price was great, these three men and others like them lived to fly. Their daring meant that they died flying.

Flying in Canada was sporadic between 1909 and 1914, but it had truly become the passion for many in every province. All too soon that passion would be spent, not before crowds at exhibitions, but in air battles over slit trenches, where weary men lived like the rats that surrounded them. On August 4, 1914, the world went to war and aviation was forever changed.

3

"The Only Way to Fight a War"

The airplane came into its own four years after the Canadian Army decided the machine was useless. By this time, World War I had started, but there was no such thing as a Canadian air force, nor would there be for some time. Thousands of Canadians were flocking to recruiting centres across the nation, and while most of these citizen soldiers were content to remain earthbound, toting a rifle, some of the young volunteers wanted to fly.

In the days immediately following our declaration of war, Militia Headquarters in Ottawa received "letters and telegrams . . . from young men wishing to serve as pilots, most of them assuming that Canada would be forming a flying service."[1] These hopes were dashed abruptly, although the Minister of Militia and Defence, Sam Hughes, did inform the British War Office that certain young Canadians would be willing to volunteer for the Royal Navy Air Service or the Royal Flying Corps. In due course, the British War Office decided to accept both Canadian and American pilots, provided they were already licensed to fly. This decision, and a later recruiting drive by the British, resulted in the formation of a number of private flying schools in Canada and the United States. Most were full the day they opened.

"I desperately wanted to be a pilot," explained Mel Alexander, a Toronto native who tried to enrol at the Curtiss School in his home city. "But they ran out of room, so I was forced to look elsewhere."

At about this time, Katherine Stinson, one of the early American flight pioneers, was looking for students for a flying school she was opening in San Antonio, Texas. Because Stinson was well known in aviation circles and had often flown in Canada, several potential pilots felt her school was what they wanted. Mel Alexander was one of them. "I signed up, and so did others from Toronto. There were lots of fellows from all over, right across Canada."

The young Canadians travelled to the south, found short-term accommodation, and presented themselves at a flying field on the outskirts of San Antonio. None of them had much money.

"We were charged a dollar a minute for air time," recalled Alexander in an interview conducted for this book. "This may seem unusual today, but learning to fly at that time was not the technical business it is now. I got my licence after 210 minutes, so it cost me $210. Very few went over the $250 deposit we had to make.

"The plane was a Model B Wright, with a thirty-five-horse-power engine. It was a pusher-type plane with two chain-drive propellers at the back. You sat on the wing with your feet out at the front, as if you were riding a kind of bobsled. The instructor sat beside you before you went solo.

"Most of our flying was done in short hops. We were in the air for five minutes and then we landed. In order to qualify for the licence you had to fly two figure eights around two pylons. Then you had to cut the motor and glide to a pre-arranged spot. At the end of the course, none of us really knew very much about flying. However, it was enough to get us overseas. I was in the Royal Navy Air Service and my rank was probationary Flight Sub-Lieutenant."

When war broke out, fifteen-year-old Clennell Haggerston Dickins, known to his friends as "Punch," was living in Edmonton and preparing to go to the University of Alberta to study mechanical engineering. He had given no thought to becoming a pilot. But as soon as he was old enough, "Punch" enlisted as a private in a reinforcing unit with the Princess Patricia's Canadian Light Infantry, left his university studies behind, and shipped out to an army reserve unit in England. An older brother was already there.

"One Christmas we spent a leave together in London," he recalls. "At the time, my brother had a commission in the Canadian Army, but had been seconded to the Royal Flying Corps. He was the one who talked me into becoming a pilot.

"He said the Royal Flying Corps needed pilots and that he thought my background and my studies might come in handy. I had always tinkered with machines, motor bicycles and so on, so I listened to his advice. Shortly after I returned from leave, I was discharged from the Canadian Army and offered a commission by the British because I had taken and passed the officer's training course while I was at university. Not long afterwards I became a pilot. I never regretted the move." Certainly not. Punch was to fly all his life and become one of Canada's legendary bush pilots.

Owen Sound, Ontario, native William Avery Bishop was another young man who was in the army when he left Canada. Billy Bishop had been a student at the Royal Military College since the fall of 1911. Three years later he was still there, and he still hated the place as much as he had when he first saw it. For him, the outbreak of war was an escape from the college's relentless examinations and the petty rules and discipline code he abhorred. But army life in England was not much better.

Bishop arrived at Shorncliffe Military Camp, near Folkestone, late in June 1915. Here he lived in a tent, and, in concert with virtually everyone in the place, grew to curse the accommodations, the boredom, and the never-ending rains that swept in from the English Channel. The stifling dust that greeted him when he arrived soon gave way to mud that reached the knees. Horses laboured through it, equipment became mired in it, and soldiers told one another that war might not be worse. Then, one day, Bishop saw a way to escape.

He was by himself, standing in a sea of mud, when a light aircraft swung down overhead and settled in an open field a short distance away. After a time the plane took off again and soon was out of sight. Bishop was enthralled.

"How long I stood there peering at the spot where the plane had disappeared I do not know," Bishop recounted later. "But when I turned to slog my way back through the mud I knew this was the only way to fight a war: there above the clouds and in the summer sunshine."[2] A few weeks later he was in the Royal Flying Corps.

W.R. May was born in Carberry, Manitoba, in 1896, but moved to Edmonton as a child. When his little sister couldn't say "Wilfred," she called him "Wop," a nickname that was to stick.

Like so many of his generation, he devoured every scrap of

news about the exploits of the Wright brothers and their attempts to get a flying machine into the air. When they succeeded, May was elated and certain that someday he, too, would fly. His chance came shortly after his nineteenth birthday.

"Wop" May had never been a great student, so when he dropped out of high school his parents enrolled him in a mechanics course in Calgary. While he was there the war began, and he ached to be part of it and join his many friends who had already donned uniforms. After a wait that seemed interminable, his parents gave their approval, and May joined the army. As Bishop, Dickins, and so many others did, he went to England and then transferred from the army to the Royal Flying Corps. There he met an old friend he had known for years. The friend was Roy Brown.

Even though he had been born in Carleton Place, Ontario, Roy Brown spent much of his youth in Edmonton and had made a name for himself there as a local sports hero. He enlisted in the army when the war started, but soon left to learn how to fly at the Wright school in Dayton, Ohio, and subsequently served with the Royal Navy Air Service in Europe, where he and May met up again. Later, in the skies over France, Roy Brown and Wop May would both be linked to one of the most famous air victories ever.

Another young man who saw service in the air war was George Howsam, a farmer's son from Port Perry, Ontario. "My family originated in Britain," Howsam explained, "and that was one of the reasons I wanted to get into uniform. I was brought up to believe that it was important to do what you could for your country. My grandfather left my father with that philosophy, so when I came along I was imbued with a fair amount of patriotism as well. England was at war and we were expected to help her.

"Anyway, we were living outside of Port Perry and I had to go into town to high school. I was not there long before my father bought me a horse to drive back and forth because I spent too much time with girls when I stayed in town." Howsam laughed and added: "But I left them all behind when I went to war." Howsam trained in Canada, but before long became a dashing and successful fighter pilot in Western Europe. The girls he left behind would have been impressed.

The young Canadian pilots who flew the wire and canvas contraptions of World War I were not all patriotic, or brave, or even highly skilled. What they were was extremely young. And, at first, because they were young, the war meant travel, adventure, romance, and, for some, a chance to dream the impossible dream. But once the fighting grew more savage, and the broken bodies of good friends had been lowered into the ground, the dream dissolved. Flying was not so much fun any more.

"At first it was thrilling," said Mel Alexander, "but the strain began to show on all of us. I lost many good friends in that war. We came together as strangers, but as time went on we all became closer. But when somebody you saw every day was suddenly not there any more . . . " Alexander's voice trailed away as he remembered those days long ago. His eyes clouded over as he pointed to the names in an old log book. "He was only eighteen. He was twenty. That fellow was twenty-four, but he seemed so much older. They all did a great job, but they died too young."

The same reflective mood hung over much of the world at the time, but it was – temporarily – lifted in London. There, the boys from Canada and other countries who had become men overnight tried to forget the war's horrors, as they sat with their girls and tried to be happy, if only for a few days.

"Musical and stage plays were packed," wrote one pilot,

> but the audience carried in the background the thoughts of France and all that it meant, with the precious days and nights of leave dropping away so quickly. The young had to laugh and not think. It was gaiety with a background of sadness. . . . The uniformed boy [and] his girl beside him were both aware of a background which had no certainty of life and the probability of death in a very short time ahead. For the boy, the hazards of war, with each day of his life, could depend on his skill, bravery, competence and above all, chances of good luck.[3]

Luck was surely with some of the flyers, and Mel Alexander told me he was one of them. One morning in an air battle his gas tank was ruptured by a German bullet. "I was pretty busy," he admitted, "but I turned toward our lines when the engine stopped. I was able to glide back to safety.

"Some planes glide like a brick," he continued, "but the glide ratio of others is so much better. Another day I was flying as a bomber escort at 13,000 feet or so over the Ruhr Valley when the cold caused the oil to congeal and the engine seized up. It was a long way back to the lines, but my only hope was to glide as far as I could. I finally landed in a little field on the side of a hill. I had no idea where I was.

"My plane was hardly stopped when a youngster ran up and stood looking at me. She watched me climb out but did not say anything. At this point I was starting to imagine German soldiers just behind the hedgerows. When that little girl spoke to me in French I was awfully relieved. She took me to her home and I got back to our aerodrome from there. I had been so lucky."

Others too, were lucky, but perhaps none more so than a quick-thinking, courageous young pilot from Stonewall, Manitoba. Allan McLeod and his observer, Arthur Hammond, were involved in an aerial dogfight over Albert, France, in late March 1918. The two were "flying a slow, two-seater, Armstrong-Whitworth bomber-reconnaissance machine which had the aerodynamics of a cow."[4]

They had almost reached their target, a German artillery battery, when Hammond noticed an enemy fighter plane below them. He shot it down, but in doing so attracted the attention of seven other fighters who had been circling overhead. They dived to the attack.

Try as he might, McLeod could not get his lumbering aircraft out of the way. The British plane was raked with gunfire; its gas tanks ruptured and the machine burst into flames. At about the same time, Hammond shot another German down.

As McLeod was making a desperate attempt to land his burning aircraft, the floor of the rear cockpit fell out and young Hammond had to scramble to a precarious perch on top of the fuselage. He destroyed a third German from that position.

By now the roaring flames of the burning bomber had forced McLeod out of his cockpit onto the left wing. With one hand holding on to the wing, his other clutching the control column, McLeod somehow succeeded in landing his crippled plane, in spite of the withering gunfire from an enemy fighter that chased them to the earth. His plane,

still bearing eight bombs and a thousand rounds of ammunition, was now blazing fiercely. Hammond had received

six wounds and was badly burnt; he was virtually helpless
but McLeod, despite his own five wounds, managed to drag
him from the wreckage, receiving one more wound from an
exploding bomb. Under heavy enemy machine-gun fire he
then dragged Hammond towards the British line and after
again being wounded, collapsed only a short distance from
the forward trenches. They were rescued by South African
troops.[5]

Some weeks later, Arthur Hammond was given a Bar to the
Military Cross he already had. For this outstanding feat of airmanship and raw courage in the face of the enemy, young Allan
McLeod received the most prestigious award in the British
Empire, the Victoria Cross. Unfortunately, he did not enjoy it
for long. Later that same year he died in Winnipeg from the
effects of influenza. He was only nineteen.

Two other Canadian pilots won Victoria Crosses in World
War I. They, unlike McLeod, survived the war.

The first and best-known recipient was Billy Bishop, the Owen
Sound native whose abhorrence for England's mud resulted in
his transfer to the Royal Flying Corps. Almost from the day of
his first flight, Bishop exhibited a daring exuberance in the air
that ultimately saw him drive seventy-two German planes out of
the sky. Although his total number of kills would probably have
merited the Victoria Cross in any event, a dawn raid on a German
airfield was the action that brought him the decoration.

The young pilot planned the raid with care, and carried it out
on his day off. He got up at 3:00 a.m. on June 2, 1917, saw to
the arming and fuelling of his aircraft, a Nieuport 17, then took
off across the lines toward a German airfield. When he got to his
destination, the place seemed deserted, so he continued to fly
around, somewhat aimlessly, hoping to find another airfield to
attack. Eventually, he did find one.

Seven German aircraft were on the ground, some with their
engines running. Bishop roared out of the sky and strafed the
field, but in doing so alerted the pilots of four enemy fighters,
who started to come after him. He shot three of them down,
then poured his remaining ammunition into the fourth, until it
turned and fled. The Canadian then headed back to his own
airfield, flying directly under four German fighters who appar-

ently never saw him. By this time, his spent adrenalin was having an effect.

The excitement, and the reaction afterward had been a bit too much, as well as the cold morning air. It seemed, once or twice, that my head was going around and around, and that something must happen. For the only time in my life it entered my thoughts that I might lose my senses in a moment, and go insane. It was a horrible feeling, and I also had the terrible sensation that I would suffer from nausea at any minute. I was not sure at all where I was, and furthermore did not care. The thrills and exultation I had at first felt had all died away, and nothing seemed to matter but this awful feeling of dizziness and the desire to get home and on the ground.[6]

The third Canadian pilot to win the Victoria Cross was William George Barker. At 8:30 one morning, two weeks before the end of the war, Barker was getting ready to fly to Britain to assume command of a training school. By his twenty-fourth birthday the Dauphin, Manitoba, native already had forty-six kills to his credit, and had won French and Italian awards, as well as many of the most prestigious British decorations, some of them more than once. Before leaving France for good, Barker decided to overfly the front one last time. As he did so, several thousand Canadian and British soldiers watched.

As he made his climb away from his aerodrome, the battlefield below seemed serene, as did the sky above it. But the peace did not last for long. A short distance north-east of the forest at Mormal, Barker spotted a German aircraft at 21,000 feet. Barker climbed up under and behind the plane and shot the machine down before its pilot had time to react.

But the German's countrymen did have time. Some fifteen Fokker aircraft swarmed around Barker, and the closest opened fire. The young Canadian's attempt to evade the enemy was to no avail. A hail of bullets thudded into his Sopwith Snipe, rocked the machine to one side, and tore into Barker's right thigh. Infuriated by the suddenness of the attack, Barker banked into a tight turn, steadied himself, and blasted his opponent from close range. The German plane burst into flames and tumbled end over end into no-man's-land. Barker then turned to two other Fokkers and succeeded in driving them away. As he did so, he was hit again.

A bullet passed through his left thigh and hit his hip bone. Barker fainted and his Snipe fell out of control. As he regained consciousness he found himself still under attack. Despite his severe wounds and the sickening pain, he singled out one of the Fokkers and under his fire it went down burning.

The Canadian was now wounded again, the elbow of his left arm being smashed, and once more he fainted. When he came to he was at 12,000 feet and was under attack by a second large formation of enemy fighters.[7]

By this time, with his plane barely flyable, and smoke pouring from the engine, Barker flew at another enemy fighter. He shot it down, then put his Snipe into a screaming dive toward the allied lines. He crash-landed safely in the British sector, a short distance back from the front. The troops on the ground were ecstatic.

"The spectacle of this attack was the most magnificent encounter of any sort I have ever witnessed," wrote the then Brigadier-General Andrew McNaughton, who was commanding the Canadian Corps Heavy Artillery at the time. "The prolonged roar, which greeted the triumph of the . . . fighter, and which echoed across the battlefront, was never matched . . . anywhere else."[8] As he watched the aerial battle, McNaughton had not been aware that the magnificent pilot was a Canadian.

Barker recovered from his wounds, returned to Canada, and formed a flying operation with Billy Bishop in Toronto. He was killed in a civilian air crash twelve years later.

One of the most famous air battles of the First World War was also one of the most controversial. It involved two Canadian flyers and the German ace of aces, Manfred von Richthofen, the man who gained world-wide renown as the legendary Red Baron. Up until the day of the battle, the twenty-six-year-old nobleman had led a charmed life, to the point that he seemed invincible to the scores of Allied pilots he faced in the air. He had already shot down eighty of them.

The Red Baron's last fight took place on April 21, 1918. That day, he had, as usual, led the elite Boelcke *Jagdstaffel* into action against the British 209 Squadron commanded by Captain Roy Brown of Carleton Place, Ontario. The sun over France that day was warm and bright as the Allied planes climbed over the Australian section of the front and went into battle against the Germans and their leader in his bright red triplane. Richthofen had already gained height, where he circled, waiting for a kill, like a vulture hovering over its prey. He did not have to wait long.

Wop May, now a lieutenant, was on his first operation against the enemy. The period of training had finally ended and he felt lucky to be part of the attack led by his old friend from Edmonton, Roy Brown. Brown had instructed him to stay out of the action, to watch and learn. May did as he was told – until he saw one of his friends falling to a certain death in a burning aircraft. Then May threw aside his captain's instructions and went after the German who had done the shooting. As he did, he knew bullets were hitting his own plane.

May cut away sharply, got out of the fire path, and turned his attention to another machine. Unfortunately, he had fired only one burst at it when his guns jammed. Defenceless and vulnerable, the young pilot now made a break for home. Richthofen, far above, was watching. Then the Red Baron swooped down for the kill.

Lieutenant May saw the red plane behind him, but was unable to shake it. He climbed, twisted, dived, cut back sharply on his track, but it was no use. The German was gaining on him, trying to get in position to fire on his quarry. By now, May was lower than the trees, heading directly for the Australian front line.

"I kept dodging, spinning, looping – doing every trick I knew – until I ran out of sky," May recalled later. "Richthofen was giving me burst after burst from his Spandau machine-guns. The only thing that saved me was my awful flying! I didn't know what I was doing."[9]

But someone else did. Far above Wop May's private war, Roy Brown had been busy fending off wave after wave of Fokkers. Out of the corner of his eye he noticed a red plane trying to drive one of his mates into the ground. It was only later that he learned the mate was also his old friend Wop May.

Brown went after the German. He was shooting as the three fighters crossed the front lines, and, as it turned out, the Australians were doing the same thing. A bullet hit Richthofen in the

back, near his shoulder, and then it entered his heart. The Red
Baron managed to get his famous red triplane down, but died just
a few seconds later.

May and Brown both landed safely. Naturally enough, Roy
Brown believed he was the man who had brought down the Red
Baron. "We shot down three of their triplanes," he said in a
letter to his father a few days later. "Among them was the Baron
whom I shot down on our side of the lines."[10]

But the origin of the triumphant bullet was to be hotly disputed.
The Australians disagreed with Brown, convinced that one of
their own bullets had killed the legendary flying ace. Several
Australians, soldiers who had been with him that morning,
claimed that the marksman was Robert Buie of the 53rd Battery,
Australian Field Artillery. For his part, Buie apparently never
bragged of the feat attributed to him by his buddies. Nor, for that
matter, did Brown. Today the question seems to have been
resolved in the Australian's favour. Indeed, in the *Official History
of the Royal Canadian Air Force, Volume 1*, the author, S.F.
Wise, states, "It is now difficult to argue that Roy Brown killed
Richthofen."[11]

Years later, Billy Bishop commented on the controversy.
"Nobody will ever convince anybody who flew in World War I
that anyone but Roy Brown shot down Richthofen. Brown was
never given official credit for the kill. Had he been in any other
air force he *would* have been given credit and would probably
have received half a dozen decorations from his own and other
countries, for to destroy Richthofen could be described as the
equivalent of shooting down fifty enemy machines – with one
bullet."[12]

Bishop's views echo the widespread respect for the great German ace. A day after his death, his body lay in state at Bertangles,
in France, and hundreds of young Allied soldiers filed by to pay
their last respects. When he was laid to rest, they fired a rifle
volley over his grave. The Germans were informed of his death
through official channels.

Even though Roy Brown never received credit for Richthofen's
death, there remains a Canadian connection to the whole affair.
Shortly after the red triplane came down that day, scores of curious approached it and removed souvenirs for themselves. In no
time, the plane had been stripped and artifacts from it were scat-

tered far and wide. Today, one of them may be found in a Canadian officers' club in downtown Toronto. There, in the Wings Room of the Royal Canadian Military Institute, is the seat from Manfred von Richthofen's aircraft. It is both a trophy and a modest monument to one of the greatest aces of the Great War – the famous Red Baron.

The war made many Canadian heroes famous, too. In addition to the Victoria Cross winners, a man named Donald Roderick MacLaren made a name for himself during the last months of the war when he shot down forty-eight enemy planes. The son of a trapper from the Peace River country, MacLaren was the third-highest-scoring Canadian ace, after Bishop and another Westerner, Raymond Collishaw from Nanaimo, British Columbia.

Collishaw was a popular flyer, and a fun-loving, wise-cracking friend to all those who knew him well. "He was probably the most comical man I've ever known," reminisced Mel Alexander, "but when he was in the air he was all business." And he had been all business from the day he left home at the age of fifteen to become a cabin boy on a Fisheries Protection Service boat on the West Coast.

Even though his formal schooling ended early, Collishaw did his utmost to continue his education. He studied hard, read everything he could get his hands on, and obtained his captain's papers while with the Fisheries people. He then enlisted in the Royal Navy Air Service and went to Europe to fight a war. His first few brushes with the enemy were uneventful, but he soon made up for the quiet beginning.

One morning in the fall of 1916, young Collishaw was ordered to deliver a fighter plane to a British base close to the German lines. Since he expected no difficulties he went alone, taking what he thought was the most direct route. Somehow, he mistakenly drifted into enemy territory.

For some time he flew along, unaware of his blunder, enjoying himself, admiring the foliage of fall in the countryside below. Here and there he saw farm animals, a few trucks, and the occasional train. The world was wonderful. Then the first shots exploded around him.

Collishaw jumped in his seat and banked sharply. As he turned to see who was near him, he was met by machine-gun fire from half a dozen German fighters. Bullets sang in every direction, crashed into the cockpit, and ripped his goggles from his head. The lenses were pulverized, and the shards of glass cut deeply into the soft flesh around his eyes. A second or two later, he realized he couldn't see. A wave of panic engulfed him, and the twenty-two-year-old Canadian was sure this flight would be his last. Rubbing his throbbing eyes with one hand, he threw his plane all over the sky with the other.

The Germans were unrelenting. They were close by, so close that Collishaw could hear both their guns and their engines as they came up to him. The shooting went on and on.

Yet, gradually, as the red film of blood washed the glass from his eyes, Collishaw's vision improved. He gritted his teeth against the pain and held on, banking his plane into turn after turn, ascending, descending, and evading his pursuers in every way he could. Then, as suddenly as they appeared, the Germans were gone, probably because they lacked the fuel to continue. Collishaw headed for home.

The young pilot kept on flying, but because he could not see well enough to use his compass he had to rely on the position of the sun to determine his course. Finally he came to an airfield. Ronald Dodds, in his book *The Brave Young Wings*, describes what was to greet Collishaw there. "Assuming that it must be French, [he] put down and taxied his machine towards the hangers, in front of which was lined up a row of aircraft. There seemed to be something odd about the aircraft and as he neared them Collishaw realized to his horror that they bore not the roundels of the French air service, but the Iron Cross marking used by the Germans. Fortunately the . . . engine was still turning over and Collishaw opened his throttle and managed to take off."[13]

Aside from the sixty aircraft he destroyed in battle in World War I, Collishaw is also remembered as the originator of the famous "Black Flight." It came about when he was attached to No. 10 (Naval) fighter squadron, formed at Dunkirk in the winter of 1917 and moved to Droglandt, near Ypres, that same spring.

"Collie decided we should do all we could to scare the Germans," laughed Mel Alexander, "so we painted our planes black. Most of the pilots in Naval Ten were Canadians anyway, and in "B" Flight, where I was, we were all from Canada. The five of us in the flight had black planes, with the name in white beside the cockpit.

"Collishaw called his plane the Black Maria. Mine was Black Prince. There was also Black Sheep, Black Roger, and Black Death. I don't know if it did any good, but it was fun for a while."

Alexander acquitted himself well in the air, although he became reticent when I asked him about his accomplishments. "I was never an outstanding pilot," he told me. "I just tried to do my job. I wasn't even a good shot."

But Mel Alexander was both a good pilot and a good shot. Ron Lowman, the Military Affairs reporter for *The Toronto Star*, paid tribute to him in a column on February 8, 1987.

Alexander, you see, was one of my boyhood heroes. He shot down 18 aircraft before his 20th birthday and wears the naval Distinguished Service Cross (DSC).

As a boy in England, I devoured every word that was written about him, his great leader, Raymond Collishaw, and their originally all-Canadian, five member "Black Flight" on 10 Squadron, Royal Naval Air Service (RNAS).

Those were the days when Alexander soared and swung in flimsy, wood-and-fabric Sopwith Triplanes and Camels with the best Kaiser Wilhelm had to offer.

His first victory in those unforgiving skies was on June 4, 1917, at 17,000 feet over Lille against an Albatross. In an open cockpit, numb with cold and without today's oxygen supply, Alexander was nevertheless sweating buckets as he watched the stricken German aircraft flutter earthward with a dead hand at the stick.

Unfortunately, Lowman was also to write an obituary for his modest hero. Mel Alexander died in October 1988, not long after he was interviewed for this book.

Today, the number of living Canadian pilots who flew during World War I grows smaller every year. Soon they, and the war

that was their war, will live on only in the history books. But
their legacy to aviation will endure. Because of their efforts and
their sacrifice, the airplane became better, and an appreciative
nation of civilians would soon realize it.

4

The Daredevil Years

When the human tragedy that was World War I finally ended, thousands of flyers had nowhere to fly. There were no more dawn patrols, no more reconnaissance and bombing missions, no more dogfights, and no more training sessions with eager youngsters at the controls. Flying fields were ploughed under, hangars were razed, and unneeded aircraft were abandoned or scrapped.

Those who were lucky enough not to be in a foreign grave came home to the farms and factories of an emerging nation. Canada had matured during the war, and the men who fought had matured most of all.

Some of the veterans forgot – and others wanted to forget – what they had done overseas for four years. They traded rifles for lunch pails and welcomed the trade. Victory medals, campaign medals, even medals for heroism would not buy bread. The camaraderie of the mess hall became a memory, as did the bayonet, the machine-gun, and the hand grenade. A nation at peace had little need for instruments of war.

But for many – perhaps most – of the men who flew, the transition was not easy. They had flown because they went away to fly; had loved flying; and had wanted, somehow, to fly forever. Flying was in their blood, in their daily conversations, and in their dreams.

''Yes, I dreamed of flying after I came home,'' Punch Dickins explains. ''I even dreamed of flying while I was flying. In the mess, in the barracks and places like that, I thought of flying in Canada. I particularly thought of flying in that great north country of ours, where the only way in was by water for two months of

41

the year and by dog team the rest of the time. I dreamed of what
the airplane would do for remote settlements, and I decided, long
before I left France, that I would fly in the North when I got
back.'' And so did many others.

Wop May was barely out of the train station in Edmonton on
his return home when he told his parents he intended to keep on
flying, as often as he could, wherever he could. Like Dickins,
May was interested in northern flying, carrying passengers,
freight, and mail. It was the dreams of such men that would open
the North in the twentieth century, in much the same way as the
dreams of the men who had built the railway had opened the West
in the nineteenth.

But, while their male counterparts were away at war, two
women had made names for themselves demonstration-flying in
this country. Both were young and attractive Americans and both
were excellent pilots.

Both before and after she opened the San Antonio school that
Mel Alexander attended, Katherine Stinson had enthralled crowds
in Edmonton, Brandon, Winnipeg, and elsewhere with her flying
skills. She did loops, rolls, and spirals in her single-seat biplane,
but her ability to recover from steep dives over the crowd became
her specialty. In Regina one day, several people near the airport
called the police because they were sure she had crashed when
her plane disappeared behind some buildings. They missed Stinson's dramatic last-second recovery. She was twenty years old at
the time.

In central Canada, Ruth Law was the favourite airwoman. She
had earned her pilot's licence in 1912, spent half a dozen years
thrilling crowds wherever she went, and broken several flying
records in the process. At the Exhibition grounds in Toronto she
even raced against an automobile. While the car roared around a
track, she flew in circles overhead.

But the dawn of the women's liberation movement was still far
in the future. When Law tried to buy her own aircraft from the
Curtiss Company, she was turned down. Years after he passed
up the sale, Glenn Curtiss explained his refusal. His reason, it's
said, ''was his concern about the young girl's life. He could not
believe that a person of such slim build, weighing only a little
over one hundred pounds, could handle an airplane with safety''[1]
– years of daredevil evidence to the contrary notwithstanding!

Wop May had no such trouble getting *his* aircraft. A few weeks after his return to Alberta, he and a friend, Fred McCall, another veteran fighter pilot, rented a plane for twenty-five dollars a month from the city of Edmonton. The Curtiss JN-4, or Jenny, was not new, and had been in storage at the local Exhibition grounds, but it was said to be flyable.

The two pilots worked busily on the machine, succeeded in getting it airworthy, and flew it to a farmer's field they had leased a short distance away. (Today, the field is the site of the city's Municipal Airport, a couple of miles from the downtown area.) There, more work was done on the engine, "May Airplanes" was painted on the tail, and the entrepreneurs waited for the money to roll in.

The money was slow in coming. Despite all the advancements in aviation since John McCurdy's day, flying in central Alberta in 1919 was still a precarious undertaking. It was the opinion of many that only the foolish and the foolhardy left good, solid prairie earth. Stable, sober citizens of the day used buggies, rode trains, or, in some extraordinary cases, drove cars. They did not fly.

Yet May and McCall intended to change all that. They flew here and there around the country, performed at fairs, took people for rides, and even taught flying in Edmonton. They had willing customers, but not enough of them. Fuel and spare parts were expensive, not to mention the necessities of food and clothing. There were risks involved in the air, but the two accepted those. They worked from dawn to dusk to make ends meet, to stay solvent, and to stay alive. But one day in Calgary, McCall ran into trouble.

Although the two rented their plane in Edmonton, McCall actually owned another machine in Calgary. Wop May was his chief pilot, although others flew his plane as well. On July 5, 1919, McCall was the one in the air with it.

He had taken off from a race track at the Calgary Exhibition, carrying two wide-eyed little boys on their first flight ever. Wop May and the youngsters' father stood on the ground, watching.

The plane arched into the sky, circled out over the crowded fairgrounds, and dipped its wings to salute the people below. The boys, by this time thrilled beyond words, cheered with delight, and waved to their father, a tiny speck in the mob below. This was flying, and they loved it!

Then the engine stopped. McCall reacted instantly: he went into a dive to try to start again, but quickly levelled off when he knew there was no hope. Then, as beads of sweat broke out on his brow, he desperately looked for a clearing where he could land.

There was none. Racing cars were careening around the track where he had taken off, a carpet of people blanketed the midway below, and every other possible avenue to safety was blocked by buildings. McCall glided in circles, coming lower and lower every second. The midway crowd, mesmerized, stood and gawked at the machine overhead. Then, as the plane dropped to treetop height, the spectators froze where they were, not knowing what to do. A few stumbled backwards in horror, but many told reporters later that they did not move because they thought the pilot's actions were part of the show.

With only seconds to act, McCall yelled at his passengers to hold on, then dropped the plane dead centre on top of a moving merry-go-round. The aircraft hung there precariously, caught in the rigging of the ride. For a few seconds, the merry-go-round continued to turn, while the riders on their ceramic steeds screamed in fear. Finally, the startled operators cut the motor.

At first, no one moved. The plane settled slightly, the two boys in it wailed, and McCall shook with relief. He couldn't believe his luck. Nor could his partner, Wop May, who had watched the whole thing.

Under the plane, the carousel riders fell all over themselves getting off the ride. Most expected the wreckage to come crashing down at any second. Several panicked, some lunged wildly into the crowd, and a few were almost trampled in the stampede. Miraculously, no one was hurt.

Within seconds, a mob of curious fair-goers had gathered at the scene. People jostled, at first two and three deep, then a dozen deep, craning their necks and pressing around the wreck. The police were called, and McCall and his passengers were helped from the plane. Half an hour later, the spectacular crash was the talk of the town.

Of course, in those years immediately after the war, even the sight of a plane flying overhead was cause for conversation. That was why barnstorming became so popular, and ultimately so widespread. Anyone who had a plane could draw a crowd. Whether it was a fall fair in Nova Scotia, an exhibition in Montreal, or a rodeo in Alberta, the airplane was an attraction in itself. If the pilot gave rides, so much the better.

Usually, at some point before arriving at a town, the barnstormer would contact a local farmer for permission to use a pasture field for a landing strip, and would promise him a free ride for the use of his property. The closer the field to the fair, the better. The roar of the low-flying planes often scared grazing cattle near the small towns, or caused horses pulling buggies or wagons to stampede. Although farmers complained at times, they generally welcomed the visiting aviators and tried to do what they could for them. More often than not, the farmer was rather pleased that *his* farm was the one where the plane landed.

"Our usual procedure," wrote Frank Ellis,

was to fly over the town and drop handbills, telling the people that we and our machine were, or would be, at so-and-so's field on a certain date, ready to do business. Also – and this to bring them on the run – the handbills stated that the first person to hand one of the dodgers to the pilot would receive a free ride. Sometimes the handbills were dropped a week ahead of time, while we were en route elsewhere to fill a date. When the great day arrived, the town was agog, and schools were sometimes closed to give the kids a chance to be on hand. Then as the roar of our engine was heard, and we dropped low, flying at roof-top level along Main Street, the entire populace and all the dogs turned out, racing to the field. In "tin lizzies," buggies, and wagons, on horse-back, on bicycles, and on foot, they poured along the high-way. Usually the first to arrive was a breathless youngster who triumphantly thrust a ragged but precious handbill into the pilot's hand.

Occasionally we arrived unheralded, and after flying over a few times at a very low level to arouse interest, we selected a suitable landing spot. A crowd arrived like magic, and soon it was all we could do to keep people from swarming all over the plane. . . .[2]

"We were treated so well everywhere we went," recalls another man who spent two summers barnstorming across the prairies. "The crowds were so damned enthusiastic. We tried to do our best for them, and it meant long hours and hard work. Still, it was fun at the time, and if I was young again I would do the same thing. We never had much money, but it was a great life."

The fascination for flying grew. The crowds on the ground regarded the daring barnstormers as the harbingers of the future. The pilots were applauded and welcomed everywhere they went. They were astronauts in a horse-and-buggy world.

But, as time went on and flying lost some of its novelty, the crowds who came to air shows grew a little jaded and looked for extra thrills to hold their interest. That was when stunt flying, wing walking, and even parachute jumping became drawing cards. The more audacious the stunt, the bigger the crowd.

Not surprisingly, there were lots of crashes: some quite accidental, others predictable, and a few that would be talked about for weeks afterward. One pilot walked away from an accident involving a farmer (who walked away, too), several fence posts, and one wing of a plane. At least one engine failure resulted in a crash on the back of cow. The unfortunate animal had to be shot.

In the fall of 1921, crowds in downtown Regina turned out to watch an American daredevil named Reese attempt to transfer from one aircraft to another in mid-air. The plan called for Reese to clamber on top of the machine in which he rode and grab a rope ladder that trailed underneath another plane. If all went well, he would go up the ladder, climb into the second aircraft, and land safely in it.

Reese had no trouble getting up on top of the plane. But then, "he was seen to grasp the bottom rung of the rope ladder, float free from the bottom of the aircraft for a moment, then lose his grip on the rope, and plunge to his death some 500 feet below."[3] Soon afterward, government regulations curtailed this type of stunt.

Another stunt that took place in Western Canada had a happier ending. It involved Wop May and the mayor of Edmonton, Joe Clarke. One afternoon, a baseball game was to be played between home-town Edmonton and a visiting team from Calgary. As usual, the long-standing rivalry between the two cities would attract a good crowd, but a local newspaper felt something extra would guarantee a sell-out. A couple of reporters went to see His Worship, the Mayor, and talked him into throwing the first pitch of the game – from an airplane. They then hired Wop May to do the flying.

The mayor had never flown, and was terrified at the thought of doing so, but he had to uphold the honour of his city. Any attempt to back out would have been unthinkable: the local papers had spread the word, and hundreds of people who rarely went to a ball game planned to attend this one. The mayor decided to give it his best.

Margaret Mason Shaw recounts the story in her book *Bush Pilots*.

> At the appointed time, Wop and the mayor took off from a field outside the city and flew low over the baseball diamond where the teams were lined up for the start. Wop went through his whole bag of tricks, diving, rolling, looping the loop. As he turned to leave the sports field, he asked Clarke whether he had thrown the ball. The mayor, shivering with fright, admitted that he had not. May insisted they go back and promised to tell the mayor when to drop the ball.
>
> Down went the plane again over the diamond, skimming the ground at a height of only about ten feet. At Wop's signal the mayor threw the ball straight across the plate where it was caught by the catcher. Then May streaked off . . . and put the machine through its paces for another half-hour. On landing, the mayor climbed weakly from the plane with the announced intention of never flying again.[4]

A newspaper in Winnipeg made use of the airplane for a story published in the fall of 1920. On October 13 of that year, there had been a daring bank robbery in the town of Winkler, some seventy-five miles south-west of the capital and twenty miles from the U.S. – Canada border. When reports of the theft and the escape by the robbers to the States reached the *Winnipeg Free Press*, the paper sent a reporter and a photographer to the scene by plane. The aircraft landed in a field close to the settlement, and the press people raced to the bank, got their story, and flew back in time to make the evening edition. In its coverage of the event, the paper told its readers that this was the first time news had been gathered by plane. Pilot Hector Dougall was praised for his skilled airmanship.

Another well-publicized use of the aircraft in the early days was in the transport of mail. Often a pilot would take a few messages with him as a favour on a cross-country junket; often, too, he would carry a bundle of letters as a publicity stunt. Then, from time to time, the post office got into the act and termed a particular journey an "official air mail" flight. There were lots of these.

The first such flight was between Montreal and Toronto in June 1918. Captain Brian Peck, a Royal Air Force officer stationed in Toronto, flew to Montreal to put on aerial demonstrations for recruiting purposes. However, on one occasion, bad weather in Quebec prevented the flights from taking place, so the pilot looked around for something to justify his trip. He managed to convince postal officials to let him carry a sack of mail on the return trip, and the letters were duly gathered, stamped "Via Air Mail Montreal," and loaded onto the plane. Peck's other cargo was a case of Scotch he was flying back to a friend's wedding, but since Toronto was dry in those days, Peck thought it best not to advertise its presence.

When Peck climbed into the cockpit and prepared to leave, he almost didn't make it. The overloaded Jenny wobbled down the field, and at the last second it staggered into the air. Almost immediately, Peck had to duck under telegraph wires, but he managed to keep the machine from crashing. Possibly the thought of losing the Scotch brought about such a superb demonstration of airmanship.

As soon as he was under the wires, Peck banked slightly, and followed a railway westward, flying so close to the tracks that if a train had come along he would have hit it. He reached the outskirts of the city before he was high enough to proceed safely. But by then, strong headwinds and continuous rain were soaking him to the skin, impeding his progress and causing the engine to spit, sputter, and virtually die. He somehow reached Kingston safely, but ran out of gas as he landed. After a refill, he completed his journey and safely delivered the mail – and the whiskey.

There were other "first flights" between Vancouver and Victoria, Edmonton and Calgary, Truro and Charlottetown, and from St. John's to Cartwright in Labrador. Some of the most memorable were flown by the young World War I pilot from Edmonton, Punch Dickins, on the prairies and in the Yukon and Northwest Territories. Dickins's exploits are a story unto themselves.

5

Punch Dickins, Pioneer

When nineteen-year-old Punch Dickins came home from the Great War with seven kills and a Distinguished Flying Cross to his credit, he pursued his dream of flying in the North. "By the end of the war I knew that flying was the only thing I really wanted to do," he says today, "so fortunately there was a reserve air force program for people like myself who wanted to maintain their flying status. It involved going to Camp Borden for twenty-eight days once a year, and it meant that I was on what was called the Canadian Air Force reserve list. In the meantime, I worked at a General Motors dealership in Edmonton.

"When the Royal Canadian Air Force was established as a permanent force on April 1, 1924, they gave me a commission in it and posted me to High River, Alberta. I stayed there until 1927 when James Richardson of Winnipeg established Western Canada Airways. I decided to see if I could get a job with this outfit, and I did so in January 1928."

At this point, Dickins was launched on the career he had wanted since the end of the war. "It took me almost ten years," he explains, "but I was finally where I wanted to be. The company planes were barely adequate for the time, but we did the best we could, and I think we made some small contributions to the opening of the North."

Dickins, who recently moved to Toronto from Victoria, is a small man with a firm handshake and a vibrant, take-charge personality. I interviewed him before he moved to Ontario to be near his family. He is now retired and working on his memoirs. Some of the "small contributions" Dickins mentioned are still regarded as being among the greatest airplane journeys ever undertaken in Canada. The first took place in late August and early September of 1928.

"Earlier that summer I was flying mining and prospecting parties into northwestern Ontario," he recalls. "Then toward the end of August I took Colonel MacAlpine up to the Barrens. And even though there had been a lot of talk about the flight at Winnipeg, I actually only had a day or two to get everything ready. We had a government map to follow, but it was really not much use in places. Printed right across a large section of the route I intended to fly was the word 'UNEXPLORED.' "

The boundless risks of going into unknown territory did not deter Dickins nor the three men who left Winnipeg with him: Colonel C.D.H. MacAlpine, the president of Dominion Explorers and the man who had chartered the flight; Richard Pearse of Toronto, editor of the mining industry paper *The Northern Miner*; and W.B. Nadin, an air engineer. The four were about to embark on a trip they would remember for the rest of their lives.

"We left Winnipeg on August 28 and flew up to Churchill," Dickins explains today. "The plane was *G-CASK*, a Fokker Super Universal. It is probably the machine that appears in more pictures of the early days than anything else I flew. It was on floats, of course."

The flight northward along the west coast of Hudson Bay was uneventful, as the salt-water waves lapped the rugged shore under the port wing. For the most part, the four men rode in silence, only occasionally shouting a comment over the throbbing roar of the engine. On the right, scudding clouds swept over the sea, their wind-driven shadows playing hopscotch to the horizon.

"There wasn't a lot of sophistication to the plane," Dickins recalls. "On that trip, and for years afterward, I flew with five instruments on the panel, one of which was for the engine RPMs and a second for the oil pressure. The other three were our complete navigational system. We had no radio, no communication, no direction-finding. Of course, there were no radio beacons anyway, so it wouldn't have mattered if you had a radio or not."

The dot in the sky that was *G-CASK* continued northward to Mistake Bay, Corbett Inlet, and finally Chesterfield Inlet, where it turned inland away from the bleak grey shores of Hudson Bay.

As they flew westward over the 200-mile-long Chesterfield Inlet to Baker Lake, the four were struck by the magnificence of the stark terrain. To MacAlpine and Pearse, the mining men on board, the mineral potential in the empty land was enormous.

In a land without landmarks, an unusually high hill near Baker Lake became a focal point for the flight. Dickins flew toward it, and when the time came to stop overnight, landed on the lake and came in to shore at an Inuit settlement. On September 3, Dickins said goodbye to those at Baker Lake, taxied *G-CASK* out to open water and took off westward, into the unknown. Years later he described the area over which he flew:

> In the summer, surprisingly, it is beautiful country with lots of brilliantly coloured flowers, although the entire area is devoid of trees and there are numerous bare outcroppings of rocks, interspersed with long gravel eskers left by the receding ice age thousands of years ago. For over three hours we wouldn't see a living creature, not even birds, but the trails made by the caribou were as plain as city streets.[1]

The plane droned westward as the men studied the terrain below. MacAlpine, the Dominion Explorers mining man, was quite excited by the mineral prospects of this stark, desolate land. He didn't seem at all bothered by the dangers inherent in the flight. Neither did Dickins.

"We were looking at land no white man had ever seen before," he explained to me. "And I knew that if we ran into trouble anywhere there, through bad weather or machine failure, we were gone for good. I can't say that any of us were scared, but we all knew no one would ever find us. They wouldn't know where to look. We just hoped and prayed the engine would keep running."

Luckily, the engine did keep running, and the lonely miles of the Barren Lands fell behind them. Dickins flew by the sun, because compass deviations made that instrument unreliable, and the government map of the area was as useless as a street sign on Mars.

From Baker Lake, the flight path had been westward over the Thelon River to Aberdeen Lake, and then south-west along the shore of Dubawnt Lake to the river of the same name. As they approached Selwyn Lake on the Saskatchewan-Northwest Territories border, the party noticed that the sun was partially obliterated by smoke "from forest fires raging in the west. In a way this was a good sign, since at least it indicated that they were now close once again to the land of trees – and trees, eventually, would mean people. An hour after crossing the treeline, they hit the shore of Lake Athabasca, flew ten miles east to Stony Rapids and landed to spend the night."[2] They had crossed the great unknown.

Dickins says he will always remember that night in Stony Rapids. "The hard part of the trip was over and we had reached civilization. However, the weather was getting colder and, because we had to chop ice away from the floats the next morning, I was anxious to get going. I checked the gauges and decided that we had lots of gas to make Fort Smith. It was about 250 miles away."

Despite the coolness of the dawn, the Fokker started easily. Dickins taxied away from the dock, increased his speed, and gradually climbed from the lake surface. Soon he was over the trees and out of sight. The day became warmer; the sun shone through the smoky haze, and the trip became pleasant again. Maps for this area were reliable, and Dickins knew exactly where he was going. His passengers sat back, lulled into a drowsy reverie by the steady droning of the motor. A carpet of green lay below them.

Then the engine quit.

"If ever silence was deafening, that was it," laughs Punch Dickins today. "Everyone was wide awake right away. I looked for a good place to put her down, while the others looked around to see where we were."

Two minutes later, Punch had expertly glided the plane to the surface of the Slave River, twenty minutes' flying time from their goal of Fort Smith.

"We drifted with the current to a mud bank," Dickins continues, "and that was when I realized we were out of gas. The gauge had apparently been frozen when I checked that morning. I never let that happen to me again."

"There was nothing to do but make some tea while we decided what to do when, out of nowhere, we heard a puffing sound up the river and, a few minutes later, a wood-burning stern-wheeler appeared, pushing a big barge loaded with freight. I don't know who was more surprised, us or the captain and crew."[3]

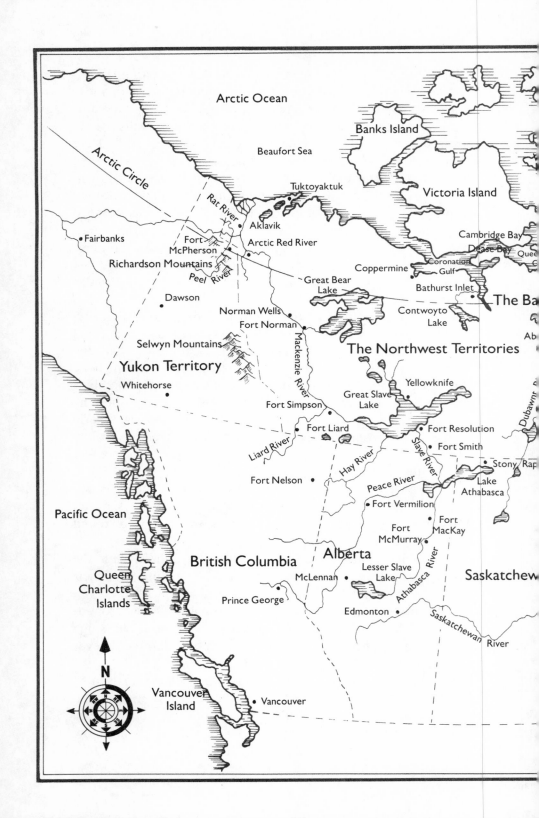

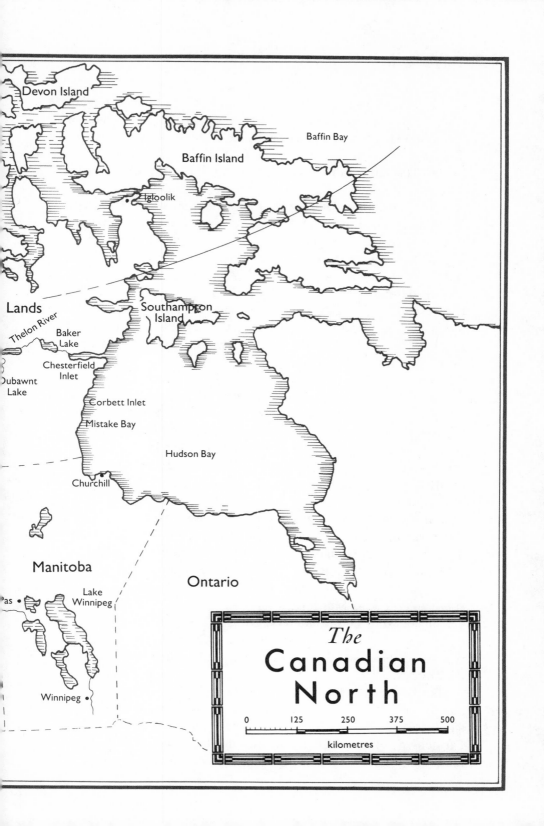

Devon Island

Baffin Bay

Baffin Island

Igloolik

Lands

Thelon River

Baker
Lake

Southampton
Island

Chesterfield
Inlet

Dubawnt
Lake

Corbett Inlet

Mistake Bay

Hudson Bay

Churchill

Manitoba

Ontario

Lake
Winnipeg

as

Winnipeg

The
Canadian
North

0   125   250   375   500

kilometres

The barge carried barrels of gasoline, so the tanks of *G-CASK*
were filled. In less than half an hour Dickins and his passengers
landed safely at Fort Smith. A few days later they were back in
well-charted Winnipeg, having travelled some 4,000 miles in
thirty-seven hours in the air – the first flight across the Barren
Lands. The same journey would have taken a good two years by
canoe and dog team.

Two months later Dickins flew another first. In 1924, as part
of his duties with the RCAF, he had been asked by the Edmonton
Post Office to examine the possibilities of using aircraft for the
transport of mail in Western Canada. He studied the matter carefully, and in his report he strongly recommended that airplanes
be considered for the job, particularly in the northern areas. Now,
four years later, he had the chance to make a test run. A temporary
route was set up between Winnipeg and Edmonton with several
stops in between. Punch Dickins flew the Regina-Saskatoon-
Edmonton section successfully.

Then, in January 1929, a much more difficult experiment
began. Western Canada Airways directed Dickins to consider
the feasibility of establishing a regular air mail service linking
Edmonton with the settlement of Aklavik, on the Mackenzie delta
near the Arctic Ocean. Such a service would test the capabilities
of existing aircraft and the pilots who flew them. Dickins was
excited by the idea, and welcomed the chance to fly "into the
real North."

At the time, the railway stopped at Fort McMurray, about 260
miles north-east of Edmonton. From there the mail had to be
taken by dog team into the outlying settlements farther north,
some of them weeks away. The post office had decided to clear
up the backlog by plane, and the first stop on the northern mail
run would be Fort McMurray.

One cold morning in January, Dickins left Edmonton in a ski-
equipped Fokker, accompanied by his engineer, Lew Parmenter;
two passengers; and bags of outgoing mail stuffed in the rear of
the aircraft.

The trip was short. Only a few minutes after departure, the
engine cut out. Dickins had to make an emergency landing on a
snow-covered field. The carburetor had iced up, and, in spite of
Parmenter's efforts to fix it, the four men had to return to Edmonton. A day later they tried again, only to be forced down by a

blizzard near the mid-point of the journey. Finally, on the third time out, they reached their destination of Fort McMurray.

The communities north of Fort McMurray were small, often made up of only a few buildings and a Hudson's Bay store. All fronted on either the Mackenzie or Athabaska rivers. In winter, they were virtually isolated from one another and from the outside world.

Dickins visited each community on his way north, until finally he and Parmenter glided out of the sky at Fort Simpson, at the junction of the Liard and Mackenzie Rivers. Because of severe winter conditions, they decided to go no further. The two men were greeted warmly by everyone in the settlement, and the mail they brought in was as welcome as it was unexpected. When delivered by dog sled, mail rarely arrived in winter. Despite the wind, fog, sleet, and blinding snow that had assailed them on occasion, the men judged the test run a great success.

"We stayed there overnight, of course," recalls Dickins. "Everyone wanted to know all the news from the south, so we did our best to bring them up to date on things. When we left the next morning, we took the outgoing mail and a shipment of furs for Winnipeg."

One of the stops on the way south was Fort Resolution, a tiny village on the south shore of Great Slave Lake. The sun was shining when they got there, but billows of wind-driven snow were sweeping across the frozen lake, obscuring the shoreline and concealing drifts and mounds of debris. Battling the wind as he fought his way to a landing, Dickins hit a hidden ice ridge.

The grinding impact tore away the undercarriage and damaged the fuselage as the plane skidded along the surface. Dickins killed the motor, but not before the ship had nosedived onto the ice, crumpling the whirling propellers out of shape. Then the only sound was the shrieking of the wind. Outside the cockpit, the temperature was forty below zero.

"I remember feeling pretty dejected at that point," recalls Dickins. "Both of us were shaken up a bit, but luckily we weren't hurt. All I could think of, though, was the fact that this one landing might put mail delivery in the North back a long time. This trip was important to me – but a lot more important to those isolated little places along the way."

The two men drew their parkas more tightly about them and

pulled on their heavy winter mitts. At first the door of the plane would not open because a drift of snow was wedged against it. When they finally squeezed out of the plane, a gust of Arctic wind swirled around them, lashing their faces with stinging ice pellets. Instinctively, they turned away from the wind, caught their breath, and began to examine their damaged airplane. At first neither spoke.

"It was worse than I expected," Dickins remembers. "At first I was sure we would never get out of there without bringing parts in from outside, and I knew that could take weeks. That was why we decided to try some repairs even though we knew that if we did get everything else patched together, the propeller would be a real problem. Both blades were bent, but one was so bad it looked like a corkscrew. On top of everything else, it was a damned cold place to try to fix anything."

They jacked up the Fokker and propped oil drums under the front end. A tarp draped over one wing gave them some shelter for working, but little comfort, since Dickins and Parmenter still only had a few tools and virtually no spare parts. Furthermore, little usable equipment was available in Fort Resolution, although a priest at the local mission found a piece of water-pipe that they used in repairing the damaged fuselage.

For hours each day the two worked, fashioning each makeshift part indoors and then feverishly attaching it to the plane, while their fingers and toes became numb with cold. As they worked, they had no guarantee that when they finished the plane would fly, or that the makeshift repairs would not tear away in flight and send them both to their deaths.

"But I don't think I was ever really scared," replies Dickins when I ask how he felt. "I had faith in that plane, and anyway, I suppose we all take chances when we are young that we would never take later on in life. I did send a fellow from Fort Resolution out with a dog team to get a new propeller, just in case we couldn't fix the one we had. But we knew he would be away a long time and we were not going to sit around and do nothing. By the time we were ready to work on the prop, we really thought the old bus would fly."

Slowly, ever so carefully, Dickins and Parmenter twisted one of the propeller blades back into shape. The work seemed to take forever, but finally it paid off. The blade was not perfect, but it would do. Then they turned to the corkscrew. "It was much harder to straighten," Dickins explains, "but we almost made it when the blade broke, about nine inches from the tip. We both cursed the damned thing, wondering what in hell we were going to do now."

The two deliberated for a while and finally got the idea that if they cut the tip off the longer blade, the two would be the same length and the plane might fly. "That was the hardest part of the whole business," says Dickins. "Somebody gave us an old hacksaw and we started cutting. When we were sawing we were sweating even though our hands and feet felt frozen. When we weren't sawing, we were cold all over."

It took most of a day, but finally both blades were about the same length, and both were bent into roughly the same shape. Then, early in the morning, on the fifth day at Fort Resolution, the men got the Fokker started and Dickins taxied out for a test flight.

The engine sputtered a bit at first. Dickins roared up and down the lake a couple of times, and then gingerly lifted off. He gained altitude and then flew in a wide circle over the village, while Parmenter stood below, watching, and listening for the first hint of trouble. None came. Finally, Dickins made a careful landing, Parmenter climbed in, and they took off for home. "We had no trouble from then on," Dickins recalls, "but I have to admit that we sure listened to the engine on the way out."

The following summer, Punch Dickins embarked on one of his longest and most memorable journeys as a bush pilot.

"In late June 1929, I left Edmonton and flew the entire length of the Mackenzie River. That flight was perhaps the most satisfying I ever made," he says. "The weather was good and I really enjoyed the whole thing. I stopped at every village on the way down the river to show the flag for Western Canada Airways. The greetings I received were always enthusiastic, particularly because the farther I went, the less chance that anyone had ever seen a plane."

On this trip, Dickins crossed the Arctic Circle, and became the first person in history to reach Canada's western arctic coast by plane. "I arrived, finally, at Aklavik [on July 1], by the light of the midnight sun. The roar of the plane as I flew over and landed brought the entire village out to greet me. There were a couple of Mounties, some priests, nuns, and local fur traders, and thirty-five or forty Inuit. None of the Inuit had ever seen a plane before, and they were quite curious about it.

"Some of them came right over to it, touched the sides, and wanted to go for a ride. Others stood back and stared, and there is a story of one older lady who would not come close because she was afraid. She is supposed to have said that she didn't believe what she had seen. Here was a bird that flew even though its wings did not flap.

"I took several Inuit up for flights while I was there, but they immediately became lost. They had never seen that great delta of the Mackenzie from anywhere above the level of a dog team or canoe, and it looks a lot different from the air. Finally they saw their village and they grinned from ear to ear."

In the first few euphoric minutes after his arrival at Aklavik, Dickins was alone with his thoughts in the middle of a crowd. "I stood on that muddy riverbank," he recalls, "and I looked north to the Arctic Ocean, and then the other way, thinking in my mind's eye of the two thousand miles I had come, and I felt very humble. Then I remember thinking of Alexander Mackenzie, who, with a few Indians and two birchbark canoes, had taken six months, and he *may* have reached the same muddy bank where I stood. I got there in about seventeen hours' flying time – and in relative ease. He battled heat and cold, flies, mosquitoes, unknown country, hostile Indians, and so on, and he did this 140 years before. That was when I truly realized what the airplane was going to do, and the effect it would have on the lives of the people who lived and worked all through the great northern region. I knew then that the airplane was there to stay."

6

The MacAlpine Expedition

One Canadian aviation story of the 1920s captured headlines around the globe. It was a tale of exploration, hardship, heroism, and luck – most of it good. At first the story involved only a handful of people, but at its end, many more were involved and, through radio and newspapers, countless others followed its unfolding.

A central figure in the epic was the forty-three-year-old president of Dominion Explorers, the intrepid C.D.H. MacAlpine, who had accompanied Punch Dickins on the history-making flight across the Barrens one year earlier.

Colonel MacAlpine was organizing and financing a second expedition into the unknown that by today's standards would be considered ill-advised if not foolhardy. MacAlpine intended a survey of mining bases in the far North, stretching from Churchill on Hudson Bay, north to Bathurst Inlet and Coppermine, along the Arctic coast to Aklavik, then south to Great Bear and Great Slave lakes. In total, the distance involved would be in excess of 20,000 miles – all in rather primitive aircraft, employing almost no navigational aids. Nevertheless, MacAlpine was convinced the trip would be a success.

In late August of 1929, his party of eight set out from The Pas, Manitoba, in two planes, a Fairchild piloted by Stan McMillan and a Fokker with G.A. (Tommy) Thompson at the controls. Both men were experienced bush pilots, and neither took foolish risks. The weather was pleasant and the trip to Churchill uneventful. But from their arrival in Churchill on, nothing went right.

A supply ship taking fuel to Baker Lake caught fire, and efforts to save it failed. Both the vessel and its cargo were lost. An equally devastating fate awaited Thompson's plane. He landed at Churchill, tied his mooring lines, and left the plane. For some reason, the lashings loosened and the aircraft drifted out to sea. As it cleared the harbour, it collided with a barge; the plane's floats were torn open, and the machine began to sink.

A hydrographic ship was in the vicinity, and the crew managed to get salvage lines onto the plane before it disappeared completely. However, the ham-handed rescuers virtually destroyed the object they sought to save. When they realized the wings would not fit on the deck at the rear of the ship, they chopped them off with axes. Thus salvaged, the Fokker would never fly again.

"We then had to sit around Churchill for over a week, waiting for a replacement aircraft," recalls Stan McMillan in an interview. "And all the while the weather was absolutely beautiful. The days were warm and sunny and the nights cool and clear – perfect flying weather. But by the time the new plane arrived, the weather was beginning to change."

Winter comes early in the North, and the time lost at Churchill was to compound the troubles they would face later on. Already, the first flakes of snow were drifting across the harbour, and the leaden skies forecast impending storms. The party reached Baker Lake without incident, in a day, but they were already ten days behind schedule. Ahead lay the trackless Barrens, called by Philip Godsell, author of *Pilots of the Purple Twilight*, "the land God forgot":

In all directions – north, south, east and west – extended the grey-white reaches . . . beneath a cold and threatening sky. Not a stick, not a tree . . . [was] there to break the dread monotony or give perspective. No shadows, not a thing with which the eye could measure distance! Like the dirge of lost souls, the wind moaned dolefully by in the same deadly, unending refrain until it nearly drove one mad. The utter immensity of this vast, illimitable No-Man's-Land, inhabited only by the migratory caribou, the Arctic hare, the sharp-eyed white fox and the gaunt wolf, dulled one's very soul and stultified the imagination. It was like a world of nothingness enveloped with[in] a winding-sheet of snow.[1]

Yet the two planes set out into this "world of nothingness." The date was September 8.

"We headed for Bathurst Inlet," explains Stan McMillan, "and we intended to navigate using a sun compass. However, we were barely under way when we flew into snow squalls, so the compass was not much help. Already we could sense a drop in temperature, and we knew ice was forming on the lakes below us. Neither Tommy Thompson nor I, nor anyone else for that matter, knew the weather patterns in that part of the Arctic, so we thought we had better get up to the straits as quickly as we could."

But when they encountered white-out conditions, they had to land on a little lake, hoping the weather would clear. When it didn't, they took off again because they feared being frozen in and marooned. "We were not sure where we were, or even which direction we were going," continues McMillan. "The snow was heavy, but we finally found a river we thought was flowing north."

The men kept the river in sight, and followed it to the Arctic coast. By this time they were low on gas, severe headwinds were impeding progress, and the storm was raging. "We followed the coast," recalls McMillan, "because we were sure that sooner or later we would come upon something. We hoped there would be Inuit along there somewhere."

By now both planes were critically short of fuel, and Thompson and McMillan strained to see any sign of life along the bleak coastal reaches below. Finally, just when they were convinced the gas was gone, someone noticed a solitary figure staring up at the strange apparition in the sky. The two planes came down.

"We had reached a place called Dease Bay [400 miles from Baker Lake]," says McMillan. "This is on Queen Maud Gulf, across from Cambridge Bay. There were a couple of others with the man we had sighted, and in the next while some others arrived. Eventually there were about twenty natives there.

"At first we wanted to get going, and we even took an Inuit up to see if he could give us directions out of there. But it was no use. We were so short of gas, we came back within a few minutes. I think the man loved the ride, though. He had no sense of fear, even though he had never seen an airplane before. He was really an amazing character."

The explorers still wanted to push on, but the Inuit convinced them it would be certain death to do so. They had almost no gas, and the ice on the Gulf was far from solid. Furthermore, it was over eighty miles to civilization at Cambridge Bay. The eight men knew they were marooned.

"We wanted to walk across the ice," McMillan remembers, "but the Inuit kept telling us it was not safe. So while we waited for freeze-up, we built a sod hut and kept warm by setting fire to anything that would burn. The fact that we were truly stranded began to hit us."

The hut the group constructed was as windproof as they could make it, but it was smoky and cramped inside. Because there was no wood available, the men burned dried moss and grass, saturated with engine oil. After a time, the Inuit loaned them a make-shift tin stove, and still later, brought them fur leggings and heavier parkas.

"But we were really short of food," says McMillan. "We had some with us, of course, but with eight people eating each day, supplies got low pretty fast. There were a few ptarmigan and ground squirrels around, and we shot and ate these, but I'm sure we would have died if it had not been for the Inuit. They were wonderful to us."

Yet, as the days went on, the eight white men were slowly starving to death. The Inuit food was unfamiliar and at times almost impossible to swallow. For days, they subsisted on chunks of dried fish, much of it rancid. Even when the men succeeded in getting it down, they often vomited it back up before it could provide real nourishment. Nor were they able to swallow the seal blubber the Inuit loved.

Not only were they starving, the men were suffering dreadfully from the bone-chilling cold. The hours spent gathering fuel numbed their hands and feet, and thawing out in the smoke-filled hut they'd constructed seemed to take forever. They tried catching fish along the nearby shore, but as often as not this resulted in a cold dunking when shelf ice broke away and the unfortunate fishermen slipped into the water. It was almost impossible to dry out completely from such a soaking. The salt spray stung their faces and left them raw, sometimes so raw they bled. And, once a fish had finally been caught, the sting of salt water burned the men's hands as the catch was cleaned.

The mental anguish of knowing they were lost was as relentless as the physical suffering. The thought that absolutely no one in the outside world knew where they were, or whether they were alive or dead, gnawed at the group constantly.

"There were times when we got depressed," understates Stan McMillan today. "But the Inuit did their best to dispel our fears. They were always laughing, joking, and playing little tricks on us to keep our spirits up. I still remember how they would run along the snow, then flip into the air and turn a somersault, with the ease of circus performers. Of course, when we tried to do the same thing we fell on our faces, and the Inuit would actually jump up and down with laughter. They hated to see our long faces.

"And we constantly bugged them to get going. We were a rather sad lot, I suppose, and we wanted to get out of there, to get across the Straits. One day, after about a week, we had the idea that the ice would be strong enough to go. The Inuit told us it was not, but we insisted. We got out a couple of miles and ran into open water, slush, and slob ice. After that, we came back and waited. By that time we realized the Inuit knew what they were talking about."

Meanwhile, in The Pas, in Winnipeg, and in far-away Toronto, the disappearance of Colonel MacAlpine and his party had become the news story of the year. At first, no one who knew of the expedition really worried. The Colonel had even given orders that if he and his associates disappeared, no search of any kind was to be launched for ten days. Now the ten days had passed without a word from the missing men. Their families began questioning the wisdom of the trip and the apparent lack of concern from those who knew most about it. Requests for a search fell on deaf ears, until a friend of MacAlpine's, General D.M. Hogarth of Toronto, went to Winnipeg and began calling business associates and others with a view to organizing a search for the lost expedition.

Then the search itself became a news story. Every bush pilot who went north kept a sharp eye out for the missing men. Every reporter who needed a story to file talked to these pilots as they departed – and just as often, updated their stories when the pilots returned without having seen a thing. Within days, several planes were brought into the effort, and the pilots who flew them were some of the best-known names in the business: Bertie Hollick-Kenyon, Punch Dickins, Roy Brown, Bill Spence, Charles Sutton, Andy Cruickshank, Pat Reid, and others. At first, search headquarters was at Stony Rapids on Lake Athabasca, and then as the weather turned cold the aircraft operated out of Baker Lake.

The searchers looked for the two planes between Baker Lake and Bathurst Inlet, the presumed direction of the MacAlpine party. They also searched the area to the west and south of Baker Lake, along the shoreline of Hudson Bay, and followed the rivers north to the Arctic Ocean. Every possible place MacAlpine might have gone was covered. But they didn't find the missing men.

"One of the search planes flew right over us," explained Stan McMillan. "We saw them, but we learned afterwards that they could not see us because of all the snow cover where we were. We could not even light a signal fire because we did not have anything extra to burn. Every scrap of fuel was used to keep warm."

And so the search went on and on – for almost ten weeks. The newspapers and radio stations all over Canada devoted extensive coverage to the quest, and speculated endlessly as to the fate of "The Lost MacAlpine Expedition." The stories were picked up by media outlets in other countries, and soon thousands of people in the United States and overseas awaited news of the fate of the missing men. Here in Canada, the immediate families of the men steeled themselves for the worst, and dreaded that the mysterious North had locked up another secret forever.

The search was a long, dangerous undertaking and spurred many pilots who had never flown over the Barrens and other unknown areas to do so in some of the worst weather conditions they had ever experienced. In all, more than 29,000 miles were flown in more than 300 hours of flying time. The Dominion Explorers' share of the search costs was roughly half a million 1929 dollars – and the search itself was the largest ever, to that time. "But all the while they were looking for us, we were trying to keep alive on the shore of Dease Bay," says Stan McMillan.

Finally, several days after their guests from the stormy heavens had first tried to walk across the ice, the natives decided that the trek to the outside could begin. Even though the sea ice was spongy in spots, it would support the weight of a human being. The Inuit insisted that the party walk in single file, each person some distance behind the one immediately in front. The whites gathered what equipment they could, and the entire Inuit community – men, women, and children – set out in the general direction of Cambridge Bay, about eighty miles of hardship away.

"We were generally a confident group," recalls Stan McMillan, "but the going was pretty rough at times. We would never have survived without the Inuit. They goaded us along, did their best to keep us smiling, and at times, almost force-fed us. They even gave up the last they had for us. Our confidence on that crossing was confidence in them."

And so the march went on – day after day, night after torturous night. The shrieking winds of the North swept over the ice and drove storms of stinging ice pellets into the faces of the walkers. The temperature was always far below freezing, but the sponge ice was treacherous in the extreme. Every so often it gave way, and someone got a wet foot. When this happened, the ice froze around the leg, and walking became still more difficult and often quite painful.

"One afternoon an Inuit woman suddenly disappeared," says McMillan. "The ice gave way and she went in, over her head in about two seconds. But she didn't panic. She swam a few strokes toward firmer ice and held on with her fingertips. One of the men near her took a line from a pack and crawled out to her. She held on and he pulled her up on the ice. At the time it was storming, and the wind was making the day seem colder than it was. I suppose it was thirty below [Fahrenheit] without the wind chill.

"The woman stood up and stripped all her clothes off in spite of the cold. Other Inuit gave her dry clothing, parka, and mitts and she was ready to go in five minutes. She never complained."

At night, the travellers slept on the ice, in hastily constructed igloos that were tiny but reasonably warm, despite the constant wind. In the morning they trudged on, wearily, warily, and with a growing anticipation that surely the march would end soon.

Finally it did. Fifty-four days after the men had last seen civilization, they topped a crest of heaving ice, and saw, through the gloom, the mast of a ship, a snow-covered jetty, and woodsmoke from the village of Cambridge Bay.

"We felt pretty good then," laughs McMillan, with the understatement that characterizes a long life of adventure and hardship in the far North.

The journey had ended. After a brief rest, the members of the MacAlpine Expedition were flown south to their homes. The trip might, in a commercial sense, have been a failure, but to the eight men who survived it, and to those who welcomed them home, it had the happiest possible ending.

7

"A Sublime Gamble with Death"

You won't find the village of Little Red River, Alberta, on the map today, but in early 1929, Canadians from coast to coast came to know its location. A Hudson's Bay Company employee there by the name of Bert Logan had become ill: his voice had gone, his throat was paralyzed, and his condition seemed to be getting worse. When Dr. H.A. Hamman from Fort Vermilion, about fifty miles away, arrived, he took one look at the sick man and knew exactly what was wrong. Logan had diphtheria, and if he was not treated immediately, he would never survive.

The diagnosis was all too accurate. Logan was dead even before Dr. Hamman found someone who could take a message for help to the outside world. When he did find a volunteer with a fast team of dogs, he scrawled a quick note, handed it to the driver, and told the man to get to Peace River as fast as he could. That was the railhead in those days, and a telegram could be sent from there. Hamman had no other way of communicating.

The musher pocketed the note, piled a few supplies on his cariole, and disappeared into the bush. It would be two long weeks before the doctor's message would reach Peace River, 300 miles farther south. In the meantime, Dr. Hamman treated several Indians in Little Red River who seemed to be suffering from the same disease that had killed Logan. Hamman knew that an outbreak of the highly infectious disease, if not swiftly checked, could devastate not only the Little Red River community, but every native and Métis settlement for miles around. He also knew that his meagre supply of immunizing drugs was inadequate for the community's inoculation and that his antitoxins were so dated that they were probably useless. If his scribbled message for help wasn't answered in time, Logan would be only the first of hundreds to die.

Meanwhile, Louis Bourassa was pushing his dog team on to Peace River, and after two gruelling weeks he trudged wearily up the steps of the telegraph office and handed the operator the desperate message from the north:

> If possible, rush aeroplane STOP Good landing and no snow STOP If snow, will clear landing strip at both Fort Vermilion and Red River . . . STOP Send intubation apparatus and several hundred units antitoxin toxoid for two hundred people . . . STOP Real emergency STOP Do all possible STOP[1]

Within seconds, it was on the wire to Edmonton, where, less than an hour later, the Deputy Minister of Health for Alberta, Dr. M.R. Bow, phoned Wop May at home. It was January 1, 1929.

May listened in silence, his mind racing, as Dr. Bow outlined the grim situation in Little Red River. May knew he was going to be asked to fly the needed drugs into the hinterland. He was ready with his answer before the doctor was finished. The doctor had only to collect the necessary drugs and May would be ready to leave with them the next morning. Then he phoned his partner, Vic Horner, who agreed to go with May in their Avro Avian aircraft, a small biplane equipped with wheels and an open cockpit.

The prospects for the 600-mile journey were incredibly bleak. The temperature the next morning was almost forty degrees below zero. The drugs had to be kept warm. The aircraft had to have a smooth runway each time it landed. The chances of flying into strong winds and heavy snow were reasonably certain – and, most of all, the terrible cold would leave the men in the plane so exposed they might perish on the way. But the young pilot who'd outrun the Red Baron faced the odds calmly.

At noon the next day, he and Horner put gas into the Avian, ran up the engine in a final precautionary check, then took the precious antitoxin from Dr. Bow and placed it in the bottom of the rear cockpit. The drugs were packed around a small charcoal heater, and the heater in turn was wrapped in coarse wool plaid blankets. The flyers were not nearly as warm. Despite heavy clothing, several sweaters, mitts, and fur-lined helmets, the bitter cold was penetrating. It was so cold that spittle would freeze into a ball before it hit the ground. But the men clambered into the biplane, and, with a final wave to a few people, May taxied away from the Edmonton hangar and was soon out of sight. The *Edmonton Bulletin*, inspired by the men's calm bravery, reported on the mission of mercy in ringing prose.

> Two knights of the skies, throwing their lives in a desperate hazard with death, riding a slender and fragile thing of wood and silk and steel; their steed a shining plane; their weapon a whirling propeller which lops off the cold, white miles, one by one.
>
> And these two knights of the skies are risking their lives to save the lives of others – behind them in their plane ride gleaming glass tubes carrying the hope of life – 600,000 units of diphtheria antitoxin and enough toxoid to handle close to two hundred and fifty cases. . . .
>
> Before the fliers is space, the illimitable skies; behind them doubts and fears. Not for the ability of the flyers but for their chance of survival in a light machine in mid-winter heading into an unknown wilderness with the ultimate risk of landing on rough ice, or making a forced landing on some nameless lake in unknown terrain with wheels.[2]

"It was a magnificent flying job," an admiring Punch Dickins tells me years later. "Wop was a good pilot and he did what he had to do. He deserves a lot of credit for that flight." "He could have refused to go," adds Stan McMillan, a man who certainly knew the perils of northern flying, "but it wasn't in his nature to do so. There were so many lives at stake. I am sure Punch or any of the others would have done the same thing."

The tiny silver Avian headed north-west, over the rolling flatland near Edmonton, past dozens of tiny lakes and rivers, all of them frozen until break-up in the spring. Over today's towns: Meadowview, Tiger Lily, and Lone Pine. Across the Athabaska River and into the desolate trackless wilderness beyond Swan Hills.

By now, the men sitting in the open cockpit were cold – colder than they had ever been. Numb, barely moving, they had frozen into human statues on a flight that went on forever. Below them, the muskeg and matted spruce; ahead of them the unknown; and without warning, all around them a winter storm that bounced the plane and lashed exposed flesh with the sting of a whip. The tiny windscreens were no protection. The blizzard was everywhere.

May descended for some minutes, trying to get under the storm, to see where he was going, to search for landmarks in a world of white. Every so often he saw a lake that looked familiar, and so he flew on – doggedly, stubbornly – in what he believed was the right direction. Then, as suddenly as the storm began, it abated enough that he could pick out the shapes of buildings, another lake, and yes, on the shore, a crowd of people looking skyward and waving. Ahead, to the left, was a frozen pond and the unmistakable markings of a landing strip between two rows of cut spruce bows. The ice between the rows had been shovelled clean. They had reached the village of McLennan.

The young pilot circled overhead and touched down. By the time he'd stopped the engine, the plane was mobbed with villagers who had heard of the rescue mission on the radio. The strangers helped them from the cockpit, and someone carried the precious drugs indoors. Two RCMP officers helped tie a tarpaulin over the engine of the Avian, while Horner drained the oil so that it could be taken inside. He did not even have to let it run into a container. The oil ran out on the snow and froze instantly into a black blob, and the blob was then picked up and removed. Inside, both the oil and the two flyers were finally warm again. After a welcome night's rest, the men were ready the next day to continue their mission of mercy. Shortly after dawn, they said goodbye to the McLennan townsfolk who lined the makeshift runway as May took the Avian off. The next stop was Peace River. There were now 300 miles to go.

The final leg of the journey into the north was monotonous and bone-chilling. Mile after endless mile passed beneath the plane. The low hills, the muskeg, and the scrubby trees were coated in snow. On the left, all the way, was the ice-covered Peace River, looking as if it were frozen in time.

Choppy air currents tossed the little plane around, but Horner and May held on, and held course. Down by his feet, Horner could feel the blanket that was wrapped around the drugs, but he had no way of knowing if they were still warm. He was incredibly cold. His face was raw, and he huddled in the cockpit, at times not sure where they were, now and then not even caring.

His partner gripped the controls in hands like claws, tried to navigate as best he could, and prayed that the unbearably long journey would end. He didn't know that just up ahead was a cleared runway, a strip of ice on the Peace, and a community of anxious northerners who feared that help would never arrive. They had not much longer to wait. Finally, sixteen days after Dr. Hamman had sent his message, the people of Fort Vermilion heard a plane overhead. They rushed to the river.

May landed, taxied the plane to where the people were waiting, and cut the motor. He and Horner sat, immobile, frozen, so cold they could not climb out. A pair of husky Mounties stepped forward and clambered up on the side of the cockpit. They grabbed Horner's arms and pulled him upward, then rather awkwardly passed him to others who stood beside the plane. One of the policemen scooped up the drugs from the cockpit floor, and a bystander took them indoors immediately. Already, a fast dog team was being harnessed to rush the medicine the final fifty miles to Little Red River.

When the Mounties were ready to pull May out of the aircraft, they had to first pry his hands from the controls. Inside the RCMP detachment there was warmth, warmth more pleasant than he had ever thought it could be. And food. Horner and May would remain with the Mounties that night. There had been two gruelling days of flying since the plea for help arrived in Peace River, and now, their delivery done, the two men still faced the trip home.

The weather early the next day looked favourable for flying, but by the time a meagre supply of fifteen gallons of gasoline had been put in the tank and the hot oil poured back into the crankcase of the Avian, it was almost mid-morning. There had been a delay in locating fuel, and the little May found was left over from the summer. As he poured it into his plane, he wondered about its quality – yet it was all there was.

Not long after they left Fort Vermilion for the south, the flyers encountered snow squalls and even occasional white-outs. Still they pushed on, because they knew for certain that a landing on wheels, anywhere amid the desolation below, would be fatal. The blowing snow stung their faces and slowly worked its way inside the flight goggles they wore. It swirled into the plane and settled on their arms, knees, and shoulders. Neither man bothered to brush the snow away. They were too weary, too cold, and too miserable. The flight became an endurance feat that seemed interminable. Then somewhere, perhaps a hundred miles out of Peace River, the engine coughed, sputtered a few times, and almost stopped.

May and Horner shook themselves alert and listened to the motor. The sputtering was repeated, so markedly that the little plane lurched in the air, like a car starting in high gear. May sat bolt upright, willing the machine to run. He knew now, as he had suspected at Fort Vermilion, that the gas was bad, probably with water in it.

Every few minutes the choking of the engine would stop, but before the two men could relax, it would resume again. Somehow, the flyers felt less cold as they listened in suspense to their erratic engine. They nevertheless were awfully thankful when they saw the Peace River buildings below. They were even more thankful when they landed, the next day, at Edmonton.

In Little Red River, the medication was literally life to those who were ill. The threat of epidemic diminished, and in the end only the one death occurred. The courage of the returning heroes was lauded in the papers from coast to coast. The *Western Tribune* of Vancouver paid tribute to the men in its January 12 edition:

> The feat, which was nothing more or less than a sublime gamble with death, on an errand of unalloyed mercy, must forever be associated with the great deeds of men since time began. It rivals the heroism of Balaclava and Lucknow. If anything it outshines them. . . .
>
> Had the tiny Avian plane foundered in its flight; had the dauntless aviators met death in the lonely northern wilds, their names would have been enshrined in the hearts of men, women and children all over the world.

As for the dauntless aviators, May and Horner were each given a gold watch and the praise of their peers. Not long afterwards, they flew to California – for a holiday; for the sun; and for a new plane with a closed cockpit.

8

Death in the Snow

Three years after his daring mercy flight to Fort Vermilion, Wop May became the first pilot to use an aircraft for police work in the Canadian North. This time events originated close to the Arctic Ocean. Again they brought May fame from coast to coast, but here the ending of the story was as much a mystery as the vaccine flight's had been a triumph.

The tale began in the summer of 1931, when a secretive and taciturn stranger arrived in the settlement of Fort McPherson, a community located on the east bank of the Peel River, more than 650 miles by air from Yellowknife. The man was a loner, a brusque, rough-hewn man of the wilderness who said little about his past and even less about his plans for the future. He came from America, said some. Others were not so sure; they thought he was from the southern prairies, or possibly the north woods of Ontario, or even from the wilds of New Brunswick. The man had money, money to pay cash for a canoe, supplies, good guns, and ammunition enough to stand off an army – or, as it turned out, several police officers, a few trappers, and a well-equipped and determined posse.

Those who met the stranger said he appeared neither young nor old, in his early forties perhaps, with brown hair and cold, piercing blue eyes. He was of average height, but tough and muscular, supremely confident in his own abilities. He travelled alone, when he wanted and where he wanted. He rarely asked questions and even more rarely gave answers. In short, he was just another oddball in a land of individualists.

Shortly after he first appeared in the far North, an RCMP officer

at Arctic Red River by the name of Edgar Millen decided to check
out the mysterious stranger rumoured to be living in or near Fort
McPherson. And, indeed, that was where Millen found him. The
policeman learned little more than anyone else, either about the
strange man's past or how he happened to be in McPherson, apart
from the information that he intended to go into the Rat River
area, a few miles away, and set up a trap line. He said his name
was Albert Johnson. Millen listened, suspicious about the
stranger, but unable to do anything more. He did tell Johnson that
he would need a licence to trap. There the interview ended. Millen
went on with his work, and in due course Johnson sailed and
portaged down the Peel River to the Rat, where, on a horseshoe-
shaped bend, he intended to build a cabin in the wilderness. For
some time no one heard from him.

But Johnson had been busy. He had selected the spot where he
would live, then set about building a home there. As he was
alone, the job must have been backbreaking in the extreme. He
dragged heavy logs to the site, laid them on top of one another,
and fashioned them into walls for a cabin some eight feet by
twelve feet. The cabin's roof was about five feet high. There was
a small door and one tiny window beside it. The building was
surrounded by water on three sides.

Late that same fall, Indians who normally trapped in the Rat
River area discovered that someone had tampered with their traps:
several had been sprung and hung up on trees. Naturally enough,
the Indians blamed Johnson, the only other person in the immediate area. They reported their suspicions to the Mounties.

Two RCMP officers trudged close to seventy miles to see Johnson
and find out what he had to say for himself. Their trip was a
waste of time. They got to his cabin all right, identified themselves
at the door, saw his face in the window, but were never invited
inside. After two hours' waiting in the cold, they departed. Without a search warrant, the policemen could do no more. Apart
from looking at them, Johnson never acknowledged their presence. His behaviour, the officers decided, would be regarded as
odd almost anywhere, but in the Arctic, such inhospitability was
unknown. The Mounties went to their headquarters at Aklavik to
report the incident and get a search warrant.

A week later, four more policemen made the long trek to the
Johnson cabin. Once again, they identified themselves by shout-

ing from outside, and one of them, Constable A.W. King, walked
to the door, search warrant in hand. He knocked and stood waiting. Smoke curled up from the chimney. Snowshoes were
propped against the front wall.

Without warning, a rifle shot ripped through the door, hit King
squarely in the chest, and threw him backwards into the snow.
His fellow officers were momentarily stunned by the cold-
blooded murder attempt, but their recovery was swift. One of
them fired shots toward the cabin, allowing time for King to get
away from the door. The other two turned to their wounded
friend.

King was placed on a dog sled and, in an incredibly swift
journey, was transported over almost eighty miles of frozen tun-
dra and wilderness terrain to a hospital in Aklavik inside of twenty
hours. Constable King survived.

A couple of days later, several police officers, augmented by
a contingent of trappers and homesteaders, went to Johnson's
cabin to arrest him for attempted murder. The trip was futile.
Johnson refused to budge, although over a period of some eighteen hours he fired several shots at various members of the posse.
The police returned the fire, but the thick-walled cabin remained
as secure as a fortress. The outside temperature was forty degrees
below zero, and a cold moaning wind swept up the Rat and chilled
the lawmen to their core. They spent as much time in a losing
attempt to keep warm as they did dealing with their quarry.

Finally, Inspector A.N. Eames, who commanded the posse,
ordered some sticks of dynamite thawed. This action was
extremely risky; under normal circumstances, no one would dare
place dynamite near a fire. For Eames, however, the situation
was far from normal. A cold-blooded madman was holed up in
relative comfort, while the man he had shot remained in critical
condition in a hospital bed – all because of a dispute over a few
animal traps.

When the dynamite was ready, Eames tossed a stick at the
cabin. The explosive went off, and a puff of smoke drifted away.
Nothing happened. Johnson's lair was undisturbed. A second
stick failed to do more.

The police drew back, discussed their strategy, and thawed
more of the explosives. This time, Eames went as close as he
dared to the cabin, lobbed the makeshift bomb, and dived for

cover. A second later a deafening boom shook the area, dislodged Johnson's roof timbers, and the fortress cabin fell about his shoulders. The lawmen thought they had won.

Two of the Mounties pried the door ajar, certain that if the destruction of his cabin had not killed Johnson, he would at least be too stunned to be dangerous.

They were wrong.

Inside, crouched on the floor, was Johnson, a gun in each hand. An instant later a withering hail of fire came through the door. The two police officers dived for cover and quickly crawled to safety. Not long afterwards, the bitter cold forced the posse to return to Aklavik. Johnson had won.

While the police were attempting to regroup, Eames ordered Constable Millen to go back and keep an eye on the cabin in case Johnson made a run for freedom. A trapper named Carl Gardlund went along.

The two trudged through three days of blizzard to reach their destination, only to determine that Johnson was gone. An Indian runner took this news to Eames, who shortly thereafter led a large posse to the shattered cabin. After several days of trying to locate the elusive Johnson, the posse was disbanded because supplies were becoming scarce. Four men, led by Edgar Millen, remained behind. It was the third week of January, 1932.

After another day or so of painstaking searches, Millen stumbled onto a faint snowshoe trail, heading west. He knew the tracks had to be Johnson's, so he and his men followed them – slowly, carefully, in the bitter cold and half-gloom of that Arctic winter.

Very early in the morning of January 30, the searchers discovered that the tracks led to a gully beside a frozen stream, into a tangle of tree trunks and large, snow-covered boulders. They also heard a man cough.

Millen's group split up, with two men approaching the hideout from either side. They moved forward slowly, a step at a time, in absolute silence. There was no sound except the mournful sawing of the polar wind.

Then Johnson saw them.

The unexpected crack of a rifle shot cut the air like a knife. A 30-30 bullet whizzed past Millen and he ducked for cover. In almost the same instant Gardlund fired into the thicket, at the shadow he knew was the fugitive. There was no answering shot.

The hunters waited, listened, stock-still in the silent wilderness. Half an hour passed, then an hour. Two hours and no movement. At last, they were sure Gardlund's quick shot had found its mark. Millen crept forward.

In a flash, Johnson jumped up, turned his sights on the young police officer, and fired. The two were but a few paces apart. Millen returned the fire, but missed. Johnson's aim was better. Millen was dead before his convulsing body hit the frozen snow.

Gardlund inched across to his friend and slowly dragged the murdered Mountie down onto the ice of the creek. There, safe behind the bank, he alerted his companions. They fired into the thicket, waited in silence, and fired again. But when they crawled closer to the matted hiding place, they saw it was empty. Johnson had disappeared.

"When we received the news that the policeman had been killed, I was asked if our company could spare a plane and a pilot to help with the search," Punch Dickins, May's friendly rival in business and in flying, explains to me many years later. "I sent Wop May up there in a Bellanca. The idea of a plane being used in police work was unknown in those days. As it turned out, the aerial part of the search for Johnson saved the ground parties a lot of time. You could cover in an hour in a plane what would take days on snowshoes."

May flew to Aklavik, despite howling winds, blowing ice pellets, and driving snow. At one point, near Fort Norman, the headwinds were so strong he was blown backwards despite the fact that the throttle was wide open. He eventually reached his destination, only to be grounded by one of the fiercest Arctic blizzards he had ever seen. When the storm ceased, he joined the manhunt. The temperature along the flatlands of the Mackenzie delta was more than $-45°$F.

The pilot's first job in the search was to haul men, ammunition, and food from Aklavik to the police base camps in the Rat River wilderness. This in itself was a tricky and dangerous business.

"In fact one of the greatest handicaps we faced throughout the search would prove to be finding landing grounds in the tangle of hills, box canyons, creeks and rivers,'' wrote May in an article describing his part in the affair. ''We were working continually over a mighty treacherous country where an engine failure made a crash inevitable, and where the slightest error in judgement, landing or getting off, would have meant a crack-up.''[1]

But the search went on and on.

May brought supplies in and occasionally took men out. On one trip, he removed the frozen body of Edgar Millen; at other times he flew frostbitten trackers for medical help in Aklavik. He brought new supplies of ammunition, dog food, and even radio equipment – the first ever used in such a manhunt. And when he was not ferrying supplies, May was searching from the air, always accompanied by two or three others acting as spotters.

On several occasions, the crew in the Bellanca were able to pick up Johnson's trail. In some spots, May brought the plane down almost to the snow surface. At other times, particularly when the snowshoe prints were visible from some distance, he flew much higher. At height, the searchers could quickly see the direction the fugitive was heading.

Just as often as they had some success, the spotters lost the trail, then had to double back and look again and again. Occasionally, Johnson's movement seemed predictable, but then he would move in a wide circle, retrace his tracks, and move on. From time to time he reversed his snowshoes, to give the impression of moving in the opposite direction. Finally, the Bellanca spotters lost their quarry in the windswept peaks of the Richardson Mountains, and they knew the killer was leaving the Northwest Territories and heading for the Yukon. The search moved there.

Meanwhile, the ground tracking continued despite the bitter cold and the frustration of the weary men. They walked for days on end, in the worst weather imaginable, through the formidable snow, ice, and rocky heights of the mountains westward to the Yukon. There, the weather was warmer, but the snow was deeper and the slogging slow.

Finally, the break everyone wanted came.

Johnson's tracks were sighted in the Yukon, and followed southward, amid the loops and whorls of the Eagle River. Here, the Bellanca was invaluable. The snow was deeper and the killer's tracks were visible from the plane. Johnson had a head start on the posse, but, because May could see useful shortcuts from the air and radio to the searchers below, the lawmen on the ground came closer. The posse was closing in.

Halfway around one of the Eagle River bends, Johnson cut back the way he had come, whether by design or chance no one really knew. When he did, he came face to face with several police officers, the first of whom was Sergeant Earl Hersey.

"He was startled when he saw me," explained Hersey. "He put on his homemade snowshoes . . . and started for the bank of the river."[2] Hersey fired one shot and apparently missed. He then knelt on one knee to steady his rifle for a second attempt. That was when Johnson fired, a quick snap-shot that caught Hersey by surprise.

The one bullet hit the policeman's kneecap, ricocheted upwards, and smashed his elbow before lodging in his chest. The impact flipped the big Mountie over backwards and his warm blood soaked the snow. Immediately overhead, Wop May watched the shootout.

"I saw a black speck on the ice in the centre of the stream," he told a reporter later.

> Puzzled, I stared at it for a second. Then perhaps 1,200 feet south of the lone speck I noticed half a dozen other specks spread out at the foot of the steep eastern bank of the river. A movement on the high western bank directed my attention to two more specks standing out clearly against the dead white of the snow background.
> A glinting flash caught my eye. . . .[3]

May circled back, craning his neck as the gun battle played out below him. There were several shots, from both the killer and the police. Finally, Johnson fell.

"When I came back the next time," continued Wop May, "I nosed the Bellanca down until our skis were tickling the snow on the river bottom. Johnson, I could plainly see as I flashed past, was lying face down in the snow, his right arm outflung, grasping his rifle.

"There is something about the way a dead man lies that is unmistakable. . . ."[4]

May landed and, with others at the site, ran to help Sergeant Hersey. He was still alive, but unless he received medical attention soon he would certainly bleed to death. While three or four of his fellow officers worked to stop Hersey's bleeding, May had a chance to have a look at Johnson.

"As I stooped over and saw him," said May, "I got the worst shock I've ever had. For Johnson's lips were curled back from his teeth in the most terrible sneer I've ever seen on a man's face. . . . It was the . . . hard-boiled, bitter hate of a man who knows he's trapped at last and has determined to take as many enemies as he can with him. . . ."[5]

Several men helped lift Hersey into the plane and made him as comfortable as possible for the journey back to Aklavik. The flight was trying for May, as he had to make his way over the mountains in weather that would have been a threat to almost any aircraft, but he arrived safely. Hersey was rushed to surgery, and he slowly but fully recovered.

As for Johnson, the man the newspapers called the Mad Trapper of Rat River was as much a mystery in death as he had been in life. No one knew if Johnson was his real name; no one knew much about his past, and even fewer had any idea where he got the $2,410 in his possession, nor the five pieces of gold dental work found in his pockets. None of the false teeth was his.

After the destruction of his cabin, the RCMP searched the place for clues to his identity. None was found. Some northerners believed his real name was Arthur Nelson because a stranger by that name had been in the North earlier, but they were unable to prove it. As late as 1987, plans were made to exhume his body from its grave in Aklavik so that certain identification tests could be run on it.[6] Even though the hamlet of Aklavik approved the move, the Northwest Territories government refused the request. So whoever he was, and whatever his background, the man the papers called the Mad Trapper would become enshrined in the folklore of the North. His story will undoubtedly outlive all those who were part of it. Wop May was one of them.

9

The Landmark Flights

In the years since John McCurdy lifted the *Silver Dart* off the ice of Bras d'Or, there have been scores of record-making flights within Canada or of interest to Canadians. All were momentous accomplishments at the time, achieved by men and women of exceptional ability, courage, and determination. We sometimes forget that it was the daring flying of these pioneering pilots that made our supersonic age possible. They initiated what we take for granted.

Here are but a few of the landmark flights over the years.

Shortly after the end of the Great War, the *London Daily Mail* announced a prize of £10,000 to the first person to fly the Atlantic, non-stop. In the currency of 1919, the prize was a substantial amount of money indeed, and it quickly attracted four teams of adventurers, all serious contenders for the prize, although it was awarded before the fourth team even took off.

The first two planes to attempt the crossing flew from near St. John's, Newfoundland. The first got farthest – it travelled for fourteen hours before bad weather and an overheating engine made a forced landing in the main shipping lanes necessary. The crew was rescued.

The second aircraft had barely left the field before mechanical failure brought an end to its flight.

The third team of contestants had better luck.

Just before 2:00 p.m. on Saturday, June 14, 1919, Captain John Alcock and Lieutenant Arthur Brown took off from Harbour

Grace, Newfoundland, in a primitive-looking, box-like biplane. Today such a contraption probably would not be given an airworthiness certificate, let alone be the vehicle of choice for a flight across the North Atlantic. In the hands of Alcock and Brown, the machine made a historic performance. Still, the trip was not an easy one.

The two flew out across Conception Bay, passed just north of St. John's, then disappeared in the grey mists over the cold ocean. Their radio failed soon after departure, so for the next sixteen hours no one heard from them; no one knew if they were alive or dead.

Anyone who has either sailed on or flown the Atlantic can visualize the magnitude of that vast, heaving wilderness of water. For two men in an open-cockpit, flimsy flying machine, the 1,800-mile trip must have taken as much courage as the astronauts exhibit today. If there was a storm, they generally had to fly through it. If there were sharp wind gusts, or snow showers, these had to be accepted as part of the situation. There were ships below them at times, but their chances of survival in the event of a crash were minimal. As it was, the plane almost did crash, but not because of the weather.

Sometime during the night, the aircraft stalled and spun dangerously close to the sea before corrections could be made to the fuel mixture. Alcock and Brown were shaken, but they gritted their teeth and flew on. Far ahead, in the mists of morning, they saw a sliver of land. The mists engulfed them again, and they were over Ireland before they realized it.

All around them, the drifting clouds from the sea obscured the land. When the clouds broke, the relief was as welcome as the revealed expanse of green below. They selected what looked like a level field and descended. The field turned out to be one of the innumerable bogs of Western Ireland, flat, covered with short, coarse grass and spongy soil. When the wheels of the plane touched, they skimmed along the grassy terrain, then gradually sank into the peat. Then the aircraft tipped forward on its nose, and, sixteen hours and twelve minutes after it had begun, the journey was over. The Atlantic had been conquered. Alcock and Brown received an audience with King George V at Buckingham Palace, and both were knighted. Sadly, just six months later Alcock was to die in a plane crash.

In 1920, a year after the Alcock-Brown Atlantic flight, the first trans-Canada crossing was made by air. Several planes were involved. All were piloted by Canadian air force flyers who wore civilian clothes because the project was supposed to be a civilian endeavour. The scheme was successful, but it was both dangerous and tiring. Weather was bad, flights were difficult, planes cracked up, and the whole thing involved a good deal of time. In all, the journey took eleven days and twenty-one hours in the air. Fortunately, no one lost his life completing the quest.

Another flight a few years later was better known when it was made and, because of a trophy that commemorates the event, is still known in flying circles today. This was the first seaplane trip across Canada, a journey made by two men, one a Canadian, one an American.

The American was Dalzell McKee, a rich, sports-loving bachelor of thirty-three from Pittsburgh, Pennsylvania. The Canadian who went with him and acted as co-pilot and navigator was Squadron Leader Earl Godfrey, a tough, no-nonsense career officer in the Royal Canadian Air Force. The two men formed an ideal team: both were excellent pilots, and both were born with a natural inquisitiveness and a belief that much could be accomplished if one tackled things in the right way. As time went on, they became fast friends.

The seaplane trip came about almost by accident. McKee had flown in this country often, and on this occasion he was preparing for a trip into the far North when he realized his aircraft was not performing as he thought it should. He took the plane to Montreal for modifications but the manufacturer, Douglas Aircraft in Santa Monica, insisted he return the plane to them for further work. McKee decided to fly first to Vancouver, then follow the Pacific coast to California. Earl Godfrey went along in order to inspect various air stations along the way. They left Montreal shortly after 3:00 p.m. on Saturday, September 11, 1926.

The first stop was Ottawa, where their recently tuned engine was checked again. The next day they went on, but not very far. While the weather in the capital was favourable, only forty miles to the west heavy rains and wind tossed the little plane around, obscured the terrain ahead, and made flying both difficult and dangerous. McKee noticed a railway line, so he dropped almost to tree level and followed it. Then the two men decided to find a lake and wait out the storm. They came down on Lake Traverse, not more than one hundred miles from where they had started that day. A forest ranger put them up in his cabin.

The days that followed were equally rough. The weather was bad, and the wooden floats of the plane had to be pumped out each day. The engine oil had to be heated each morning, and because the machine was water-cooled, it had to be drained to prevent freezing. Fortunately, any of the thousands of lakes across northern Ontario could provide landing places – as long as gasoline was available somewhere close by. As it was, the gas often had to be brought in cans to the plane and poured in by hand. The work was both hard and slow. As often as not, after the plane had been gassed up, the trick engine refused to start. Getting going became a chore.

Yet the two persevered, from lake to lake and river to river. Finally, on September 18, a week after they'd set out, they had reached Lake Wabamun, a long, rather narrow body of water nestled in the slightly rolling country a few minutes' flying time west of Edmonton. Today the lake is ringed with scores of cottages, and hydro-generating plants rise above its surface, but when McKee and Godfrey were there they had little company. The lake itself would become a footnote in aviation history because of their visit.

At about 10:00 a.m. the next day, McKee and Godfrey took off from Lake Wabamun on what would be the first ever non-stop direct flight between Edmonton and Vancouver. The sun was shining, there was little wind, and the engine gave them no trouble. The flying was a delight, as they went through the mountains by way of the Yellowhead Pass, the North Thompson River, and then the Fraser. "When they reached Hope, they could see the waters of the Pacific in the distance, and were overcome with a sense of exhilaration,"[1] wrote one author in describing this historic leg of the journey. By dinner time they were in Vancouver. The trip had been completed successfully.

McKee was always appreciative of the help he had been given by Canadians, and in particular the RCAF, on his record-making flight. As a token of this appreciation, he donated a trophy in his own name to be awarded to the person who had contributed most to aviation in any particular year. The award, called either the McKee Trophy or the Trans-Canada Trophy, now rests in a place of honour in Canada's Aviation Hall of Fame in Edmonton. Its first three winners were Doc Oaks, a veteran bush pilot and, later, the founder of Western Canada Airways; Punch Dickins; and Wop May. As for Dalzell McKee, the trophy was to be his last contribution to aviation history. He was killed in a plane crash in the Laurentians the summer after his record flight. The plane was a Vedette flying boat. He had never flown it before.

Many other Americans visited this country while on record-making flights both before and after McKee's trip.

In 1924, for instance, the men of the United States Army Air Service were here as part of their flight around the world. Four planes left Seattle and flew north through the Rockies and then west by way of the Aleutians to Japan and China. From there they touched down in what is now Pakistan, followed by Austria, Paris, London, and eventually Iceland, Greenland, and Nova Scotia. The final leg of the journey took them across the continent and back to Seattle. Not all of the planes made it back, but the two that did had covered more than 26,000 miles in 175 days. The globe had never been circled before.

At 7:15 on the morning of May 20, 1932, a tousle-headed, outgoing young American woman climbed into a Lockheed Vega at Harbour Grace, Newfoundland. She waved to a clutch of bystanders, started the engine, and within a couple of minutes was airborne. The thirty-three-year-old pilot had crossed the Atlantic as a passenger four years earlier, but this time Amelia Earhart was determined to make the flight alone.

Fourteen hours and fifty-six minutes and 2,026 miles later, a startled farmer near Londonderry, Northern Ireland, looked up from his chores to see an airplane landing nearby. He rushed over to it just as a young woman was climbing out. "I just came over from America," she told him.[2]

The man stared in speechless wonderment at the first woman in history to fly the Atlantic alone. The feat made Earhart the darling of a world sunk in the midst of a depression more crippling than anyone had ever known. And no wonder! The feat had been entirely magnificent – even though the young woman who accomplished it would relish it for all too brief a time. Five years later, Amelia Earhart disappeared in the South Pacific while attempting to fly around the globe.

Charles A. Lindbergh, of course, made the very first solo flight across the Atlantic from New York in 1927. Four years later he came to Canada with his wife Anne while on a round-the-world flight. They travelled north along the coast of Hudson Bay and then to Baker Lake and along the Arctic coast to Alaska.

Archie Hunter, a Hudson's Bay Company trader at Baker Lake, remembers Lindbergh. "I liked him," Hunter told me, "but he could be rather abrasive at times. He always treated me well, though, even when I was climbing all around his plane taking pictures." Hunter, a modest, kind gentleman who has since passed away, wrote of the Lindbergh visit in his memoir *Northern Traders*, published shortly before his death.

> My most vivid recollection of Lindbergh was that he was brusque to the point of rudeness. This gruff manner even extended to his wife who was, in contrast, an exceptionally charming person.
>
> They spent much of their time checking over their airplane. One conversation I overheard went like this:
> "Anne, I want the pliers."
> "Which pliers, dear?"
> "The only damn pliers that are there."[3]

Hunter wrote about the fate of the photos he had taken:

> The Lindbergh flight was a world news event and . . . a news syndicate in Toronto . . . were offering 60 per cent of the world's gross sales of any pictures we could supply. As I had taken about 120 pictures, I set to work and developed the film. A government plane which had been doing survey work . . . was on its way back to The Pas. My negatives were handed over to the pilot and that was the last I ever saw of them. Where they ended up I never did find out. I had kept a couple of the negatives and that's all I got out of it.
>
> It's hard for young people today to realize just what an event that Lindbergh trip was. When our famous guests were

leaving they asked if there was any mail to go out. They promised to have it postmarked at each stop and then mailed when they reached their destination. I hastily scribbled a note to my sister in Scotland telling her that when this arrived she should hang onto it as it was going to be worth something. It had no sooner been delivered when a man was at her door asking if she'd sell it. He must have been from the Post Office.[4]

Another American, Wiley Post, came to Canada several times. In the summer of 1931 he was here twice, within the space of a week, on either end of a frantic flight around the world. That summer he and Harold Gatty circled the globe in eight days and fourteen hours – from New York to New York – by way of Newfoundland (not yet a part of Canada); England; Moscow; Nome, Alaska; and Edmonton. The only night spent on the ground was in Edmonton, where they had to sit out poor weather before continuing. The epic journey brought the flyer world acclaim.

Post came back two years later while on a solo flight around the world, and he returned again in 1935 with American humorist Will Rogers in tow. The media dogged them at every stop, in such places as Dawson and even Aklavik. In Dawson City they toured the town, visited the local radio station, and posed for pictures everywhere they went. More photographs were taken in Aklavik. Then the two men took off and never returned. Both were killed when their plane crashed and came to rest in two feet of water near Point Barrow, Alaska. They were heading for Siberia at the time of the crash.

Canada was also involved, at times rather peripherally, in several other historical flights. In April 1928, three men, one Irishman and two Germans, made the first flight westward over the Atlantic from Dublin, Ireland, to Newfoundland in a Junkers monoplane called the *Bremen*. Two years later, the Australian flyer Charles Kingsford-Smith and his crew made the same flight in their *Southern Cross* to Harbour Grace, and Jimmy Mollison flew solo from Ireland to Pennfield Ridge, New Brunswick, in 1932. The first Canadian to fly the Atlantic was Erroll Boyd from Montreal. He and an American friend, Harry Connor, flew from Newfoundland in a Bellanca to a beach on the Scilly Isles in just under twenty-four hours in October 1930.

But whether it was because of the Boyd flight, or the Lindbergh travels, or the Mollison journey, the world of the 1920s and '30s was shrinking. There were many other air "firsts," of course, and each of these was startling in its time. By 1935 the world which had suffered depression was not far from a world that would be racked by war. When the interlude of peace ended and the guns began to fire again, flying, like everything else – everywhere – would change. Canadians were involved in a manner and with a record second to none. For the next few years, achievements in aviation would be made by the men and women in uniform.

10

Adventure, Heartache . . . and a Chance to See the World

When the Second World War began, there were fewer than 300 aircraft and slightly more than 4,000 personnel in the Royal Canadian Air Force. At least half our planes were old and slow, and many of those who flew them wanted a pension instead of a paycheque. We were poorly equipped for Hitler's war.

In the years after the 1918 armistice, all three services had been allowed to decline. Formed in 1924, with no one to fight, the RCAF had turned to other pursuits: search and rescue, aerial photo mapping, and patrolling in the losing battle against rum-running. There'd been some bombing and air combat practice, but the edge of readiness was just not there. The mood of the services was the mood of the nation: if there was a threat, it seemed remote, of minimal importance, and less than alarming. The Great War was over, and surely its like would never recur.

Few warned of war. Indeed, when Mackenzie King went to Berlin to see Adolf Hitler in the spring of 1937, our prime minister came away believing the Germans wanted peace.

In the weeks that led up to our declaration of war on September 10, 1939, we had begun to strengthen our armed forces. The building would be too little and much too late – we would spend the next six years struggling to produce a war machine, and the years after that trying to pay for what we had built. But, in the beginning, first and foremost, we needed people in uniform.

"I had been at university in Saskatchewan, and after I got my geology degree in 1939 I took a short service commission to learn

91

to fly,'' recalls Bob Norris. "I thought that by combining flying and geology, I would have a future in my field. Later I intended to go back to university and eventually get my Ph.D. However, the war came along and things didn't work out in the way I intended. The next thing I knew I was on a ship at Halifax, heading for England as a pilot in the RCAF.''

Norris was only one of thousands who left his country to go to war. The upheaval of war brought to his life, as to thousands of others', adventure, heartache, lasting friendship, and a chance to see the world – albeit under anything-but-normal circumstances. For some, the circumstances were unpleasant from the very beginning.

"Our ship, the *Duchess of Athol*, was an old, flat-bottomed passenger vessel that would be unsteady in a bathtub. I had never been on the high seas before, and neither had my cabinmate, Chuck Trevena. When he saw that ship, he was pretty unhappy about it. He said, 'I even get sick in a rowboat.' He also suffered from claustrophobia, so he asked if he could sleep in the bottom bunk. It didn't matter to me, so we settled in.

"The next morning when I wakened, Chuck was standing at the sink shaving. He said good morning to me, and then added: 'My God, this thing rolls. I know I'm going to be sick on this trip.' At the time I couldn't detect any movement, but Chuck was sure the ship was rolling badly. He was swaying back and forth as he talked. Anyway, I went over and opened the porthole and, hell, we were still in Halifax Harbour.

"Chuck then announced: 'Okay, that's it.' He dropped the razor, climbed back into bed, and stayed there for the entire seven days of the crossing. I brought him all his meals and looked after him.

"As we were sailing to England, we knew the Allies had been badly trounced by the Germans in the period leading up to Dunkirk. We actually thought it would be a hell of a good idea just to turn around and go back. Everyone thought the Germans would be in England in no time. However, we went on, of course, and landed at Liverpool on June 15, 1940.''

Jack Wells was born in Liverpool, but had gone with his parents to Saskatchewan in the November that he turned four. "I was raised on the prairies,'' he explains, "after I got over the shock

of arriving there from England in my short pants so late in the
fall.

"When I turned eighteen, in 1940, I joined the Air Force with
the intention of becoming a mechanic. Actually, I was trained as
a mechanic at a mental hospital the Air Force had taken over in
St. Thomas, Ontario. A year later I was back in the West working
on Bolingbrokes, Fairey Battles, Ansons, and so on. I wanted to
be a pilot, but we all knew you had to be God to be a pilot, but I
remustered anyway, and found that it was true, you did have to
be God.

"I was accepted, took my training, and some while later got
my wings. As a newly minted officer, I was one of many who
were sent to Halifax to wait for a ship to take us overseas. At that
time, however, the wolf packs were torpedoing the convoys off
the east coast, so they sent us down to Taunton, Massachusetts,
to an American Army camp. Finally we were told we would go.

"The ship that took us was the *Queen Elizabeth*, and we
boarded her in New York. At the time I weighed about 125
pounds, and as an officer I had a big suitcase, a haversack, and
a kit bag. I remember standing on the dock beside the ship and I
thought it was at least twenty-seven storeys high.

"They were filling her from the bottom up, and as my name
started with a letter at the end of the alphabet, I was in the last
group to go on board. After an entire day travelling to the ship,
and then waiting to get on it, I was so tired I could hardly drag
all my belongings up the ramp and then up all the levels to my
cabin. But I was lucky. I only had to share space with half a dozen
guys. The chaps at the bottom were jammed twenty or more
together. In all, there were over 12,000 American servicemen on
board, and 300 Canadians.

"We did not get along too well with the Americans because
they were never sure just who we were. For example, if they
wanted to take over an area, a lounge or something, they just
announced that it was the location of a meeting, with only Americans involved. They simply took all the seats and the rest of us
either sat on the floor or left. I got sick sitting up, so sitting on
the deck was okay.

"There were boat drills, of course, with life jackets. On my
first of these, I asked another guy where my muster station was.

'The same place it was on the last drill at four this morning,' he replied. After the travelling and the suitcase-carrying, I had slept through the entire drill. If we had been torpedoed, I would have sunk with the ship.

"They fed us twice a day; for me it was ten o'clock breakfast and eight o'clock dinner. Being near the end of the alphabet helped here because I could sleep in every day. We were able to use the officers' lounge, so that was pleasant, particularly so because there were 300 American nurses on board and we got along quite well with them."

Another of Canada's pilots who went overseas and distinguished himself during the Second World War and after was a young, clean-cut kid who grew up during the Depression in Victoria, British Columbia. His name was Reg Lane.

"My father was an engineer at the dock yard in Victoria," Lane says, "and he wanted me to go into the navy. However, I wanted the air force instead, so I applied there soon after the war started. It was not until May 1940 that I got anywhere, though. I had my medical but was put on hold until that September. The British Commonwealth Air Training Plan had been under way for some time and they had more recruits for air-crew training than they could handle.

"I went through the normal pilot air-crew training in Regina, Vancouver, and Dauphin, Manitoba. We were among the first at Dauphin, and at the same time there were no blacktop roads, but there was lots of mud. We were slogging around in flight boots, and the mud covered them. It was a terrible mess.

"I had trained in Harvards, but I asked for bombers – and for no good reason. That was why, as soon as I got to England, they sent me to an Operational Training Unit [OTU] where I learned to fly the Whitley bomber, a real flying cow, a lumbering old aircraft that took off at 110 miles per hour, climbed at 110 miles per hour, and stalled at 110 miles per hour.

"I was almost killed on my first night flight at the OTU, and I wasn't sure if I was ever going to actually be in the war. I was coming in for a landing in this bloody big Whitley, with just flare pots for guidance. We were controlled at the time by an Aldis lamp at the end of the runway. There was no radio, of course. Anyway, as we came down, we received a red light, or a wave-off, from the controller with the lamp. This meant overshooting because I was on final and down to about 200 feet.

"I opened the throttle and started the undercarriage coming up. The procedure was for the second pilot, or whoever was in the right-hand seat, to bring up the wing flaps, in short steps, and not all at once. But when I said 'flaps up,' he was close to panic, I guess, and he brought the flaps up all at once.

"That just about stalled the airplane and we were falling out of the sky. The only way to recover was to slap the flaps down again very quickly, which I did. By this time, the engine is wide open and roaring like crazy, and the undercarriage is just coming up. That was when this character froze on the control column. I was having a hell of a time just trying to fly the aircraft. Finally, in sheer desperation, I hit him across the mouth and nose with the back of my hand. This forced him to let go of the controls, and now I was able to fly the plane. I came around, landed, and refused to ever fly with that man again. He was an absolute menace!"

Jim Edwards was a kid in his last year of high school in Battleford, Saskatchewan, when the war began. He tried to enlist in the air force right away, but was finally called in October 1940. In his biography of Edwards, J.P.A. Michel Lavigne writes: "Up until then, young Edwards had never driven a car; he had never seen the cockpit of an airplane, or even stepped within a hundred yards of one. But he was determined to become a pilot."[1]

This man, who would later be better known as Stocky Edwards, would have an admirable flying career ahead of him – after he learned the trade in such places as Edmonton; Brandon, Manitoba; and Yorkton, Saskatchewan.

Leaving home was not easy.

"The railway platform was crowded with relatives and friends saying goodbye to their loved ones. As the train slowly began to pull out of the station one of the troops, who had a beautiful tenor voice, began to sing 'I'll Be Seeing You.' He sang it with such feeling that the result was contagious and almost catastrophic,"

Jim recalls years later. "Everyone on the platform joined in. As the train pulled away into the night, there were many men with tears in their eyes and sobs in their throats."[2]

Edwards sailed to Europe on a converted merchant ship, along with hundreds of Australians. In England he began training on Hurricanes near Newcastle.

Buzz Beurling was born George Beurling, on December 6, 1921, in Verdun, Quebec. He was brought up within the confines of a religion known as the Exclusive Brethren, a small, very strict sect where Bible study, Sunday worship, and absolute adherence to the dictates of the faith were expected. With such a background, it is surprising, to say the least, that the man would become one of the top ten fighter pilots in the Allied cause during World War II.

Beurling had little formal education, although he did have a facility with languages. After he learned to fly he even studied German on his own so that he could understand what German pilots were saying on the radio during air battles. He felt that if he knew what they intended, he would have an advantage in fighting them. He learned Italian for the same reason.

Even though he spent hours and hours hanging around airfields, Beurling's limited education prompted the RCAF to turn down his request to become a fighter pilot. The Royal Air Force was not as particular, however, and accepted him for pilot training. He flew a variety of aircraft, from the trainer called a Miles Master, to the Hawker Hurricane, to the Spitfire, undoubtedly the finest fighter aircraft in the world in its time. His first air combat was on Christmas Day, 1941. Apparently this first taste of fighting was less than he expected: when asked about it, he replied that it had been as "exciting as Toronto on Sunday."[3] The boy with the puritanical beliefs must have been bored indeed.

Violet Milstead was a builder's daughter in Toronto who, in her free time, worked at her mother's wool shop on north Yonge Street. As a teenager, Violet had already decided she wanted to fly someday.

"One afternoon," she recalls, "I was watching a high school

football game when a small airplane 'shot up' the field. This was probably in the autumn of 1936, when the Great Depression was becoming old and grey and tired, but was still hanging on. I never learned who the pilot was or where he came from. I also never learned whether or not he was reported for low or dangerous flying. But I owe him much. The sight of that airplane diving on the field, racing across it, then departing in a long, graceful, climbing turn gave me a thrill I have never outgrown. I decided, then and there, that I would fly.''

Milstead began saving money, a little at a time, for the flying lessons she knew would come. She went to ground school for a couple of hours a week and then, finally, the day came for her first-ever trip in a plane. This was from the long-gone Barker Field on Dufferin Street in Toronto. For her, flying was fun. It ''confirmed everything I had dreamed,'' she says today. ''As soon as the airplane's wheels left the ground, just as the earth began to fall away, I felt alive in a way I had never before imagined.'' She was nineteen at the time.

In due course, Milstead obtained her private pilot's licence, her commercial licence, and, a few months later, her instructor's rating. By this time, the British Commonwealth Air Training Plan was in operation and the need for military pilots became acute. Civilian flying training ceased.

Another young woman who was flying in Toronto at this time became and remained a close friend of Milstead's. Her name was Marion Orr, and today she is one of the few women to have been inducted into Canada's Aviation Hall of Fame in Edmonton. When World War II began, however, she was still a starry-eyed teenager who flew and flew because she loved to do so. And this love would lead her, along with Milstead, to England where they joined the Air Transport Auxiliary.

''The ATA was a paramilitary organization of civilian pilots who, because of age or other reasons, were unfit for military service,'' Milstead explains. ''Their principal work was ferrying military airplanes within Great Britain wherever and whenever required. Mostly, this meant flying fighting aircraft from factories to maintenance units where they would have radios and guns installed, from the maintenance units to the operational squadrons, and back again when extensive repairs were needed. This released large numbers of military pilots for combat.''

"Vi found out about the ATA somewhere," laughs Marion Orr today, "so we two adventurers decided to fly away with them. First we were sent to Montreal, and we waited there to get sent overseas. The wait seemed so long that there were times when we thought we would be in Montreal forever. I remember two things about the city at that time: the shopping and the cold. It was in the late winter, and it seemed as if the wind off the St. Lawrence was determined to go right through you. There were lots of guys around, of course," says Orr, her eyes twinkling. "We had a great time for a while, but finally we were on our way."

The two young women arrived in England on May 9, 1943.

In the weeks leading up to the German invasion of Poland, a young Polish air force fighter pilot named Jan Zurakowski was attending officer's school in his home country. He had been flying for some time, and had become a fighter pilot because he had been told that fighters were the flying elite. "Lots of people will probably dispute that," he admits today, "but when I was asked what I wanted to fly, I asked for fighters. I remember that some of my friends tried to talk me out of it, though, because they thought the day of the fighter was over. I told them they were crazy."

Young Zurakowski finished his education in Lublin, and went to the air force from there. He had dreamed of flying since he was a small boy. As a teenager, he flew gliders, once remaining aloft for more than fifteen hours on one flight. When the war came along, he was well prepared for his calling. Unfortunately, his country was not. When Hitler's Blitzkrieg rolled across so much of Europe, Poland fell, but despite the loss of 333 aircraft and hundreds of pilots, many got out before the ultimate collapse. Zurakowski was one of them. He spent time in Rumania, then went by ship to Beirut, and finally arrived in England in the summer of 1940, just as the Battle of Britain was about to begin.

Gerry Bell was a bomber pilot during the Second World War, but he had already been flying recreationally and commercially for ten years when war came. The Hamilton, Ontario, native had intended to become a doctor, and no doubt his father, who was a foreman at National Steel Car Company, wanted the same thing. But neither as yet understood the lure of the air.

"I was home for the summer from the University of Western Ontario," he explained to me in an interview from his hospital bed shortly before his death in January 1989. "I had a summer job, of course, because we didn't have much money. But one day I was walking along the street and a plane flew over. I stopped and stood, just stood, looking at it and kind of dreaming in the daytime. The plane landed not too far away, so I went and asked how much for a ride.

"A bit later on, when I saved some money, I started spending it on flying lessons. I didn't let on to my parents because I knew they would never approve. The plane I learned on was an old Tiger Moth biplane, and I used to hitchhike out to Mount Hope Airport to fly."

Bell got his licence in 1929, and for him personally his dream almost ended a day or so later.

"I was at home one afternoon," he said in the rapid staccato speaking voice he used when warming to a good story, "and the doorbell rang. I looked out a window and saw these two big guys standing there. They had rumpled grey suits and hats, and they looked pretty stern. I'm thinking to myself 'they're cops,' but I couldn't think of what I'd done. Anyway, my mother opened the door and one guy says: 'Does Gerry Bell live here?' I'm sure my mother was close to a heart attack, but she managed to tell them I did. 'We're from the newspaper and we want to interview him about getting his pilot's licence,' the other guy told her. My mother started to tell them they must have the wrong Gerry Bell when I came to the door. I told them I was the guy they wanted and, yes, I did have my licence. My mother didn't know what to say. That was how my parents learned I'd been flying."

Bell did the interview, and his parents, even though they now knew he would probably never become a doctor, admired him and gave him their support. The reporters had the right Gerry Bell, and they got the story they wanted. It was the story of the first black man in Canada to become a pilot.

One of the many other Canadian pilots to fly in World War II, Gordon "Robbie" Robertson, descended from some of the earliest settlers on Vancouver Island. His path to the cockpit of a plane was long, laborious, and unlike that of many of his peers. "I was born in Cumberland, B.C., in 1916," he says. "When I was sixteen, I began working in the coal mines there at fifty cents an hour for an eight-hour day. I stayed at this for almost seven years, but when it looked as though war was coming, I paid my own way to England and joined the RAF as a flight mechanic. I was there all during the Battle of Britain and after, and then I got the idea I would like to be a pilot.

"I was married by this time," he points out, "and my wife was an English girl. The Powers That Were decided I would have to be shipped either to South Africa or back to Canada to learn to fly, so I naturally chose Canada. I had to leave my wife in England because wives were not allowed to come over at that time. This was in 1942.

"I was shipped to Alberta for training, and, when I could, I would try to get home. One thing that stands out in my mind was the fact that I was broke all the time.

"One of my good friends at Medicine Hat was a guy named Arthur Hailey. He was an ambitious fellow, even then, and as we lived in the same building, we became good friends. I flew a lot with him, both in Medicine Hat and at Lethbridge."

Contacted in the Bahamas during research for this book, the best-selling novelist says he well remembers those days in the Canadian West when he and Robertson were learning to fly. He had joined the RAF in England, but did not have the education to be a pilot. His wife, Sheila, takes up the story in her book about her marriage to Hailey.

His shorthand and typing, however, eventually tunneled him to a desk job and soon after, as a corporal, he was working as a clerk to the station administration officer – an elderly wing commander who loved nothing better than to fly. He loathed the time he had to spend in his office. Desk work has always been child's play to Arthur and he took over more and more chores – reading the mail, typing the letters in reply and presenting them as a *fait accompli* for his superior's signature.

The wing commander was delighted with this bright young chap who relieved him of so much time-wasting office work.

He relied on Arthur more and more. Some days he barely glanced at letters he was signing – until one day his assistant overreached. Arthur had typed the wrong answer to one of the incoming letters and it went out, signature and all, to the commanding officer. The wing commander was in deep trouble. How could he admit that it was his clerk whose judgment was in question?

He admonished Arthur with a never-to-be-forgotten line: "Yes, Hailey . . . you're clever all right . . . but in a *night school* sort of way."[4]

Hailey still wanted to fly, and, after the RAF lost so many of its pilots, academic standards were lowered and he was given the chance he so desperately wanted. The RAF sent him to Americus, Georgia, to be trained by the United States Air Force. Sheila Hailey continues:

Right from the beginning, he was chronically airsick. The students flew in open-cockpit planes – Stearman PT-17s – and wore heavy flying jackets. Each time Arthur put his on, the smell of stale vomit on the sheepskin collar wafted up to his nose, making him queasy even before climbing into a plane. Occasionally, he'd have to wash out the entire cockpit to clean up the mess. Airsickness slowed his progress in learning and he failed his first flight check. He was bitterly disappointed, because this automatically disqualified him from further training.

He was sent from the U.S. to a personnel depot in Nova Scotia, Canada, and from there to western Canada and, miraculously, another crack at flying. In a confidence only given pillow-to-pillow, he told me, "A strong recommendation from my flying instructor reached my new posting. He said anyone who had spilled as much of his guts as I had, and then had some left over, should be allowed to take the course again."

Occasional airsickness continued, but Arthur adjusted to it, finished his training successfully, and became a sergeant-pilot in 1943. Later that year he was commissioned. He reminisces: "That was another turning point in my life. When I entered the Officers' Mess, I encountered a new world. From that day on, no one ever asked what my education was or where I went to school. It was assumed because I was an officer I was an educated person."[5]

Hailey was subsequently transferred to England, where he embarked on what he describes today as an "unadventurous and unspectacular" flying career.

The same cannot be said of the flying career of Len Birchall, one of Canada's real heroes of the Second World War. Birchall was born in St. Catharines, Ontario, and like so many men and women who went on to become pilots, was fascinated by airplanes from his earliest youth.

"When I was a kid, we had a little grass-strip airfield just outside of town, and I went there as often as I could – just to watch. But then when I got to be fifteen or sixteen or so, they would let me do odd jobs, cleaning up the place, or washing planes. I wasn't paid in cash, but in air time. I'd get to fly for five minutes or so, for so much work done. Then, with some paper-route money, I would buy another few minutes. I eventually got up to five hours there."

Birchall went from high school to the Royal Military College in Kingston and subsequently was sent to Trenton, where he got his wings and his commission.

"There were thirteen in my class," he says today, "and we were the only thirteen who became pilots in the entire air force that year. Actually, my officer number is 775, so up until the time I got there, the RCAF only *had* 774 officers before me.

"I can still remember my first solo. It was thrilling – as it is for anyone the first time, I suppose. There was this tremendous exhilaration and then the great fear of whether you were going to get the damned thing down."

There were flying boats at Trenton in those years just prior to the outbreak of World War II, and Len Birchall began flying them. The pilots sat side by side, hooked to the floor of the aircraft by a cable. Up in the front was an observer who was not even strapped in. The plane had an open cockpit.

"These were the old Vickers Vedettes, and we operated on the Bay of Quinte. Up until that time, they had been used in the North, for aerial photography and so on, and as patrol aircraft. I enjoyed flying them."

Birchall finished his training at Trenton and then went to Dartmouth; to the Gaspé; back to Trenton; to Rivers, Manitoba; and then to Winnipeg, where he flew senior officers on inspection tours. Eventually, he would go away to war – a war that was to test his stamina, his courage, and his inner resolve in a way that few Canadians were ever tested.

But Birchall was not alone. World War II changed everyone who was involved in it. That included all those who flew.

11

The Wings of War

Twenty-four hours before Bob Norris walked down the gangplank at Liverpool on June 15, 1940, goose-stepping soldiers of the Third Reich had marched into Paris. The fall of the City of Light was a terrible blow to the Allied cause, and fears of a similar fate for London became acute. In Britain, home defences were strengthened, slit trenches were dug, anti-aircraft batteries were tested, and shopgirls practised wearing gas masks. Thousands of children, particularly the children of the poor, were placed on lorries and trains and taken to country accommodation where German bombs were less likely to fall. In an untold number of ways, the great island nation prepared itself, and watched for something that might be worse than death. The wait was brief.

On July 10, 1940, the Battle of Britain began.

As far as can be determined today, there were 103 Canadian pilots involved in the Battle of Britain,[1] one of whom was Bob Norris.

"I started out as an Army Co-Operation pilot," Norris explains, "flying Lysanders. The job was enjoyable but it was not terribly exciting. Then one day some of us were asked if we wanted to transfer to fighters. The RCAF #1 Fighter Squadron based at Northolt had lost pilots and they needed replacements. Four of us from my squadron volunteered to go. I took the course on Hurricanes and reported soon after."

Northolt was on the north-west outskirts of London. The flying field was a well-camouflaged grass strip that, from the air, looked as if it had a river running through it. The planes had nets over them so that they, too, would be hard to see from above. The

Canadian squadron there had acquitted itself well against the Germans – indeed, it had been the first RCAF squadron to engage the enemy. The place was busy.

"We were on the go pretty well all the time," recalls Norris, "and even though we could get into London easily, there just wasn't time. We were either flying or we were sleeping, and we needed everyone we had."

The daily routine was hectic for the Northolt pilots. They were up at 4:00 a.m., had breakfast in the mess, and reported to the dispersal hut immediately afterwards. There were a few cots there, and often it was possible for the pilots to grab a few minutes of fitful sleep, even though they were wearing flight suits and ready to go.

"When the siren went, we were out the door," Norris continues. "This was generally a bit after seven. Our ground crews were already at the planes, so we just had to climb into the cockpit, get strapped in, and go. The guys on the ground were so good, they could have us in the air within two and a half minutes of the time the siren went. I have the greatest memories of and respect for them. Those ground crews were absolutely wonderful – always. And they have never really been thanked.

"Generally, twelve aircraft took off together, and we flew a V formation in those days, mainly in groups of three. I found this hard for a while, as I had really little training in formation flying. Hell," Norris says with a laugh, "the only formation flying I ever had was flying line astern under the Bristol Bridge. You'd be shot for doing that today.

"Once we engaged the enemy, we'd break off," he says. "Our job was to get the German bombers, and the Spits looked after their fighters. We tried to climb to 20,000 feet or so in order to get the drop on Jerry. This was because the Germans staggered the height of their bombers. The Spitfires were up at 30,000 feet or so."

Other pilots in other places also found that the war was a kind of coming of age for them, a time when each takeoff could well have been the last.

With Battleford, Saskatchewan, far behind him, Stocky Edwards became a war hero above the sands of North Africa. He flew 195 operational sorties with the RAF there, and was officially credited with destroying twelve enemy planes in the air and as many on the ground. He also made other successful kills in Germany and Italy. Edwards, who became a Wing Commander at age twenty-three, came home from the war with a chestful of decorations, among them the prestigious Distinguished Flying Medal and the Distinguished Flying Cross. He won the latter twice.

But Edwards was not the only Canadian fighter pilot who won several decorations in the air.

Buzz Beurling won his glory in the skies over Malta. In one two-week period he shot down twenty-seven aircraft and won the Distinguished Service Order, the Distinguished Flying Cross, and the Distinguished Flying Medal. He later received a bar to the DFM when it was awarded to him a second time. By the end of the war, he was the leading Canadian air ace. Unfortunately, he was killed in an air crash in Rome in 1948.

The fighters were in the air five and six times a day, for days, and toward the end, utter fatigue set in. Jan Zurakowski arrived in England following the fall of Poland, with the knowledge that his homeland was under Hitler's control. He was particularly anxious to do everything in his power to thwart the Germans.

"I was twenty-six at the time," he says, "and that was older than the average. If a guy was thirty, he was an old man. My English was not good then, and I had a hard time because of it."

Zurakowski was a Spitfire pilot, and a good one – but his not-so-good English made radio communications very difficult. The radio had a manual adjustment, and all pilots had to have the volume loud enough to hear ground control over the noise of the engine.

"I would be flying along, with the volume turned up, trying to figure out whatever was being said from the ground. Because the volume was up, another pilot breaking radio silence was like an explosion in my ears. But even though I generally could not tell what was being said, I knew that when the voices sounded excited the Germans were near. Then I just switched the radio off and got ready."

Zurakowski was based at Middle Wallop for some time, and from there flew in the defence of the Portsmouth-Southhampton area. He had several close calls, and his Spitfire was shot up on five separate occasions. One of them resulted in the loss of the plane.

"One day I was attacking a formation of Dornier 17s over

Portsmouth, but they got me instead. My tail was badly damaged and I had no use of either the ailerons or the rudder. Because I could not control the plane, I bailed out. This was at 18,000 feet or so.''

As Zurakowski left his aircraft, the machine began falling in tight circles around him. The free fall spun him around, tore his breath away, and once or twice almost swept him into the path of the plummeting plane. He escaped death by inches.

''Each time the plane brushed near me,'' he says, ''I was afraid to open the damned chute. I knew if I did the plane would likely get tangled in the chute and finish me off.

''Finally, when I was so low I knew I would die *unless* I opened the parachute, I pulled the cord. The plane hit the ground with a great racket, and I hit a second later. It was that close. The plane did not catch fire.

''Almost beside me was an old gentleman holding a shotgun. He was Home Guard or something, and he was terrified. I'm sure the crash scared him, and now he didn't know whether I was a German who would kill him or not. He looked at me and then asked if I spoke English. Imagine! The way I spoke English at the time would not help. He would likely think I was a German who was *trying* to speak English.'' Zurakowski laughs now at the man's predicament. ''I decided he was too scared to shoot me,'' the pilot adds.

''I took out my identity card and tried to hand it to him, but he couldn't take it. His hand was shaking too much. Fortunately, a young lieutenant showed up in a car and the standoff ended. I was driven back to the base. I felt sorry for that poor old man, though. He could have had a heart attack.''

When Reg Lane first met one of his commanding officers in England, the man looked as if *he* had had a heart attack.

''Shortly after I had completed my training in the OTU in England, I was posted to #35 RAF Operational Squadron. When I arrived there, I got in late in the afternoon, checked into the mess, got my room allocated, and so on. The next morning, fairly early, I went down to the flight line and walked into the flight office. I wanted to get to know who my flight commander was, and look around a bit.

"But when I walked into the Flight Commander's office, I found the guy unconscious, sprawled across his desk. At first I thought he was ill; then I decided he was drunk. I thought to myself, 'My God, I have a drunk for a Flight Commander,' and I wondered what kind of a place this was going to be.

"Anyway, I shuffled my feet and coughed a couple of times, and this body finally sat up. He looked at me, rather bleary-eyed, and then apologized. 'I'm sorry,' he said, 'I'm writing a book and I have a deadline with my publishers. It's only four weeks away and I still have a lot to do. I have been writing all night and I guess I fell asleep. I'm sorry.'

"Well, I stood there, not knowing what to say. Here I was, a brand-new pilot officer and I was talking to a squadron leader. The man was the famous Leonard Cheshire, vc, and I was quite ill at ease.

"We shook hands, and he asked if I had ever flown in a Halifax. I told him I hadn't, so he said he would take me up for a flip. He called another member of the squadron, and it was decided we would do a formation takeoff.

"We got into the airplane, and Cheshire was going to format on this other fellow, a Flight Lieutenant Wilkinson. We taxied out. Wilkinson opened up, Cheshire opened up, and we went charging across this grass airfield.

"I don't know what happened, but Wilkinson cut his power a bit sooner than he should have, just after getting airborne. We were tucked in under him and were about to overtake him. In order to avoid a mid-air collision, Cheshire cut power very severely, and we dropped about fifteen feet, hit the ground with an awful bump, and bounced back into the air again. I was sure we were going to stall and crash, and I decided this would likely be my first and last flight in a Halifax, because I was sure we'd be dead soon.

"We broke formation, of course, and I pulled the undercarriage up. But then we had a warning light indicating that it wasn't up on one side. We tried to put it down again, but the light was still on. We knew then that when the plane hit the ground the under-carriage must have been damaged.

"Cheshire decided he would come around and land, which he did – on one wheel. We did a wild ground loop around the field, tearing up dirt and finally coming to a stop. There was no fire, but Cheshire was furious at himself for pranging a perfectly new airplane. I was just thankful to walk away from it.''

Lane remained with 35 Squadron and did his first tour of operations from there. All of his trips were dangerous, but some were more gut-wrenching than others.

"We did two daylight raids on Brest in early 1942, and we were pretty badly shot up. The Spitfires that were to escort us had only enough range to get about halfway across the Channel, so from there on we were on our own. On the way back the squadron commander had to ditch because his plane was so badly damaged. The air-sea rescue launches were able to reach him.''

Later that same year Lane was involved in low-level attacks on the *Tirpitz*, the great German battleship which at the time was tied up in a Norwegian fiord. Because of the topography of the area, bombing runs were virtually suicidal. The planes had to come in low and get their bombs away before being obliterated by the enemy or piling up on the steep slopes of the fiord itself. At least one 750-pound bomb penetrated all the decks of the ship, yet she remained afloat.

"That exercise was deadly," Lane admits today. "There were three attacks. We took twelve crews in there and we had only four left when it was all over. I was only able to do two of the three attacks because my plane had been blasted all to hell by twenty-millimetre shells, which had even cracked the main spar. We were very lucky to get out at all, and there was no possibility of going in the third time. My plane just would not have taken the load.

"In the summer of 1942, just after I had finished my first tour, the Pathfinder Force was formed. Our squadron was chosen to be a part of it, so we went down south to begin the training. Ordinarily I would have been posted to an Operational Training Unit, but I received permission to go with the squadron.

"The Pathfinders were, as the name indicates, the people who would lead the way to the target, and mark it for the main force of bombers that was coming in behind. The aiming point for the bombers would be marked with various types of coloured pyrotechnics. We were supposedly chosen because of our experience.''

Reg Lane is modest and low-key when talking about the two tours he did with Pathfinders, undoubtedly one of the most dangerous and nerve-racking types of work imaginable. These men went in over Occupied Europe, flying long distances in terrible weather; battling enemy fighters and flak from ground defences, not to mention personal crises, loneliness, fatigue, and bitter cold; coping with mechanical deficiencies and the ever-present chance of being lost, shot down, burned alive, or maimed for the rest of their days. Yet because of the Pathfinders' work, Allied bombing improved considerably. "A number of those flights were pretty hairy," is about all Lane will say concerning this work. That he was a squadron leader at age twenty-two and had won both the Distinguished Service Order and the Distinguished Flying Cross speak to both his skills and his courage. He was also one of the few selected to be part of a Pathfinder Force Training Unit, the elite of the elite, who flew with Pathfinder pilots and trained them on the job – in the flak-filled darkness over the burning cities of the Nazi empire.

There were some 20,000 Canadians who were Bomber Command aircrew during the Second World War. They flew with Englishmen, Americans, Poles, Norwegians, Australians, New Zealanders, Dutchmen, and a host of other nationalities. They endured hardship and faced sudden and terrible death. Don Charlwood, an Australian navigator who trained in Canada, believed that the men he flew with accepted their lot with a stoicism that was remarkable: "After a time the most timid of men can become accustomed to the most threatened of lives. We became accustomed to seeing planes disintegrate beside us and to learn on our return that in them were probably men we had known and admired; we even became accustomed to the idea that . . . home was a place for which we could afford no longings."[2] The loneliness was pervasive.

Charlwood continues.

"Against the roar of climbing revs our voices sound distant and unreal, as though, instead of sitting close together we were separated by many miles in the outer emptiness. Out of the east night is rising, majestic and overwhelmingly lonely. Jupiter hangs pale above us. We are England's no longer, but creatures of the void. About the edges of our consciousness lap waves from our other life, memories of places and persons and spoken words. Even as

I glance out at the chill host of stars, I see with another eye the faces of those very far away, further away in time and spirit than the stars themselves.''[3]

But the pilots and those who flew away with them were not the only ones who were lonely. At home in New Zealand, in Canada, in Poland, or even on the airfield itself, there were many others, who waited, hoped, and prayed for a safe return. Among them were those in the uniform of the Women's Auxiliary Air Force.

> At the end of the runway
> The WAAF corporal lingers,
> Nervously threading
> A scarf through her fingers.
>
> Husband? Or Lover?
> Or friend for a night?
> Her face doesn't tell
> In the dim evening light.
>
> The Squadron is airborne
> But still the WAAF lingers,
> Nervously threading
> A scarf through her fingers.[4]

In far-away Toronto, in Regina, and in Charlottetown, young recruits were singing a ribald ditty with few clean verses, one of which went:

> Around her leg she wore a purple garter
> She wore it in the springtime and in the month of May
> And if you ask her why the hell she wore it
> She wore it for an airman who was far, far away.[5]

The theme of waiting was everywhere, and many of those with loved ones waiting never returned.

For every one of the thousands of Canadians in the Second World War, there is a story. Many of the stories are now long forgotten. But by the end of the war, we had the world's fourth-largest air force, and the tales out of it are legion. Douglas Harvey, a Canadian bomber pilot, in his book *Boys, Bombs and*

Brussels Sprouts, recalls that crippled aircraft always had priority on landing, whether after a fight over Germany or a short training trip to the Devon coast.

> One dark and miserable morning a pilot called the control tower just as I was entering the final landing leg. I had the wheels and flaps down when I was told to overshoot. I poured on the power and yanked the wheels up before asking the tower why.
>
> "We have an aircraft on three engines," the controller said. A moment later another voice called the tower asking permission to land. The tower told him, "We have an aircraft on three engines. He has priority."
>
> The pilot shot back with, "Well, I've only got two engines."
>
> Immediately the tower gave him number one position, and directed the poor bastard on three engines to stand by. I watched, fascinated, as a Wellington bomber landed. A Wellington aircraft *had* only two engines![6]

Harvey also tells the story of an eighteen-year-old farm boy from Moosomin, Saskatchewan, whose disdain for military regulations was appreciated by those closest to him. Ken Davidson was his name, and, according to Harvey, the kid's uniform

> was mostly his own creation – usually a thick turtleneck sweater, no tie, and battledress with the blouse open. Rarely did he wear his hat, and he often wore brown leather loafers in lieu of the standard black oxfords. He did do something about the shoes by dabbing on a small amount of black polish. Which fooled no one.
>
> Late for briefing one afternoon, he was running full tilt past the station headquarters when he was stopped by a roar coming from a ground floor window.
>
> "You there, that man!" roared the voice. "Stop where you are!" Davidson stopped. A form flung the window wide open and stepped through onto the grass. A Wing Command staff officer, British, and very correct, marched up to the puzzled Davidson.

"Where is your tie, sergeant?" he barked.

"I don't know, Sir."

"Where is your shirt, sergeant?"

"I don't know, Sir."

"Where is your hat, sergeant?"

"I don't know, Sir."

Then staring down at Davidson's shoes, the Wing Commander bellowed, "By God, those are brown shoes you're wearing!"

Davidson was tiring of the harangue.

"Your eyes," he said, "are damn near good enough for aircrew."[7]

We are told little of what happened to the unfortunate Davidson following the exchange, but there is little doubt that such a dressing down was commonplace. The boys who did the work of men over Fortress Europe would grow up in a hurry and would also develop a mature sense of what really counted. Still, in times of crisis, most were damned scared.

Dave McIntosh was a navigator with 418 Squadron, which was formed at Debden, Essex, in November 1941. Squadron 418, the top-scoring unit in the RCAF, flew the twin-engined Bostons and Mosquito aircraft on night-intruder missions. McIntosh claimed he was always frightened.

"It was said that if you made it through the first seven trips you had enough experience to give you a pretty good chance of surviving a whole tour, which was at least thirty trips, and usually thirty-five on 418, but often more because some of the trips were pretty short. All a short trip meant to me was that I was scared for a shorter period of time than on a long trip."[8]

One night McIntosh and pilot Sid Seid were on their way back to England after they had shot up a German train. "We were comfortably out over the North Sea on our way home when the English coast failed to show up," writes McIntosh. "Another five minutes and still no English coast. Even with my navigation you could hardly miss England altogether. It should be there, a great big island, right in our path."[9]

The two eventually got home, after several nervous minutes over the grey waves far below. Their compass had malfunctioned during the attack on the train.

Soon after Marion Orr arrived in England with her friend Violet
Milstead, she began her flying with the ATA, ferrying various
types of aircraft to and from factories, to various squadrons and
so on. "The work was interesting," she says today, "and you
got to fly a lot of different planes. In the morning we would arrive
at work and pick up our orders for the day. There were sometimes
only a couple of flights to do, depending on where you were
going, and sometimes as many as seven. They could be in seven
different kinds of planes. One day I flew two Wellingtons, a
Dakota, a Spitfire, a Hurricane, a Lysander, and a Ventura.

"They gave you this little book called *Ferry Pilot's Notes*, and
it listed all the different types of planes in use in England at the
time. Each plane had a page and it gave the type of engine, the
grade of fuel, and all the flying particulars for the plane. It told
you how to start the thing and the speed for takeoff, for cruising,
and for landing. I tell you, that little book was wonderful."

To the uninitiated, the pilot's book is a myriad of facts presented
in the most basic and straightforward way. For example, starting
instructions for the Avro Tutor were given as follows: "Starting
handle stowed in locker. Priming pump in each cockpit. After
priming, set all ignition switches ON (front and rear) and switch
ON starter magnets. Wind mag. with handle on right whilst engine
is being turned. After starting, switch OFF starter mag."

The handbook page for the Spitfire is both detailed and com-
prehensive. Consider for example, the comments on the pressure
cabin: "There are two kinds. Some aircraft have a detachable
hood which is lifted on after pilot is seated. Four cam levers must
be forward. When hood is located, push levers back and connect
two rubber tubes at sides. Keep cabin pressure control lever at
left elbow OFF. Two red lights show if it is ON. Automatic control
may be fitted. To jettison, push forward two front levers and push
hood upwards. Other aircraft have a sliding hood. Pressure lever
to starboard and sealing cock to port must be OFF. To jettison,
pull red knob on left dash and push hood upwards. On both types
two air cocks by front windscreen panel must be OFF."

No wonder the men and women who flew these planes became
versatile!

"It was all part of the job," insists Marion Orr. "You just went
out to the plane, did a walk-around and climbed inside. If you
had never seen that kind of aircraft before, you took a bit longer

with the notes. Then you started up and away you went. It was fun most of the time.

"My first Spitfire was a thrill of a lifetime. It was a pilot's dream; the most wonderful aircraft I've ever flown. It was light, sensitive, easy to handle, smooth as a kitten's wrist. I remember looking at the little wings and wondering if they would hold the plane up.

"Just before I got into it, a fellow I knew who was an old hat on the plane said: 'I would advise you to taxi and do your check while you're taxiing, and get off the ground as quickly as possible.' But he didn't explain to me the feeling I'd get on takeoff. Anyway, I wheeled it out and touched the throttle. The next thing I knew, I was pushed back in the seat and I couldn't *move*. That thing just shot off the ground like a bullet. My God, I was up to 6,000 feet before I knew it. The plane just purred. It was like a beautiful dream!''

Marion Orr still flies, and today has in excess of 25,000 hours in the air, but the Spitfire to her was the best plane ever.

"Flying the Spit was such a pleasure; you never wanted to damage one of them. That was why we used to fly them at the height we said before takeoff, and according to the flight plan. One day, however, I was taking one somewhere, but the day was so hazy you couldn't see much. We had to use the map and not the radio, so when I was where I thought I should be, I began the letdown.

"Then I realized I didn't know where I was. There had been a strong headwind and my gas was almost gone. I was away out on my timing and I could *not* find an airfield. But the more I looked the worse things got. That Spitfire was brand-new and I was more worried about bending it than I was about myself.

"I thought to myself that I had to get down somewhere, but I didn't want to hit someone's house either. Finally, I noticed this gold streak through the haze and I knew it had to be a river. I decided that maybe if I set the plane on the water as gently as I could it wouldn't be smashed too much. But then I remembered I couldn't swim so I had to keep close to shore.

"I was sweating, I'll tell you. I had the top open, my scarf undone, the flaps up, the undercarriage up, and I was ready for the splash. Then, just before I touched, I saw these little yellow dots nearby. I couldn't believe it. There was a landing strip!

"So I put on the power, roared back up again, and was over the little field before I knew it. Then I had to do a 180° turn, put the flaps down, the wheels down, everything I could drag. When I landed, I just sat there, so thankful I could hardly move. I didn't have to learn to swim after all. And I never have."

One morning, Diane Ramsay, who also flew with the Air Transport Auxiliary, ran into trouble flying a fighter aircraft from Langley to Henlow, England. Somehow, after a normal takeoff and climb, the throttle of the plane stuck in the open position. Ramsay tried climbing to reduce speed but to no avail. When she was near her destination, she climbed again, got the wheels down, and cut the motor in order to slow to a landing speed. She was still going too fast so she attempted to start the engine and overshoot. The engine would not respond.

With no alternative now, she was forced to come directly in to the airport. She did not make it.

"I saw a small field," she explained afterwards, "and I tried to get in through a gap in the trees, but the starboard engine touched one of them and everything happened so fast. I think I hit another tree and then a ditch, and went over the ditch broadside and into some trees."

E.C. Cheesman, who wrote the history of the ATA, completed the story:

> The aircraft almost completely disintegrated, but by some miracle the cockpit escaped damage and the pilot, though bruised, was almost unhurt. She climbed out of the wreckage and began to cross the field in search of help. When the ambulance and crash crew reached the scene, somewhat to their surprise they found that the pilot had returned to the aircraft and was sitting in the cockpit.
>
> When she afterwards was asked what caused her to retrace her steps, she admitted reluctantly that the field was full of cows and she was terrified to cross it until some male help arrived![10]

In the same volume, Cheesman related the story of a Scotsman, beloved by many Canadians, named Douglas Fairweather. A big, bluff man of 225 pounds or so, Fairweather was fifty when the

war broke out and he joined the ATA. His chief difficulty flying
was that

[o]wing to partly defective eyesight he could only see the
ground *without* his glasses and could only read the map with
them on.

As with all his life, his methods were unorthodox, but
pilots were at that time so urgently needed that much was
forgiven. . . .

He quickly learned all England visually and preferred to
fly without the aid of a map. This led to other pilots complaining that his methods were likely to lead to their losing
their way and getting off course.

Not in the least daunted by their complaints he proceeded
to fix up his map in front of him in the Anson and started to
refer to it in a normal way while flying. One day one of his
passengers took a closer look at it.

It was a map of Roman England.[11]

Douglas Harvey related a story of a man who needed more than
a map when he bailed out.

We had a crew on our squadron who landed back at base
minus their mid-upper gunner. They had encountered heavy
opposition over Germany and, in escaping from German
fighters, had used up most of their fuel. The skipper decided
to take a shortcut over London to save some gas.

Unfortunately, they got caught in the middle of a German
raid on London and took a severe pounding from their own
flak guns. The skipper ordered everyone to prepare to aban-
don aircraft, but the mid-upper gunner didn't wait for the
actual order to jump. He bailed out immediately. Meanwhile, the pilot managed to escape the barrage and fly on to
base.

As soon as the gunner got back to base he . . . refused to
fly again. When he had landed in London by parachute he
had been set upon by irate Londoners who assumed he was
German. He had to be rescued by air raid wardens and
police. He said that if his own people would do that to him

he could imagine what the Germans would do if he ever
bailed out over Germany. That ended his flying career.[12]

During the final days of the Second World War, Battle of Britain
pilot Bob Norris, now with 424 Squadron, led 120 Lancaster
bombers on a raid to Wangerooge, one of the Dutch Frisian
Islands. The Dutch had been badly treated by the Germans who
controlled the area, and the raid was an attempt to force the
occupying army out.

"We were supposed to be bombing through clouds," recalls
Norris today. "I was flying the lead Lanc, and we carried smoke
bombs with us. When we were coming up to the target we turned
on the smoke to mark the target for the planes who were following. As it turned out, there wasn't a cloud in the sky.

"Up ahead I could see the eighty-eight-millimetre anti-aircraft
shells coming up, zeroing in on us, so I yelled at one of my guys
to turn off the damned smoke. You could *see* the target, and the
smoke only made it easier for the Germans to see us.

"Anyway, one of the fellows had trouble getting the smoke off,
so I told my flight engineer to go back and help. Just as he started
to do so, we were hit. He got a piece of shrapnel right through
the thigh. We later found the steel. It was a couple of inches
across, razor-blade sharp, and it had been spinning. The guy was
lucky not to lose his leg or his life."

The German ground fire was deadly accurate. Two of Norris's
engines were hit, flying Perspex from a shattered windscreen
struck the pilot in the eye, and the big Lancaster bounced around
the sky. Luckily, he and his crew managed to jettison their bombs
over the target and limp back to base. Others were not so fortunate. The bombing raid was a success, but thirty-seven of the
huge bombers – almost a third of them – did not return.

This had been the story for days and nights on end in Europe,
North Africa, the Far East, over the Atlantic, in virtually every
theatre of war. The Allies lost planes, men, and billions of dollars
in equipment. Gradually, however, the losses became smaller,
the Axis forces drew back, and the bloodletting came to an end.
And while it is impossible to tell every war story involving pilots,
or even a tiny fraction of the tales, there is one that is special.
This story took place far from Europe, out over the Indian Ocean,

and it was, according to Winston Churchill, one of the most heroic of the entire war. This time, the hero was that young Canadian from St. Catharines, Ontario, flying boat pilot Len Birchall.

12

"The Saviour of Ceylon"

Today Len Birchall is seventy-three years old, a man with an easy laugh, a salty vocabulary, and a direct manner. Gracious with his time, he works with cadets and is a frequent guest speaker at military functions. Retired and living in Kingston, Ontario, he is miles and years away from the days when he found himself in Bermuda, then in the Shetland Islands, and, finally, by April 1942, in Ceylon, the beautiful island nation now known as Sri Lanka. The journey to the then British colony in the Indian Ocean was uneventful, but the postings that led up to it were not. "Both were interesting," he says today, "but Bermuda was the pleasant place. My time in the Shetlands was hell on wheels."

Birchall was in Bermuda during his time with the Trans-Atlantic Ferry Command. He stayed there for a short time immediately prior to and during the Japanese attack on Pearl Harbor and the American entry into the war. "There were a lot of Americans around," he recalls, "and they used to give us the gears about fighting a European war. 'Those people over there are not worth it,' they'd say. 'Canada is a big country; you have everything you need at home. Why are you trying to protect the Europeans?' This type of teasing went on and on.

"Then one night we were sitting around the lounge in a hotel there, and a radio was playing in the background. Suddenly, an announcer came on and said that there had been a terrible disaster, to please stay tuned for an important news bulletin. The thing turned out to be President Roosevelt's 'Day of Infamy' speech about the Japanese attack on Pearl Harbor.

"Well, I'll tell you. I've never seen a group of guys turn tail faster. The Americans in the room were absolutely stunned. They didn't know what to say or do. They were just shocked. Of course we began to lay it on thick. 'So, are you going to let this thing pass, or are you going to do something about it? The fight is over there; why bother getting involved? Let someone else fight!' It was fun watching them squirm because they had sure given it to us all the time we were there. We were glad the Americans were finally in the war, of course, because it had been hard going alone.''

Birchall's next posting, doing coastal reconnaissance work out of the Shetlands, was so frightful he will never forget it. He arrived there just before Christmas in 1941, and remained all that winter, flying the big, nine-man Catalina flying boats over the North Sea, up the coast of Norway, and into the Arctic Ocean to the Barents Sea and Murmansk. The weather was terrible all the time. Wild ocean storms, lashing salt spray, and waves higher than tractor-trailers rolled across the surface of the grey seas.

"Our normal patrol was twenty-four hours non-stop," he says, with a chill of remembrance, "but we could stay up for thirty-six hours if we had to. The Catalina had three big tanks in the hull, and there was a little electric pump for pumping gas up to the wing tanks. We just flew on and on, on the lookout for submarines, escorting convoys on the Murmansk Run, and, for a period of time, looking for the two battleships, the *Scharnhorst* and the *Gneisenau*. Most of the time we were half-frozen.

"It was so cold, they finally installed a heater in the Cats, a thing called the Southwind. It had a little spark plug at the top and it burned gasoline. The only trouble was, when it was on, the compass went out of whack. Then you'd have to turn off the heater, let your compass settle down, find out where the hell you were going, and then relight the heater to get a little warmth. In the end, the whole procedure was such a nuisance, we just threw the goddamned things out and went from that time without them. There were lots of times when the situation made us pretty miserable, though.

"Sometimes when we came back from a patrol and the weather was lousy, it was damn near impossible to get out of the plane onto a little pinnace that was used, more or less, as a tender for the plane. The wind would be blowing, the boat bouncing, and if you fell into the water you were dead. After one patrol, we just couldn't get out of the plane. We were heaving up and down and from side to side. The pinnace was rolling and we sat there for twenty-four hours waiting for the storm to stop. We had no heat; the guys were all sick and cold and dog-tired after the patrol. It wasn't much fun. Often when we arrived back at night, you couldn't see much, but the pinnace had a searchlight on top. We'd home in on the light and come right above it, then try to settle in. Half the time, though, the winds were so strong that the power would be full on and we would be going backwards."

The first Canadian commanding officer of 413 Squadron after it was formed at Stranraer, Scotland, was Wing Commander R.G. Briese. Birchall relates the Briese story and points out how similar his own could have been.

"One day Dick Briese got an order to do a daylight reconnaissance in an area near Trondheim, Norway, because there was a rumour that the Germans had just moved in some fighter planes. He was to take pictures of whatever was there for the RAF. He objected to being given orders by the British, but then asked for volunteers for the flight. Briese and everyone else knew it was a suicide mission. What was the point of sending a Catalina, which flew at about ninety knots and lumbered along like an old truck, up against fighter planes?

"Anyway, Briese took the flight, and he and his crew left on what they were certain was a one-way mission. It was. They were shot down and none of them ever came back.

"Not long after I was in the Shetlands, a similar call came in to Jack Twigg, the new 413 CO. He was asked to do some night photography up around Narvik, because it was thought the Germans had moved some night fighters there. This was a bit tricky because you had to have special cameras and so on, and you had to drop a flare. The camera was made in such a way that you could keep the flare out of the picture. Anyway, we didn't have the right camera, but they wanted us in there anyway. This was also a one-way mission, particularly in a Catalina.

"Jack said he would fly the plane. I was the second in command, although we took only a skeleton crew. All of us were sure we would never return, so there was no need to waste more men. We did have a damned good wireless operator, because if we were going to die, we were going to break radio silence and at least report what we found. The best we could hope for was to be shot down and become prisoners of war. Just before we left, we made sure our personal belongings were in order. Then we took off.

"The weather on that trip was something else. We flew through the worst blinding snowstorm I had ever seen. Up the coast, then in through that long fiord to the town. The snow was so bad we couldn't take pictures, but the Germans couldn't send up their fighters either. There was flak all over the place, and all around us, but we got out okay. The weather was the only thing that saved us. We later got hell because Jack and I had flown together. If we had been shot down, the commanding officer and the second in command would have been lost."

A few weeks later Birchall was sent to Ceylon.

"No one told us where we were going," he recalls, "but they did pull us out of the Shetlands and begin to equip us with tropical clothing. At least we knew the destination would be warm. They told us where we were going on the morning we left."

Two aircraft left Britain together, with Birchall in command of the first. The journey took the men south to Gibraltar and then across to Cairo. The original intention had been to put in at Alexandria, but a raging sandstorm was sweeping northward from the Sahara, so the Catalinas both landed on a bend in the Nile as it passed through Cairo. The sultry heat, the stench, and the noise of the ancient Egyptian metropolis provided an unbelievable contrast to the bitter cold reaches of the North Sea they had so recently left behind. Even today, a Canadian accustomed to winter warmth in a heated home is stunned by the heat and the cacophonous vitality of the sprawling city beside the pyramids. How much more so did Birchall and his men appreciate the contrast! Indeed war was different here.

The planes flew on: to Abu Qir, to Basra on the Euphrates, then down over the Persian Gulf and the Gulf of Oman to Karachi, the principal seaport of modern-day Pakistan. The last leg of the journey was south along the west coast of India, then across the Gulf of Mannar to a place called Kegalla, near the city of Galle, on the southern tip of what is today Sri Lanka. To Birchall, and to the hundreds of men and women based there during the war, the place will probably always be Ceylon.

"We had to land on a tiny lake," Birchall says, "and doing so was quite tricky. The thing was filled with coral reefs, although a landing path had been dredged through them. The shores were ringed with tall palm trees, though, and none of them had been removed. We got in okay, but I was told not to try a night landing until I got used to the twilight. Our arrival was shortly after the noon hour.'' The newcomers were given the afternoon to rest and look around their new base. The date was April 2, 1942.

"Things were in a great state of confusion," Birchall wrote later on, "and nobody seemed to know what was going on. All we did know was that the war was really getting close and we were not winning. There was a very sad deficiency in long-range patrol aircraft and hence we were a very welcome support. I was given a fair briefing by the Station co, especially as it concerned our squadron at this place. He also asked if I could do a trip the following morning to a secret Royal Navy base to carry messages and also bring back information on the location of our ships and their future intentions. With radio silence there was no information on our ship movements. Since the trip was in daylight I accepted with pleasure."[1] A Dutch aircraft would leave at the same time to do a patrol toward the south.

Sometime after midnight, the commanding officer came and woke Birchall and told him there had been a change in plans. The Dutch did not want to do the southern patrol; would the Canadians do it instead? When I asked Birchall to explain the change, his answer was characteristically forthright.

"The Dutch simply refused to go," he explained. "They thought it was too dangerous. There had been rumours that the Japanese fleet was out there somewhere, and everyone in the camp knew this except us. The Dutch were not going to take the risk. I found out much later that everyone else knew more than we did, but I did agree to do the patrol. We were to leave at first light, come back late in the day, or after dark, then circle over Ceylon until we could see to land the following morning. This was okay with the co, so I left word for an early call for breakfast.''

At this time during the war, the Japanese were gobbling up more and more territory in the Pacific. Their ''war effort had two purposes. The first was actually to capture the rich and coveted lands of South-East Asia and the Netherlands East Indies. The second was to secure and fortify their outer defensive line and to extend it southward so as to threaten communications between the United States and Australia."[2]

The attack on Pearl Harbor indicated both their objective and the speed at which they planned to move toward it. Guam, Wake Island, Hong Kong, Rangoon, and Singapore had all fallen in the three months after Pearl Harbor, and the city of Darwin, in Northern Australia, was under attack. The Japanese then planned to take the Netherlands East Indies (indeed, Djakarta had already come under their control) and Ceylon. Later, they would go on to the Philippines. If the Allies had any hope of thwarting the enemy drive in that area of the world, Ceylon had to be defended under any circumstances.

But on that spring morning in 1942, when Len Birchall and his crew were lifting off the little lake at Kegalla, the mighty and hitherto victorious Japanese fleet under Vice Admiral Chuichi Nagumo was steaming toward Ceylon, its carriers bristling with fast fighter planes. Soon these planes would go to battle with a nine-man, lightly armed, lumbering flying boat. The fight was less than fair.

"We were called about three that morning," recalls Birchall. "We had breakfast and then went for a briefing about the flight and about what we were supposed to do."

The briefing was less than candid. "They weren't sure what the hell was out there," Birchall continues, "and they weren't telling me the truth about the fact that we could run into the entire Japanese fleet. I found out afterwards that Admiral [James] Somerville, the British Commander in that part of the world, knew the Japanese were headed that way, but when they had not shown up by the end of March, felt that they might have gone somewhere else. Anyway, we were to go out and check."

The British had moved their fighting ships around so that there would not be many vessels tied up in one place vulnerable to a Japanese attack, as had been the case at Pearl Harbor. Two cruisers were at Colombo, Ceylon's capital, while others were tied up at Trincomalee, on the Bay of Bengal. The rest were being refuelled at an atoll in the Indian Ocean.

"We were to positively identify anything we found, even if it was British," continues Birchall. "We were to keep absolute radio silence, of course, so away we went."

The Catalina flew on and on, at about 2,000 feet, sweeping an ever-greater area of the Indian Ocean. The sun beat down from a cloudless sky, and the shimmering waves looked both beautiful and peaceful. The world at war seemed far away.

"We went about as far south as we intended to go," Birchall says, "and by this time it was about dusk. However, the navigator asked me if we could hold course a bit longer. The moon was just starting to come up and he wanted to get a good astral fix so he would know exactly where we were. I told him to go ahead, because we would have to stooge around over Ceylon until morning anyway in order to land in daylight back at Kegalla.

"After he plotted our position, we realized we were about 500 miles south of Ceylon, and 200 or so farther than we intended. However, he got his fix and we were ready to turn for home."

At this point someone noticed tiny specks on the southern horizon. The specks were several miles away, and from the flight deck of the Catalina they could not be identified. Birchall decided to get closer and have a look.

"As we flew farther south, the specks got larger and gradually began to take shape. We knew then that we were onto something," says Birchall. "I alerted the others and told the radio man to get ready. I knew we'd get one chance only and we couldn't afford to blow it. In the meantime we started counting ships."

There, spread out below them, was the vast array of the enemy fleet. The sight was chilling. Unknown to the Catalina crew, Japanese zero fighter planes were far above. As yet, they had not noticed the lumbering flying boat down nearer the surface.

"We came in under their fighter screen," says Birchall, "and luckily, we were able to get the exact number of what was there. The fact that we had just done an astral fix meant that we could pinpoint the exact location for our transmission back to Colombo. Our radio man was ready and we started our count. I was looking out with binoculars and checking the numbers, types of ships, their speed and direction. I'd call the information to the navigator, he would write it down, and the first message to Ceylon went out. The message was repeated three times before waiting for an acknowledgement."

Suddenly the radio compartment of the plane was blasted by cannon fire. The Catalina lurched to one side and more tracer bullets cut into the hull, tore off the leg of one man, and set fire to the interior. Burning gasoline poured down from an upper tank, and the plane was filled with flames, acrid smoke, and sweating, cursing, terrified men. Birchall went into a desperate dive to get the plane down in one piece. Fires spread wildly, ferociously.

"They shot the hell out of us," says Birchall. "We never really had a chance, but we got our message back to Ceylon. A few seconds after the bombardment started we knew it was all over for us. We had no self-sealing tanks, so when the ones we had ruptured, the gas poured down through the tunnel between the wing and the hull. The explosive shells started the fire.

"You know, we got the fire out twice, but the third time there was just no way. Everything started to blow up inside. I bounced the plane down onto the water, and the guy whose leg had been blown off went down when the Cat sank. Two other guys were badly wounded so we put Mae Wests on them and threw them into the water. The rest of us grabbed Mae Wests and jumped. We had no time to get them on."

The bleeding, desperate airmen swam for all they were worth away from the stricken aircraft as the zeros circled for yet another strafing. Cannon fire cut the water in straight, deadly accurate lines. Bullets thudded into the burning hulk of the flying boat and into the prostrate bodies of the two wounded men. Both were shredded to bits.

"The poor buggers could not escape the bullets," says Birchall, "and they never had a chance. The six of us who were still alive were able to dive under the surface, and doing so saved us. You could see the splashes of the bullets on the water. Three of the guys were wounded and bleeding so we knew the sharks would soon be around. Finally, the strafing stopped."

The Japanese came closer in a destroyer, lowered a small boat, and collected the survivors.

"They hauled us up on the deck and started to question us, pound us around, and question us some more. The wounded guys were in bad shape. One had collected a whole burst of shells right up one leg; another's arm was torn open and a third had been shot in the hip. We might have been a sorry-looking bunch but we weren't saying much.

"Then one Japanese, who spoke perfect English, asked who the senior officer was. I identified myself and he started to pound me around again. He wanted to know if we'd sent a signal back to Ceylon. We denied it, of course, and he kept slugging me. Finally, just when we almost had him convinced, they picked up a radio signal from Colombo asking us to repeat our last message. That was when we knew the game was over.''

Birchall and his men became prisoners of war, in a series of hell-hole prison camps that they endured for three and a half terrible years. The message they sent got to Colombo in time, and Ceylon was ready for the attack that came. The Japanese failed to achieve their objective so they left the area.

Years later, Winston Churchill said that Air Commander Len Birchall was truly the Saviour of Ceylon. Birchall received the Distinguished Flying Cross for his heroics in the air, and the Order of the British Empire for his leadership and selfless courage while in prison camp. Both were richly deserved.

Above, from left to right: Glen Curtiss, Dr. Alexander Graham Bell, John McCurdy, and Casey Baldwin, the members of the Aerial Experiment Association, formed in 1907 at Mabel Bell's suggestion. (National Archives of Canada/C-28213)

The *Silver Dart*, piloted by John McCurdy. It made its historic flight over Lake Bras d'Or, Baddeck, in February, 1909. (National Archives of Canada/PA-61741)

Ruth Law, *circa* 1913, in a Curtiss biplane. Although Curtiss couldn't believe that "a person of such slim build . . . could handle an aircraft with safety," this popular airwoman spent years thrilling crowds across Canada with her daredevil stunts. (Canada's Aviation Hall of Fame)

When the engine of his Curtiss Jenny failed, veteran pilot Fred McCall landed it on the only spot available at Calgary Exhibition's crowded fairgrounds: atop a carousel. (National Archives of Canada/C-59783)

Texan Katherine Stinson (centre) enthralled crowds across the prairies with her loops, rolls, and spirals in her single-seat biplane. Her ability to recover from steep dives became her specialty. (Canada's Aviation Hall of Fame)

Mel Alexander learned to fly at Stinson's San Antonio school in an amazing 210 minutes, in the Model B Wright pusher-type plane shown here. He was soon to distinguish himself in World War I, shooting down eighteen enemy aircraft before his twentieth birthday. (Courtesy Mel Alexander)

Wop May with his Moth aircraft, 1933. After flying with the RAF in World War I, May returned to Canada where he performed at fairs and taught flying. In 1929 he and his partner Vic Horner became national heroes when they rushed antitoxin from Edmonton to the isolated village of Little Red River, where diphtheria had broken out. It was a 600-mile journey, flown in an open cockpit biplane through blizzards and 40-below weather. Because of their courage, an epidemic was averted and the village of Little Red River saved. (National Archives of Canada/PA-120773)

Stan McMillan, piloting a Fairchild, was one of the eight-member MacAlpine Expedition whose disappearance in the North – and the resulting ten-week search – became the news story of 1929. The group had set out from Churchill, Manitoba, in late August with the ambitious plan of making a 20,000-mile survey of mining bases in the far North. Fifty-four days later, they made their way back to civilization, having survived with the help of the Inuit. (Courtesy Stan McMillan)

Above, the author interviewing veteran fighter pilot Jan Zurakowski. Zurakowski learned to fly as an officer in the Polish air force. Years later he was the first to fly the most exciting airplane ever built in Canada – the Avro Arrow. (Father Wally Mucha)

Right, Group Captain J. D. "Red" Somerville, #1 Fighter Wing, Marville, France, 1955. When, in 1948, the RCAF purchased several de Havilland Vampires, Somerville wanted to be the first to fly one. Unfortunately, when he lost his engine three miles on approach, he was also the first to crash one. (Courtesy J. D. Somerville)

Marion Orr is one of the few women to be enshrined in Canada's Aviation Hall of Fame. While still a teenager, Orr joined the Air Transport Auxiliary in World War II, where she flew just about everything, including her favourite, the Spitfire. Later, she was manager of Aero Activities Ltd. in Maple, Ontario. (National Archives of Canada/PA-125931)

Buzz Beurling in Malta, 1942, adding another "kill" to the hull of his aircraft. In one two-week period he shot down twenty-seven enemy planes, and by the end of the war he was the leading Canadian air ace. (Canada's Aviation Hall of Fame)

As a kid growing up in St. Catharines, Ontario, Len Birchall hung out at the grass-strip airfield outside of town doing odd jobs in exchange for a few minutes' flying time. Years later, Air Commander Birchall won the admiration of Winston Churchill as "the Saviour of Ceylon" when he managed to radio a warning that the Japanese fleet was steaming towards Ceylon, before being shot down. (Courtesy Len Birchall)

Lt.-General Reg Lane during his time as Deputy Commander of NORAD. During the Second World War Lane flew with the RAF as part of the Pathfinder Force, undoubtedly one of the most dangerous and nerve-racking types of work imaginable. That he was a squadron leader at the age of twenty-two and had won both the Distinguished Service Order and the Distinguished Flying Cross attest to his exceptional skill and courage. (United States Air Force)

13

From the Bush to the Boardroom

In Canada, the histories of bush flying and commercial flying are intertwined because one, to a large degree, has been the outgrowth of the other. Successful single-plane bush operations expanded, became even more successful, and so continued to grow. With the expansion came competition, amalgamation, more competition, and success – or failure – on a commercial scale the first pilots could never have imagined.

Many of our most illustrious aviation pioneers went from the bush to the boardroom, and were equally at home in both. Punch Dickins was an early success story.

"I was lucky," he admits today. "When I returned from overseas, I was fortunate to get picked up [as a pilot] by Western Canada Airways, because I certainly did not have the money to start my own airline. It was really a case of being in the right place at the right time." That was in 1927, and Dickins's career had barely started. It was just a year later that he won the McKee trophy, as we have heard, for his historic flight over Canada's Arctic Barren Lands, mapping large areas of the region en route and charting airways over 4,000 miles of wilderness not flown before. He later was an executive with Canadian Pacific Airlines and de Havilland Aircraft of Canada. Today, at ninety, he is regarded by many as the greatest living bush pilot in the country.

Russell Baker was another success story. At the age of twenty-five, he left his home town, Winnipeg, and flew bush planes all over the West. In 1946 he formed Central B.C. Airways with a partner, another bush pilot, Walter Gilbert. Their fleet consisted of three war surplus T-50 Cranes and two old Junkers from CPA.

In 1953 the company was renamed Pacific Western Airlines.[1] At
the time of his death in 1958 Baker was making plans to transform
his company into a national airline. Pacific Western has since
merged with Canadian Pacific to become Canadian Airlines International, the second-largest airline in the nation. Recently, what
is now called PWA Corp. has acquired Wardair as well.

Pierre Berton, in his book *The Mysterious North*, remembers
flying with Russell Baker in the North:

> Over these mountains and through these canyons for about
> a dozen years a pilot named Russ Baker had been bringing
> mail, beefsteaks, tinned beans, mining machinery, new
> brides, policemen, priests, prospectors, beaver pelts, gold
> samples, and almost anything else you can name, including
> upright pianos, in and out of the country. . . .
>
> . . . Baker . . . had no instruments to fly by and was his
> own navigator and weather forecaster. His weather gauge
> had always been a cabin's smoke, his barometer the sky at
> dawn. His only landing strips were the choppy lakes or the
> snow-choked rivers. . . . He had long since learned to
> improvise in a country where you can't always buy aircraft
> parts. When he blew the exhaust stacks off a plane, he
> replaced them with stovepipes. When he ripped the bottoms
> from his floats on a shallow river, he pumped them out,
> stuffed them with rags, and flew on.[2]

Max Ward traces his airline to very humble origins during the
days after the Second World War ended. Ward had been in the
Canadian Air Force and had learned to fly there. However, like
Punch Dickins following the Great War, Ward longed to get out
of uniform and fly in the Canadian North. He got his chance in
1945, flying a wartime aircraft on bush operations with Jack Moar
in the Peace River-Yellowknife-Hay River area. The following
year he decided to go it alone with a little de Havilland aircraft
called a Fox Moth, for which he paid $10,500. Ward called his
one-plane operation the Polaris Charter Company. According to
one source, "young Ward, operating single-handed from dawn
until dusk, hauled prospectors and supplies into the mining exploration camps that were springing up in the area. In addition to

flying the Fox Moth, he maintained it, cleaned it, loaded it, and ran the business all by himself.''[3]

The company lasted for four years before Ward left to fly for other companies and begin building houses in Lethbridge. By 1953 he was back in Yellowknife trying to keep his new four-plane outfit, Wardair Limited, aloft. He did so, in spite of several brushes with bankruptcy, and has never looked back. By 1976 Wardair had grown from a fleet of four to become the country's largest international charter airline, while today Wardair Incorporated is our third-largest scheduled air operation.

In his sixties, Max Ward is now more businessman than pilot. He has a home in Edmonton, a condominium in Toronto, and several honorary university degrees. He's built up a commercial fleet of some of the most modern, long-haul jet aircraft in the skies. He's a long way from his days of flying the Fox Moth, yet flying is still his first love.

"Yes, I suppose that will always be the case," he admits, and adds with a trace of wanderlust in his voice, "I still get up north to fly every summer. That's the way I relax, and I love it. I have a Twin Otter, and I put in over one hundred hours in the summer. I go alone with my family, and I do the maintenance, the loading and unloading. This takes me back to some of the most wonderful days of my life.

"Flying in the North is a tough job, but it's exciting, and there is never a dull moment. It was great for me when I came out of the Air Force and went up there. I had to face up to the challenges – and that is all part of being in the great outdoors. This is a massive country, and I never fail to be amazed at just how big it really is. Even today, most Canadians do not have a clue about just what there is in the North. Nor do they really understand the life of the bush pilot, particularly the early bush pilots. Of the guys who flew with me in the early days, at least sixteen of them died in air crashes. It's a dangerous life at times."

One of Max Ward's most pleasant memories seems, to an outsider, surprising, almost out of character for a man both sophisticated and urbane. But the early pilots, like Wop May and Punch Dickins, would have no trouble understanding.

"Just being warm was a pleasure beyond words," he recalls. "When you were flying up there, and you were gone for three or four or five days or more, you had to stay with the airplane all day long. From the time you took your blowpot down to start it in the morning until the time you put it to bed and took the oil in in the evening, you had to be with your machine. You couldn't leave it. That was why, at the end of the day, when you arrived at the Hudson Bay post, or the RCMP detachment, and you sat by the fire and let the heat soak in, that was total contentment. It was so nice to be warm,'' he laughs.

"But you have to be alert to fly in the North," Ward continues. "Because it is not always the first thing that gets you into trouble, or even the second thing, but, rather, those things in combination with the third, with the others. When you are flying up there you have to know where you are going at all times, but after a while you recognize certain things and you are guided by them.

"For example, going to Bathurst Inlet there were two or three hills just beyond Contwoyto Lake, and there was this structure and that structure. Pretty soon you learned to know where you were by looking at the land, the contours of it. Of course, in the winter time as you approached the Arctic Ocean where the water was warmer than the land, there would be a haze, ice crystals in the air, and sometimes white-outs, although these were not too common. You had to remain alert always."

Max Ward continues, describing his life bush-flying, in the days before he bought his 747s, his DC-10s, or his Airbus Industrie A-300s.

"I was down in the Arctic for five days in November 1949. I got away with it, but I was awfully lucky to come out of that one.

"I was flying from Yellowknife to Bathurst Inlet and I had a passenger by the name of Neil Murphy, a northerner who was with the Hudson's Bay Company. We had a full load of supplies on board but not much extra fuel. The plane was a Bellanca Skyrocket, and the tanks would only carry enough for the trip with perhaps enough for an extra half hour or so. Because November is a terrible time of year to fly up there, Neil and I left before dawn in order to have as much light as possible."

Neil Murphy wanted to visit his father along the way, so they landed at the elder Murphy's cabin, some 200 miles out of Yellowknife. The father was not at home, but Neil insisted he would have heard the plane and would soon arrive. Unfortunately, it was some time before he did show up – and by then the short day had become even shorter.

"I should not have let him talk me into waiting," says Ward today. "But it was such a reasonable request, I couldn't say no. Anyway, Neil saw his Dad, dropped off some mail and picked up some furs, and away we went. By this time, we had just enough fuel to make it."

The men flew north-east, in the general direction of Bathurst Inlet, but the weather turned bad; they encountered headwinds, and the aircraft navigational system acted up. Finally it quit altogether. "From then on, I was feeling my way," admits Ward. "I had a general idea of where I was, but I knew things were going to be pretty chancy. We couldn't see much and the headwinds were getting stronger."

As the little plane drove onward into the gloom, the situation began to look more and more desperate. The windswept barrens below them were almost impossible to see, and even when the land was visible, there were so few landmarks that a forced landing anywhere would be dangerous. Even if the men survived the landing, the chances of someone finding them would be remote. "The terrain was so flat, I knew no one would ever locate us if we ditched," recalls Ward. "For that reason alone, I kept going. I knew there were a few hills nearer the coast, so I flew in the direction I thought would take us to them. In that sense, we were lucky."

The Barren Lands finally gave way to low hills, and from time to time the men noticed glaciated valleys leading off toward the snow-swept horizon.

"Just when I knew the gas was about gone, I saw a little lake down by the foot of a long rocky ledge," says Ward. "I decided that we would be wise to make for it. Neil opened the window on his side and I did the same thing on mine. As I came down, I told him to watch with me, and yell if there was a problem. I dropped the plane as gently as I could.

"Suddenly Neil screamed: 'Pull up, pull up!' I did as he said, but it was too late. We ploughed into a little hill, well down the valley, and we both could hear the undercarriage tearing away. We skidded for a short distance and then everything was quiet. We were not going anywhere but at least we were down safely."

Heavy snow swirled around the stricken plane, but the men scarcely minded. They were on the ground and they were uninjured. Ward recalls looking up out of the valley and seeing the driving snow far above them. Things were more sheltered by the plane.

"We set up light housekeeping under one wing," Ward continues. "We had a tent, lots of furs, sleeping bags, and plenty of food. It was about 45 below [Fahrenheit] at the time, though, so the tent was not that warm. We slept on the furs, in our sleeping bags, and made ourselves as comfortable as we could. At about seven that night I decided to see if we could contact Yellowknife on the radio. I knew transmission would be a bit dicey, so I waited until I thought our chances of getting outside reception were best. When my first call went out, I almost cried when Yellowknife boomed right back to us." The stricken flyers relayed their position as best they could: near the west side of the Burnside River, in a small canyon, close to a lake. The location was noted and the exchange ended.

"At the time, there was only one other aircraft in that whole northland equipped for winter flying, and that was a Beaver, back at Yellowknife. The next morning they gassed it up and came to look for us. Unfortunately, they got lost in the storm and also had to put down for three days. In the meantime, we were reasonably comfortable," says Ward. "We ate a lot of snow because it's easy to become dehydrated up there; the air is so dry. The storm continued, and we waited for five days in all."

When the skies finally cleared, Ward and Murphy put on snowshoes and walked several miles up and out of the valley where they had crashed.

"When we finally got to the top of the ridge," continues Ward, "the plane was as insignificant as a black dot against the snow. I couldn't believe it! You could hardly see the thing at all. I knew then that anyone flying over would have to make a lucky sighting or they would never see us. We got a signal fire ready to light in case they couldn't find us."

The men trudged back down the valley to their airplane. The next day hope arrived, preceded by the far-away drone of an aircraft.

"Suddenly there was a big, twin-engined RCAF Search and Rescue Dakota up there," Ward says, reliving the relief he felt then. "We were awfully glad to see that thing – but we couldn't communicate with it with our radio. So we hitched up the radio again and called Yellowknife. They heard us and they called the Dakota. The guys in the Dak couldn't see us, so here we are giving them directions right over our heads, but the directions had to go all the way down to Yellowknife and back, 700 miles or so, round trip. The Dakota flew over us and went on, and we told them they had gone too far. Then they circled back and when they were right over us we were screaming into the radio: 'You're there, you're there!' Finally they came right down to the tops of the cliffs and saw us. That's how insignificant you are when you are down in the middle of nowhere. We were only a dot in the snow."

The Search and Rescue people marked the crash site, and the next day the Beaver from Yellowknife finally arrived. Ward's broken plane was repaired and flown to safety at Bathurst Inlet.

Several years later Max Ward was involved in another air crash, this time during the summer and only a few miles from his Edmonton home.

Late on Sunday morning, June 14, 1981, he and his wife, Marjorie, and five friends left Edmonton International Airport, en route to the family fishing lodge 150 miles north of Yellowknife. They took off from Runway 01 at the International Airport, then banked out over the North Saskatchewan River in the direction of Edmonton, some thirty miles away. Max Ward was flying the twin-engine red-and-blue de Havilland Caribou. "The day was beautiful," he recalls. "The sun was shining and it should have been an easy flight. However, sometimes things just don't work out the way you expect."

As the group flew over the western outskirts of his home town, Ward called the control tower of Edmonton's other airport, the Municipal Airport, and received clearance to continue north. The tower gave an affirmative. The Caribou was at the 4,500-foot level.

Suddenly, with no warning whatsoever, the left engine of the aircraft began giving trouble. The propeller started to race, and the roar of the motor became a scream. At the same time, the engine temperature shot up alarmingly, forcing Ward to cut the motor and feather the prop, letting it spin uselessly in the air. The starboard engine would keep the plane from crashing, but the pilot knew he had to land as soon as possible. No one, in such a situation, flies any farther than necessary. As well, the idle engine was now smoking dangerously.

Just as he made the decision to attempt a landing at Canadian Forces Base Edmonton, on the right and a few miles to the northeast, the second engine of the aircraft quit.

Down on the ground, a farmer named Philip Oatway saw the stricken plane approaching, a stream of smoke pouring from the left engine. He knew that a crash was imminent unless the pilot could somehow get the big plane down. "By now the plane was half a mile north of his farm and heading east. It was visibly descending. . . . Suddenly the plane went silent. 'It was eerie,' [Oatway said later]. 'There was no sound in the sky. You could see it so near. But it was quiet like a lake on a summer evening. And now the plane was coming down faster than ever.' Mr. Oatway jumped in his pickup truck, eyed the falling airplane, estimated where it would hit, and set out along the road at top speed."[4]

In the plane above, Ward radioed a quick "mayday" to the Edmonton Municipal Tower, yelling at his passengers to brace themselves, and look for the nearest level ground where he could land – and spotted a grain field that had recently been sown. A minute later he had the machine down. No one was hurt, and two hours later, in another plane, the party was again airborne. Max Ward was, of course, at the controls.

Marjorie Ward did not try to take credit for the remarkable landing, but she did get the last word about the adventure. Of her husband's flying skills she said: "He's made rough landings before this, you know. In fact, I've seen him do a worse job when nothing was wrong at all."[5] Fortunately, there have not been many of them.

Don Braun, one of the bush pilots who later flew for Wardair and who now has one of the company Airbus 300s named after him, remembers a close call on a flight from Fort Smith in the days when radio transmission was less than reliable. Braun is an American from Saint Cloud, Minnesota, who started to fly by towing gliders on lengths of clothesline behind his father's barn. When

World War II started, he came up to Canada and joined the RCAF, so much of his flying was done in this country.

"That trip from Fort Smith was one I would rather forget," he says today from his home in Saint Cloud, "but it ended okay, and I'm still here to talk about it. A friend of mine named Pat Ivey, who was my co-pilot, and I were in an old Lockheed 10, heading for Norman Wells, N.W.T. We left Fort Smith one night, and by the time we were up to Fort Simpson we were on top of the overcast, and things seemed to be going well. However, the guy we called at Simpson gave us the weather, but he forgot to mention that Norman Wells was off the air. We flew on, down the Mackenzie, not knowing about the radio. By this time, we were in so much overcast that we would not have been able to see the ground even if it had been in the middle of the day.

"Anyway, along about that time I noticed that we seemed to be using a lot more gas than we should have. Both of us knew the tanks were full when we took off, but the main tanks were virtually empty, long before they should have been. The engines seemed to be running okay, and we could not figure out what was wrong. Then, when we tried to call Fort Norman to advise them of our location, the station didn't respond. We had a maximum fuel range of 450 or 500 miles or so, and the distance to Norman Wells from Fort Simpson was only about 300 miles, but the gas problem was giving us some worry.

"Up along the river there, the hills are on the west side, and we could make out Sugar Loaf Mountain at a place called Wrigley. Fortunately, there was a small radio station there, and they finally told us Norman Wells was off the air. Well, here we are: no radio ahead, dense cloud cover, and losing gas quickly.

"We switched to the reserve and decided to turn around and try to get back to Simpson, but for the longest time we couldn't even raise them on the radio. When they finally came in and said the weather was good there, we were relieved, but we weren't sure if we had enough gas to make it. The first reserve tank had run out and the second was really low.

"Finally we came south of the overcast and could see Fort Simpson some distance ahead. Pat was smoking, and I had even taken a cigarette he offered. Normally I didn't smoke, but I was pretty tense. I called the tower and came straight in and got the plane down. We taxied over to a stop and the gas was virtually gone. The next morning we found a few ounces in the last tank – no more." Braun was never so happy to be back on the ground. A hose connection had worked loose, and raw gasoline had drained from the tanks. "To this day, I don't know why there was no fire," he says, thinking back on the flight. "But if it had started to burn, it would have been all over for both of us. It was that close."

One of the most colourful characters in Canadian aviation was also one of the most successful. Like Max Ward and Russ Baker, Grant McConachie went from flying bush planes to being an airline executive, and the legacy he left will remain an enduring monument to his initiative, skill, and unbounded ambition. Like the others, McConachie made his name in the West, although he was born in central Canada, at Hamilton, Ontario, in 1909. He died at Long Beach, California, fifty-six years later. He spent most of his life in the airline industry.

From his earliest years, McConachie had the reputation of being a wild and crazy pilot, but one who lived to talk about his exploits. Take the time he flew from Edmonton in the fall of 1932 to a small lake 150 miles into the bush to pick up two injured trappers. The two had been badly burned when the stove they were lighting blew up in their faces, and needed medical attention urgently. McConachie decided to go to their rescue.

McConachie knew that the lake closest to his destination was partly frozen, rendering it useless for either a float or a ski-equipped landing. The ice that had formed was not thick enough to support an aircraft, but could tear apart even the sturdiest pontoons. McConachie decided to land on the shore instead. But the shore, though reasonably flat, was so narrow only one wheel of the plane could sit on it. The plane's other wheel would have to skim along the ice that fringed the land. One end of the tiny beach was overgrown with tall clusters of bulrushes, and the nearby trees left little clearance for the wings of the plane. Nevertheless, McConachie wanted to give landing a try.

He took off in an old blue Fokker, accompanied by a mechanic named Chris Green, and headed north from the Edmonton airport.

The 5:00 a.m. temperature was above freezing, but the harsh slipstream was cold in the open cockpit. The two men sat huddled against the wind, their helmets and goggles tightly fastened, their thoughts on the precarious venture ahead.

When he saw the lake where he was to land, even the normally ebullient McConachie was subdued. The beach was not only very narrow, it was terribly short, bumpy, and much more overgrown than he had expected. But there was nowhere else to land. He circled the lake a couple of times, judged his distance, and carefully watched his airspeed. The Fokker did not have brakes, but would instead come to a rolling stop. McConachie hoped this stop would not be in a fiery heap among the trees at the end of the beach. He came lower, almost to a stall, and touched down.

Almost instantly, a loud bumping, tearing, scraping sound came from the fuselage. The plane bounded into the air, thumped down again, and careened wildly forward, cutting a swath through the bulrushes, and finally came to a lurching halt near the injured men that McConachie had come to help. He cut the motor and climbed out to tend to the men. Green crawled under the belly of the plane and examined the fabric torn in the landing. When McConachie saw the severity of the men's burns he knew that any repairs his mechanic had to make would have to be done quickly. Green set to work.

The torn skin of the bottom of the Fokker was patched together, the weeds ploughed up by the landing were untangled from around the undercarriage, and the plane was hauled back to a spot where a takeoff could be attempted. A trapper who was with the injured men helped McConachie break down the bulrushes along the makeshift runway. Finally, the three men cleared away odds and ends of debris, bits of tree branches, larger stones, and anything else that might hurt the Fokker.

There remained one serious problem. McConachie knew that, without brakes to hold the plane as the motor was run up, the takeoff would probably end in the trees. He therefore decided to tie the Fokker to a tree, and then, once he and Green were aboard and the motor was racing wildly, the trapper would untie the machine and let it go, like a stone shot from a slingshot.

The men quickly realized that it would be next to impossible to untie the rope with the plane straining against it. Instead,

McConachie directed that the rope be laid across a tree stump
that would function as a chopping block. Later on, he described
his intentions:

> I told the trapper to stand by with his axe while I ran up the
> engine to full power, then to chop the rope when I waved
> my hand. . . .
>
> We were taking off into the wind, and I figured that . . .
> we had a good chance of making it. I pushed the throttle
> wide open, waited for the engine to pick up full revs, then
> gave the signal. The trapper swung his axe, the rope parted
> and away we went, rumbling through the bullrushes. . . .
>
> With full power from the start, the blast of the slip stream
> over the rudder gave me full control, so it was not too difficult
> to thread the needle of the narrow beach between the trees and
> the lake. We didn't seem to hit any obstructions, but suddenly,
> just before the wheels left the ground, there was the most
> terrible vibration. I thought it would shake the plane to pieces.
>
> I throttled back as much as I dared but by this time there
> was no other choice. We had to either take off or crash, so
> I manoeuvred the Fokker out over the lake, just skimming
> over the tree-tops, figuring it was better to crash through
> the ice than into the trees if we had to go in.
>
> The shuddering continued. It increased when I put on
> more power, diminishing as I pulled the throttle back, but I
> couldn't figure out what it was.[6]

Somehow the plane kept flying, and the mercy mission succeeded. After several months of hospital recuperation, the
injured trappers returned to their wilderness home. The old
Fokker had continued to fly, for the day the rescue mission
ended, McConachie and Green found that the aircraft vibration
they thought might bring them down was caused by a damaged
propeller – damaged by cutting through bulrushes along a beach
that should never have been used as a runway.

Grant McConachie continued flying, of course – in the North-
west, on the prairies, in central Canada, and, finally, around most
of the world. When he died of a heart attack in 1965, he was
president of Canadian Pacific Airlines, and his airline circled the
globe. Some said he was one of the last of a breed.

14

Flying Folklore

Every occupation has its own folklore, and flying is no exception. In any hangar, at any airport, find two pilots together and they are likely to be swapping flying stories. There are thousands of pilots and so there are thousands of stories – stories of romance and adventure, of courage and heartbreak. And, since pilots revel in recounting the embarrassing incidents, too, there are plenty of funny stories. Here are just a few of the stories pilots have told me.

The first pilot hired by Trans-Canada Airlines, now Air Canada, was Zebulon Lewis Leigh. Lewie Leigh joined the fledgling operation on August 20, 1937, and over the years participated in many of the company's early flights to destinations in Canada and overseas. Most of these trips were without incident, but every now and then things happened that Leigh, and those who were with him, would not forget. One such incident occurred on the night of October 26, 1938, on a flight from Vancouver that was supposed to terminate in Winnipeg.

"The plane was a Lockheed 14," he explains, "and I was doing a check ride with the captain, whose name was Maurice McGregor. The co-pilot was Don Brady. On board were a number of Department of Transport [DOT] people from Ottawa, and a load of mail. We were to leave in the early evening, shortly after seven o'clock."

Before they departed Vancouver, the pilots had been alerted to a potential weather problem over the Rocky Mountains. A mild

141

occlusion, the front formed by cold air overtaking and pushing warm air upwards to cause rain and clouds, had been predicted, but was not supposed to pose any serious threat to air travel in the area. The flight crew acknowledged the advisory, but decided there should be no problem. The plane took off.

"We left at 7:15," says Leigh today, "and climbed up to 13,000 feet, which was to be our cruising altitude for the first part of the trip. It was raining and there was a good deal of cloud. I was in the right seat, Maurice was doing the flying, and Don went back to sit with the passengers. There were a few bumps during the climb, but nothing serious. The plane was not equipped with oxygen in those days, so we had to watch our altitude fairly carefully."

The silver twin-engine Lockheed headed east into the mountains as the black October sky grew ominously darker: the weather was changing. Driving rain lashed at the plane, and then as the temperature abruptly dropped, the rain turned to sleet and ice began to form on the plane. Captain McGregor struggled to hold his course as vicious updrafts tossed the aircraft about. The plane's de-icing equipment kept the wings and carburetor ice-free, but every so often chunks of ice from the props broke loose and slammed into the fuselage. In the back, passengers were starting to feel queasy.

"We were bouncing around a lot," says Leigh, "so we decided to get a bit higher and see if things would be better. As it turned out, they weren't. The radio reception was bad because of static, and the turbulence was terrific."

Somewhere near Grand Forks, British Columbia, the situation became desperate. In his book *And I Shall Fly* Leigh described what happened next.

Just as we thought we were near the cone of the Grand Forks radio range station, which we had much difficulty hearing through the heavy static, we hit a real belt of turbulence, one jolt flinging the aircraft about violently and causing us almost to roll over. At this moment Maurice was trying to re-tune our main radio receiver, the handle of which was on the roof of the cockpit. In the upheaval the gear train to the tuner of the receiver broke. The main receiver was not tuned now to the station, nor could we alter it further. By coinci-

dence a tube burned out in our standby receiver, causing it
to fail. These things we did not know at the time but were
told later by our technicians. Finally, the only receiving set
left for radio range operation was a small emergency one
powered by dry cell batteries. We tried for some time to
pick up the ranges on our main sets but couldn't. Later we
turned on the emergency set.

We knew now that we were in real trouble. The icing was
getting worse, so we climbed to 17,000 where it seemed a
bit lighter. We also decided to return to Vancouver.[1]

Violent turbulence continued to buffet the Lockheed, sometimes pushing it up to 19,000 feet, far too high for a plane not
equipped with oxygen. On the flight deck, the lack of it made
work and concentration a chore, and gradually the pilots realized
they were lost. With the fuel gauges indicating a dangerously
diminished supply of gasoline, the situation was becoming more
desperate by the minute.

"We decided to turn south, to the United States," recalls Leigh.
"We knew there were more radio stations there, and we hoped
we could find out where the hell we were. It was getting harder
all the time to concentrate, and finally we had to write down our
direction and both of us kept referring to it. We knew if we didn't
find an airfield soon, we would almost certainly crash."

Back in the cabin, the passengers were feeling the effects of
hypoxia, or oxygen deprivation. Many had been sick, but the
nausea had given way to drowsiness and an inability to think
clearly. A few had been injured in the turbulence, and were
bleeding. Don Brady, the young pilot who had been sitting with
the DOT personnel, managed to get out of his seat and laboriously
make his way to the flight deck to tell McGregor and Leigh of
the passengers' condition. McGregor and Leigh were much better, but they fought to carry on. They called for help as they went,
but had no way of knowing if their appeals were received on the
ground.

In fact, the frantic transmissions from the storm-tossed airliner
were heard, and Vancouver ordered all traffic cleared on the
Lockheed's radio range. At the same time, appeals went out to
people living in British Columbia and in the northern United
States to report any information on the stricken aircraft. By this

time, wild headwinds of up to 200 miles per hour buffetted the plane and, in effect, drove it backwards, so that when the pilots believed they were far south into the United States, they were actually north of their starting point in Vancouver. The emergency transmissions from the plane were garbled, sluggish, and at times barely coherent. Both pilots had turned blue and were desperately fighting unconsciousness.

"Then suddenly we could hear Vancouver calling on our emergency radio," says Lewis Leigh. "We came lower and saw the lights of a strange city, and then an airport. We were almost out of gas when we finally touched down after over four hours in the air. We could hardly believe we were back in Vancouver, because, until we had actually landed, we had no idea *where* we were. We thought we were away down in the States, but we had come in from the north. There were a number of reports from people who lived in the B.C. interior who said they had heard airplane engines that night. We were very lucky to be alive. The high winds had blown us all over the sky."

After a short rest, Leigh and the rest of the crew set out again for Winnipeg. This time they flew over the mountains without incident.

Those same mountains provided the backdrop for another kind of tale, this one of survival at a strange cost. Even today, some pilots find it hard to believe, but the aircraft commander on the flight stands by his story. He is Norm Cairns, a former military pilot with thousands of hours on the flight deck.

"I was flying a C-119 Boxcar and I was to take a couple of engines out to Comox [B.C.] from Summerside [P.E.I.]. This friend of mine said, 'Norm, I understand you're going to Comox.' I said yes. He said, 'Is there any chance of putting a convertible on board?'

" 'A convertible what?'

" 'A car.'

" 'Why would you want to do that?'

" 'Well, I'm transferred to Comox and we have two cars, but my wife doesn't drive. It would really help me if you could do it.'

"Even in those days that wasn't quite kosher, but we got away with things you wouldn't get away with today. So I said, 'If you want to load the thing at night and make damn sure it's tied down, I'll have the sergeant check it in the morning. It's okay with me, but I'm *not* responsible.'

"To make a long story short, we ended up with our last refuelling at Edmonton, and we took off, but we lost an engine over the Rockies. I said to the flight engineer, 'Everything goes. That airplane just does not stay on one engine very long at any height.' He said, 'You mean the car, Sir?' I said, 'Any damned thing that's moveable goes, and that includes the car.' So we opened the back door and threw the car out.

"It was a brand-new red Buick convertible. I can still see it doing beautiful cartwheels as it left the airplane.

"When we got to Comox, my friend called me up. He said, 'I'll be out tomorrow, where did you park the car?' I said, 'Don't bother. I don't have it.' He said, 'Okay, you've had your fun, where is it?'

"I said, 'I don't have it; you're not listening to me. I had to throw it out over the Rockies.'

" 'My God, you're serious.'

" 'I've never been more serious in my life. It was a case of your car going, or the airplane not staying in the air, and there wasn't a hell of a lot of choice.'

"He said, 'What do I do now?'

"I said, 'Well, was it insured?'

"He said yes.

" 'Well, I guess you tell the insurance company you can't find it.'

"I don't know what he told the insurance company, and I didn't want to know," Cairns laughs as he recalls the incident.

Sometimes apprentice pilots run into problems that, while embarrassing at the time, are the stuff of good stories in retrospect. Linton Read has had his private pilot's licence for several years, and he recalls one early flight with his wife as a passenger.

"My wife, Gerry, is a 'white-knuckle' flyer in a small aircraft. But, loyal lady that she is, she flew twice with me: once as my first passenger after I passed my flying tests for my licence, and once in Muskoka on a very beautiful summer day.

"On the second occasion, I had persuaded her to join me in a rental plane so that she could view our summer cottage property from the air and also enjoy a flight over the three spectacular Muskoka lakes.

"It is a required procedure that the supervising pilot of a plane-rental organization check out a pilot renting an aircraft. So that the instructor could do the checking from the right seat as I flew from the left (pilot) seat, my wife sat in the back seat for the check flight. After we landed and I was given the okay, she moved from the back to the front. We then closed and locked the door, completed the pre-flight checks, and took off.

"Scarcely were we at the levelling-out height of 1,600 feet when a most unearthly banging began in the aircraft; it was a regular, pounding, boiler-factory sound that hinted ominously of a blown cylinder or a crack in a propeller shaft. Despite my sinking heart and rapidly shattering nerves, I immediately moved into the emergency mode required by engine failure. A check of all instruments revealed no oil pressure drop, overheating, or other frightful possibility. The RPMs remained constant and our air speed seemed unaffected. Quickly I moved into a tight pattern for an emergency landing on the airstrip and radioed to base my fears and predicament. Since we were still within sight of the field, we landed safely despite the blood-curdling banging. Interestingly enough, as our speed and altitude declined, the noise lessened. As we taxied to the hangar and a group of worried personnel, the noise stopped.

"We tumbled quickly from the aircraft as the mechanics checked it over. The explanation was a wonderful anti-climax to our few minutes of terrible fears and apprehension. When my wife had moved from back seat to front seat, the rear seat belt had fallen part-way out through the open door; the part outside was the half with the steel tip on it. The door had been closed over the belt, leaving the steel tip loose against the hull. At 1,600 feet and 90 miles per hour, the air turbulence had set the tip vibrating against the hollow aircraft hull – thus the tremendous racket!

"Game lady that she is, once she understood the problem, my wife re-embarked for a continuation of our air tour. But she never flew with me again!"

Read, who by his own admission is somewhat rotund, once executed a landing that was less than perfect. In fact, he bounced down the runway as a bemused air traffic controller watched. The tower waited for the plane's run-out, then asked: "Was that a landing, Sir, or the dance of the sugar-plum fairy?" Some time earlier the same controller watched the same pilot ignore instructions and take off in the wrong direction on his first solo. The controller has since taken up another occupation . . .

Arnold Warren was an instructor at an elementary flying school in Windsor, Ontario, in 1940. On the final day of class for the first group of students there, the weather was miserable, but several flights were made anyway.

"At the time, there was a United States Air Services elementary flying school on an island in the Detroit River," Warren says. "On that last day someone got the idea that it was a shame that the Americans were not having any fun. There was no war going on for them, of course.

"We were going to have a graduation party and we thought someone should invite the Americans. One thing led to another, and we found a container somewhere, put a message in it, and tied a long ribbon to it. Then three of us took off in formation, roared over the U.S. flying field, and shot it up. Then we came down, really dragged the tarmac, and dumped out the message.

"Well, the Americans all showed up at our party, even the commanding officer. They had a great time, and so did we, and just before he left, their CO made a little speech. 'Come over anytime,' he said. 'Shoot the place up, roll your wheels on the tarmac, but for Christ's sake don't land, because if you do it will take an act of Congress to get you out.' We loved it."

Later on, Warren was posted to an RCAF elementary flying instructor's school at Arnprior, Ontario, where he became part of what was called the Pilot's Pool. He instructed at first and then became an examining officer. "The Pilot's Pool was an odd sort of arrangement," he says, "because I was the only person in the pool. It really meant that when any senior officer came around for a category upgrading, he was my pupil.

"I only had three students and I remember flying one beautiful day with one of them. As we went along, right beside the Ottawa River, he said to me over the intercom: 'I say, there's an airplane beating up that beach.' I told him I had noticed the same thing.

"I went down to have a look at what was going on, but the guy in the other plane saw me. Well, we got into a bit of a ring around the rosy, and the next thing I knew there was a chunk of yellow in a tree. The other pilot was so determined not to let me see his number that he got lower than he planned. He hit some trees, tore a wing off, and crashed to the ground. I never felt so sick in all my life.

"The guy lived, though, and I was called later to testify at his court-martial."

Tom Horne is not a pilot, but in a series of jobs over a number of years he has worked with pilots and has developed a great respect for them. On one occasion he almost became one. At the time, he was in the Royal Canadian Navy on the aircraft carrier *Magnificent*.

"We had been at sea for about three weeks without a break," he explains. "This was part of an exercise called 'Operation Mariner.' For five days, aircraft had been coming and going on the deck, twenty-four hours a day, and all of us were terribly tired. This was on the North Atlantic, in the late spring of 1953. I was one of the deck crew, a naval seaman.

"Anyway, this one night about midnight, just before the end of my shift, we were waiting for some planes to come down. As they landed, the aircraft would taxi forward and stay there until all the planes were on board. Then they would be towed back toward the stern to wait for the next takeoffs, or taken below decks to the hangars.

"When this Sea Fury came in, the pilot got out and went below, and I climbed into the aircraft to hold the brakes on until the fellows tied it down. It had been cold outside, and I was so tired, and that pilot's seat was pretty comfortable. So I settled back, locked my feet on the brakes, and fell sound asleep. The guys tied the plane down.

"I was rudely awakened after a time when I heard a loud crash and the ripping of metal, and I thought the plane I was in was falling overboard. I stamped hard on the brakes, pushed the hatch cover open, and yelled out: 'Have you guys got this thing tied down yet?' There was no answer, of course, because one of the last aircraft to land had crashed on the deck and torn itself apart.

"This was now after midnight. The deck shifts had changed, and the guys who worked with me couldn't find me. They thought I had fallen into the sea, so our carrier radioed a destroyer behind us to look for a man overboard. The ship had to be searched as well.

"When I finally climbed out of the plane and went below, the guys were happy to see me, but they were more interested in learning what my punishment would be for falling asleep on duty. As it turned out, I was reprimanded and had to help clean up the mess after night flying. I also lost some merit points and some of my pride."

Although he has never flown, Tom Horne once took some pains to learn how to do so in an emergency. In 1982 he was working with an oil company in Alberta dealing with problems relative to fire protection. One day, he accompanied a drilling crew in a small, six-passenger aircraft. The drillers started playing cards to pass the time while Horne sat in a jump seat with the pilot.

"As we were going along, I noticed that the pilot was a lot older than I had realized, probably in his late sixties or so. Then I got to thinking about what would happen if something went wrong and this guy suddenly slumped forward over the controls. None of us had any idea how to fly the plane, and without the pilot all of us would die in a blazing crash.

"I decided that maybe one of us should at least know how to keep the thing in the air until we could radio for help, so I started asking the old guy to explain the various controls. 'What's this for?' I would ask. 'What does that do?' and so on.

"Finally the pilot – he was a tough little grizzled character – turned to me and growled: 'Look, you sonofabitch, I'm not going to have a heart attack; you won't have to fly the aircraft. Now settle back and enjoy the flight!' I did as I was told."

In 1961 Jack Wells, the skinny kid who sailed to war on the *Queen Elizabeth*, was flying for CP Air when John Diefenbaker dissolved Parliament on April 19 and called an election for June 18. Between those dates, Wells flew the Prime Minister's campaign plane into forty-three airports across the country, and took off and landed seventy-two different times.

"The whole experience was interesting," remembers Wells. "We were to be as precise as possible insofar as our arrival and departure times were concerned. However, the schedule was extremely hectic, weather permitting. In all that time, we had only one twenty-hour break in Vancouver, where I was living at the time. That was the only time I saw my family during the campaign. Mr. Diefenbaker was certainly an easy person to deal with. He never bothered us at any time, and didn't demand anything from us. The whole thing went without a hitch."

Wells was unable to say the same thing about his next assignment with CP. It involved flying a Britannia on any of its various routes, particularly in the South Pacific.

"We used to fly out of Vancouver to the Far East, to Hawaii, to Sydney, Australia, to Auckland, New Zealand, and so on," Wells explains. "An old friend of mine had a dairy farm south of Auckland, and I was able to see him quite often. It was on a flight down there that I ran into trouble.

"We were in a Britannia, about 150 miles out of Fiji, when we hit what is called a sharp-edged downdraft. I had thirty-five people on board."

The unusual air current gripped the airliner and, in a matter of seconds, virtually flipped it over and dropped it from the 17,000-foot cruising altitude. Inside the plane, screaming, crying, terrified passengers were tossed around like clothes in a dryer. Four passengers smashed through the inner ceiling of the plane; several others were flung across the cabin where they became wedged against other passengers' seats. A stewardess was thrown headlong into the bulkhead, while a purser was somehow stabbed in the neck with a knife. One woman slammed into a wall, then slid down it and lay crumpled across the back of a seat, her neck broken by the impact. People near her received wounding blows to the head from heavy carry-on luggage that was hurled about the cabin. On the flight deck, neither pilot was hurt, but the navigator sustained a concussion when he went through the ceiling and his head hit the plane's water tank.

Then, just as suddenly as it had begun, the turbulence stopped. The plane had dropped several thousand feet, but it was flyable, and after a landing in Fiji and emergency medical treatment, most of the passengers and crew continued their journey. Only four passengers, all of whom had their seatbelts fastened, escaped injury.

"It was not long before Lana, my wife, heard about the whole thing," says Jack Wells today. "She was in the kitchen getting breakfast for our two girls when the news flash came on the radio. The bulletin referred to a CP airliner over the South Pacific that had plunged thousands of feet, and that there were many injured on board.

"This was traumatic for her, of course, because she knew that the only Canadian Pacific aircraft in that area of the world was the one I was flying. I contacted her as soon as I could but, until she knew, it was hard. By the time we arrived in Auckland, the newspapers had the story in two-inch banner headlines."

Jack Wells, on duty in that Britannia, might well have felt that he was in the wrong place at the wrong time. But in this story, twenty years before Jack Wells's adventure, a pilot by the name of Cliff Fielding *did* find himself flying at the wrong time – quite by accident.

Fielding, a Canadian military veteran who has flown all over the globe, is also an inveterate raconteur.

"In the summer of 1961, I was flying for Eastern Provincial Airways on contract with the Royal Greenland Trade Department, flying up and down the west coast of Greenland carrying passengers, freight, and mail. We went to eight different communities there, and we built up a lot of hours, mainly in Cansoes. In the summer season we probably had 10,000 passengers, operating out of Søndrestrøm. I think it was probably the most interesting flying I've ever done, most of it off water.

"By the middle of August that year, I had put in 300 hours in two and a half months, and the limit they allowed you was 300 in three months, so I couldn't fly for a couple of weeks. I checked with SAS, the Scandinavian airline, and wangled a free pass with them to go to Copenhagen. They flew in and out of Søndrestrøm on the polar route on the way to Los Angeles.

"Anyway, I went to Copenhagen, saw some friends there, and

had a pleasant holiday. Then one day I received a telegram asking me to come back early because one of our pilots had to be away – his father had died – and we were short of people.

"I hitched a ride on a DC-6 SAS charter going to Greenland, but in that type of plane the trip looked as if it would be long and boring. Because it was a charter, there was nothing in English to read, and very few of the passengers spoke English. Fortunately, there was a good supply of cognac on board, and one of the stewardesses knew me and kept me pretty well supplied. I also knew the guy next to me, a Dane going to Godthåb. The combination of cognac, the conversation, and the long trip made for a pleasant flight, so by the time we got to Greenland I was feeling no pain.

"When we landed at Søndrestrøm, somebody from the company approached me and said I would have to change and get my uniform on. I would be taking the passengers who had just arrived down to Godthåb because there was no room for them in the quarters at the terminal. There were no other pilots available.

"Well, this presented a bit of a problem. I wasn't staggering by any means, but I sure had more than the legal amount of alcohol. I protested, but got nowhere, so I decided I'd better make the best of it. I showered, changed, shaved, had something to eat, and made my way out to the aircraft.

"In those days, the captain was expected to greet passengers as they were boarding, so I stood by the ramp, steadied myself with one hand, and welcomed the people as they came to the steps leading up to the plane.

"Things were going quite well until my seatmate on the flight from Copenhagen appeared. He took one look at me, ran up the steps into the plane, put his seatbelt on, and stayed *very* quiet. I'm not sure what he thought, but we never heard a thing from him for the entire trip. It was uneventful, fortunately."

Fielding remembers another incident later that fall that also involved the consumption of alcohol.

"One day I was flying out to Godthåb, but the weather was poor, and there was a lot of cloud and rain and cold. We were well into the icing season, and ice build-up on the wings and props was a problem. On top of that, the de-icing boots on the plane were not in great shape, and it took them longer than it should have to inflate and break the ice away. As the ice got thicker, I increased power, but after a while the engine began to overheat. We couldn't descend below 10,000 feet because there was no radar, and the minimum altitude for that leg of the trip was 10,000 feet over the western part of the ice cap.

"It wasn't long before the ice build-up became a real concern, particularly on the props. Then the de-icing fluid went dry so I told the engineer to add more right away. That was when he gave me the bad news: 'Sir, there is no more fluid on board.' I looked at him in amazement and wondered what in hell we were going to do now.

"Luckily, we just happened to have some Danish friends farther south, and because booze was so expensive for them they had us bring it down from the American base at Søndrestrøm. On that flight we were carrying a case of Scotch. It probably saved our lives.

"We poured the Scotch into the de-icing tank and got the props cleared off. The whiskey worked well – even though we hated to waste it on the airplane. Three bottles got us to Godthåb."

Don Clarke joined the Air Force right after he completed high school in Nova Scotia. "The base at Greenwood was near my home," he explains, "so I was always keen on the military. I have never regretted joining."

Now, after almost twenty-eight years in uniform and countless moves, Clarke calls Trenton, Ontario, his home. Here he is chief check pilot on the Boeing 707 with 437 Squadron, though he has flown scores of different aircraft over the years. One of these was the Dakota.

"Several years ago, when I was on the Dak," he recalls, "another guy and I flew into Camp Borden to take several nurses up for a familiarization flight. Most of them had never flown before.

"Things were going well for some time, and I was flying along at 6,000 feet or so. My friend was in the back with the nurses, showing them around the aircraft and telling them how it worked.

"Suddenly the aircraft started doing things on its own, and I was having trouble controlling it. We were all over the sky and I was damned worried. But then, just as I was about to call Borden and declare an emergency, the plane seemed to fly properly. At that point, my friend came up from the back, and I told him what had happened.

"He just looked at me, then laughed and said: 'Oh, there was nothing to worry about. It was just us in the back. I was pulling some of the cables and showing the women how the plane worked.' "

As do most of his colleagues, Clarke sings the praises of the men and women in Air Transport. He is particularly happy about the types of pilots who come to the 707: "By the time they are flying the big jets, they are pretty competent," he says. "Air Transport is the backbone of the military, and the people who stay in it are good. We take passengers all over the place, and every so often haul relief supplies after floods, earthquakes, and so on. Unfortunately, we are now losing a lot of pilots to the civilian airlines, but I suppose that can't be helped."

North Bay, Ontario, native Paul Baldasaro is now in the Canadian Forces, but before putting on a uniform, he was a bush pilot out of his home town. He made lots of memorable flights, but one stands out more than the rest.

"This one day we got a call to pick up an Indian couple who lived a little over a half hour's flying time north of us," he explains. "I was new, so I was told to take the job. The couple lived in a log cabin on a little lake, about a quarter of a mile from a railway. Once a month they would come into town and expected us to go for them. Their names were John and Annie, so the flight was always referred to as the John and Annie run.

"Anyway, when I was first given the John and Annie run, there were a lot of smirks around the office, and the other guys were telling me I was a natural for it, and so on. By the time I was gassed up and ready to go, I didn't really know what to expect. I was briefed to the point that I knew the lake where I would land was small, and that you had to be careful taking off from it, but no one wanted to tell me much about the couple I was to fly.

"I found the lake all right, and I circled around a couple of times to size it up. There were exposed rocks, a few deadheads here and there, but if you were careful, there was no problem. I landed and taxied in toward the only cabin on the lake.

"Well, after about twenty minutes, this little, withered, stooped old character came limping down to the shore to meet me. He had a big smile on his face and bits of tissue paper sticking to it. The guy told me in great detail that he and his lady had just been making love, but that he had decided to shave afterwards. He knew the plane was coming but he had been so busy, he just lost track of time. When he shaved, he'd cut himself all over the place, and the Kleenex was stopping the bleeding. But he was sure happy. He just kept grinning.

"After some time his wife came out of the cabin. She was enormous! I think I must have showed my surprise, but she ignored it, and slowly waddled down to the shore. All the while I'm thinking, 'How in hell do I get her up into the plane?'

"Finally, I waded out into the water and pulled the aircraft around and backed it into the shore. Then John handed me all these gas cans, kerosene cans, and so on, and said he had to take them with him. There were lots of fumes around, but I tossed the cans in and got ready for Annie. The whole thing didn't bother her a bit.

"I got the door open first, then helped her out onto the pontoon, as the plane tilted away down on her side, and I slipped and slithered into the water. She just couldn't get up. She held onto the plane and tried but there was no hope. Finally I got under her and pushed her rear end up over my head, all the while trying to stand on the stones at the bottom, which were slippery.

"I lifted for all I was worth, while she sat on my shoulders and grunted and pulled at the door jamb, as the old guy watched. She was such an enormous dead weight that I thought I'd never get her in. At last I heaved for all I was worth, she popped through the door, and I fell in the water. The old guy grinned. It was no problem loading him.

"Away we went, on a tilt, and finally I got airborne, but with only a small bit of lake to spare. When I got back, the guys were breaking up laughing, because they all knew what I had been through.

"As time went on, I did the John and Annie run often, and I really liked those two people. They were real characters. They would stay in town overnight, get all their supplies and go home by train. I often wondered how she ever made it the quarter of a mile from the railway to their cabin."

Paul Baldasaro did a lot of flying fighting forest fires in Northern Ontario, but he is modest in his assessment of his role. When fighting rapidly spreading bush fires, he and his crew made countless trips, hauling freight, supplies, pumps, axes, and other equipment to the fire sites. Every so often they flew in great arcs over the bush, pinpointing new outbreaks, charting fire progress, and helping to lay the groundwork for the firefighters below. The work was exhausting, and sometimes hours of unrelenting work had little effect. But, for Baldasaro, fighting fires was flying at its most exciting.

"Training flights were just as interesting, though," he says, "depending on where we were going. Back in 1983, I think it was, I was the first officer on a long-range trainer down through the Pacific to Hawaii, Tahiti, Fiji, American Samoa, and back to Edmonton. This was on a C-130, a Hercules transport.

"When we got to Hawaii, there was a hurricane alert. We were to be there for two nights, but because of the alert we stayed overnight and left before the storm hit, deciding to go to Tahiti, spend two nights there, and stay on schedule. The Hawaii-Tahiti leg was no problem, and we arrived there, looked after the aircraft, finished our work, and checked into a hotel.

"Well, the place was pleasant, and it wasn't Edmonton, so we settled in fairly quickly. Before long we had a drink, then another and another, and some of us became rather creative, as often happens to people in such situations. The creativity was fun while it was happening.

"We drafted a message for the folks back in Edmonton, telling them that the flights had gone well so far, but that we liked Tahiti so much we had sold the plane and bought a mai tai plantation with the money. We included our hotel address, and made the request that any pensions or other allowances coming to us were to be forwarded to our new residence. We also asked that our families be informed, and that all mail from the squadron was to be forwarded to us at our plantation.

"Then we addressed the message to the squadron and no one else. We knew it would go into the squadron Operations and they would know exactly who it was from and get a laugh out of it. We paid for the telex ourselves, because it was only intended as a joke.

"However, the telex went into the Edmonton message centre,

and an overly keen guy got it, saw that it was from Service Flight 540, or whatever, and noted that we had forgotten to indicate the other places where such communications were to go. Apparently the guy didn't even read it, but sent the damn thing all over the bloody world – and that included our headquarters. We sure had to do some back-pedalling when we returned.''

Another military pilot who spent time far from home is Captain Al Mornan, a specialist in air-to-air refuelling using the big 707 transport planes. When asked to talk about his most interesting flying, he tells you about a year he spent in Kashmir as part of the Canadian involvement with the United Nations.

"Back in the summer of 1971 we took a Twin Otter to Kashmir from Trenton, Ontario, by way of Søndrestrøm, Greenland, to Keflavik, in Iceland, and so on to Lahr, Bahrein, Karachi, Rawalpindi, and finally Srinagar. That flying was fantastic. The job involved carrying UN Observers, mail, supplies, and food all over the place in that area of the world. We landed at dirt strips, paved runways, and gravel, and you often had to fly a couple of passes over the runway first to chase away the water buffalo and the kids playing soccer.

"One of our Canadian planes, an Otter, was blasted to hell by the Indian Air Force, and we later got into some hot water when we said who had done it. The plane was on the runway at the time, and fortunately no one was near it. War had broken out on December 3 between India and Pakistan, and two days later the plane was a casualty. Not long afterwards, Canada had a replacement aircraft there.''

Reg Wild is from Western Canada, but he spent several years in Tripoli, Libya; London, England; and Calgary before joining the Canadian Air Force in 1978. His father, who was in the oil business, had been a pilot and had his own plane, so it was not surprising that Reg would gravitate to flying as well. He had his pilot's licence when he was sixteen, but spent two years studying medicine and some months in dentistry before deciding that a career in flying would be more fun. He has never regretted the

move, and now flies Hercules transport planes with 426 Squadron
out of CFB Trenton. One of his more bizarre adventures took place
a number of years ago, but the gory details have not faded.

"You may remember," he begins, "that back in October 1984,
about 10,000 caribou drowned trying to swim across the Cania-
piscau River up in Northern Labrador. Well, six months after that
happened, several of us were sent up to Fort Chimo to haul the
corpses away. Some small helicopters and a couple of private
companies had tried to do the job, but I guess it was too much
for them.

"They had us hauling dead caribou out of there on large pallets,
25 to a pallet, for a load of 125 bodies. By the time we got there,
the damn things stank, they were half-rotted, and blood and everything else was pouring out of them. They sure weren't a beautiful
sight. We had to bring them all the way down from Fort Chimo
to Dorval at Montreal, where they were eventually made into
fertilizer.

"Now, we were flying Hercs, of course, and down below the
floor of that plane there is a large cavity, perhaps two to three
feet deep. On one particular trip we had flown all night, so the
fluids from the corpses had drained down below the floor and
were sloshing around, overflowing and leaking outside. We
arrived in Montreal, landed, and pulled off the active runway. A
light aircraft landed just after us, and followed us along the
taxiway.

"We didn't say anything because we sure as hell didn't think
much of our cargo. Then the tower called: 'Canadian Military,
you are losing fluid out of your aircraft at a great rate.' We
responded: 'Roger, we know that. No problem.'

"The tower came back again: 'Canadian Military, you are
losing a *great deal* of fluid. Do you want us to call emergency
vehicles? Is the fluid flammable?' We acknowledged the transmission and told the tower the answer was negative to both
questions.

"About two seconds later, the tower called again and asked:
'Canadian Military, what is the fluid?'

" 'It's blood,' was all we answered. I guess the civilian behind
us was concerned and so was the tower. The tower called: 'Where
have you guys been? What have you been doing? There's an
awful lot of blood coming out of there.'

" 'Yes, tower, the airplane is full of it,' we answered. I can still remember the blank stares we got when we pulled to a stop. The fluid was pouring out, all over the place. That was the only remotely pleasant part of that exercise – seeing those faces.''

While pilots exchange anecdotes about their adventures – and misadventures – in the air, there are other flying stories that capture the imagination of the public. The public remembers the stories that tell of disaster – of loss of aircraft, loss of life, loss of loved ones.

The public remembers the crashes.

15

The Crashes

Even though our skies have always been, statistically, safer than
our highways, air crashes do happen. Some of those involving
the big passenger airlines have been horrific beyond description.
The men and women who walk away from the wreckage of any
accident are lucky, though they will probably remember the
events leading to the crash in vivid, almost slow-motion detail
for the rest of their lives. Some crash survivors feel that the
accident was the most traumatic thing to ever happen to them.
Certainly, any air accident is serious, and pilots as much as their
passengers want to avoid them. But, to the pilot who lives to tell
about it, there is such a thing as a ''happy-ending'' crash.

Paul Apperley has had several happy endings in a lifetime of
flying, in both civilian and miliary life. In his earlier days in the
Air Force during World War II, he was, in effect, given a plane
and told to try to crash it. ''Three of us volunteered to fly a funny
little aircraft called a Beaufighter over the Bristol Channel during
the later stages of the war. It had two big engines and a short
nose. All we were told at the time was: 'Get as low as you can,
and fly as fast as you can.'

''This was fun for a while, but after a month or so we were
posted out of there to Bomber Command, because they didn't
need fighters any more. As we were leaving, we told the guy
who signed our log books how much fun this had been, but then
we asked him what it was all about. As it turned out, they had
installed radar equipment in the noses of the planes, and then

160

covered it with a fibreglass shield. This was for the night fighters, and not for us at all. If we flew them low and fast and the nose did not come off, then it was okay for the experienced pilots to use them. The designers weren't sure if the new design would stand up to high speeds and the occasional splash of water. We proved that it would, and we never crashed a single one doing this stuff. I guess we were more or less expendable."

Later on, after he returned from overseas, Apperley was flying a crop-dusting plane near Windsor, Ontario. The work was interesting, but to someone with Apperley's experience, not particularly exciting – until one morning when he was spraying a field of peas for a local canning company.

"I had dusted about half the field one evening," he recalls. "The next morning, just after sunrise, I took off again with a full load. Because I knew the field, there should not have been a problem. I made one pass down over it, then turned to come back, but I forgot about a big elm tree at one end. I was flying into the sun when suddenly the tree was right in front of me.

"I kind of gulped, I guess, but then I pulled the plane up, closed the throttles, and settled into the top of the tree. The plane just stuck there, so I got out, climbed down, and went to Windsor and hired a big crane.

"The guy came out to the farm with the crane, and I got on the ball at the front where there was a big hook, and he lifted me up to the plane. Then I took the two panels off where the wings join the fuselage. I put a rope around the plane there; the guy hauled me down, and I was flying again that night." Apperley laughs as he describes the accident, but dismisses it as "just one of those things." For many people, such an occurrence would likely mark the end of a flying career, but to Paul Apperley, and to most of the pilots who have walked away from crashes, such accidents are just part of the job.

Dennis Bradley, the president of the Canadian War Plane Heritage Museum in Hamilton, Ontario, would certainly agree. To hear him describe a crash he was in is like listening to someone else describe falling off a bicycle. The incident has both tragic and comic elements, but the humour was not so apparent when the accident was happening.

"Our museum's first North American P-51 Mustang came from 417 Squadron at Rivers, Manitoba," he recalls. "On July

4, 1984, I was flying it back to Hamilton after having had some maintenance done on it in Minneapolis. Up on the top edge of Lake Huron, south-west of Sudbury, I had a crankshaft break. This makes it awfully quiet in the airplane. I had a mechanic named Ken Kline with me, and we both were pretty surprised.

"As somebody said, 'What's that thing on the front of the airplane?' The answer, of course, is, 'Oh, that's a fan that keeps the pilot cool. When that thing stops, the pilot really sweats.' Well, when the propeller stopped, I was sweating. So was Ken.

"Anyway, not far from the town of Massey I saw a dirt road in that barren, nothing country, and I decided that road was the only chance I had. I landed on it."

The fighter touched the narrow roadway, raced forward, hit a bump the pilot could not see from the air, and veered to one side when a wheel dropped into a shallow ditch. With the wheel off the road, one wing of the plane clipped several fence posts. Bradley fought to keep the Mustang going on a straight path, Kline held on for dear life, and both of them saw a farmer's storage shed that was a lot closer to the road than it seemed from the air.

"Because the one wheel had dropped into the ditch," says Bradley, "the plane swung to one side and a wing hit the storage shed. When this happened, we could hear electrical wires snapping and see the shed start to burn."

On the other side of the barn, the farmer who owned the place was startled when he looked up and saw two men in flight suits racing around a corner toward him. He had not seen the plane come down, but within seconds he saw his storage shed in flames. With no fire-fighting equipment around, and no hoses long enough to reach the flames, the three men had to stand and watch helplessly as the fire raced through the tinder-dry frame structure. Then, almost as an afterthought, the farmer mentioned the stored propane somewhere inside the conflagration.

"When he said that, we all took off," says Bradley. "In no time, the propane exploded and the shed was levelled. So was our plane. The accident investigator later told me that the temperature in that shed got up to 3,000° F during the fire. Our Mustang melted.

"I suppose it must have made the farmer wonder what in hell was going on when we ran toward him. The crash also startled a lady in a house nearby. She had been doing her dishes and the airplane went right by her window.''

As for Bradley: "Just before we hit the ground, all I could think of was: 'Damn it all, now I've got to get a truck and get the plane out of here, because I know I'll never be able to take off on this road.' I also was wondering how I'd explain the fact that I hadn't cleared customs. That Kline and I could be dead a minute later never occurred to me.''

Jack Hamilton, another pilot who survived a crash, had even less time than Bradley to assess the situation.

"I had been flying the Canadair CF-104," says Hamilton, who today resides in Munster, Ontario, on the outskirts of Ottawa. "After my time on the 104, I went on an exchange tour with the United States Air Force, flying the F-4D Phantom, out of Nellis Air Force Base in Nevada. On December 18, 1967, we flew six planes to Tucson, where our navigators were undergoing simulator training. It was late that day when we were ready to return.''

The Arizona weather had been wet for several days that month, and when the twelve men were ready to leave for Nevada, cold rain was falling, dark clouds streamed across the sky, and the runway lights shone drearily in the darkness.

"The weather was marginal, but one of the fellows had to get back to Nellis, so when one went, we all went. We took off in two flights of three. I was number two in the second flight.

"We rolled onto the runway, did our checks, called for burner, released the brakes, and away we went. As soon as we were airborne, it was gear up, flaps up, and out of burner. When I came out of burner there was a horrendous loss of thrust, and I took a look down and everything was unwinding. I just said, 'Flamed out.'

"Before I could say another word, the Lead yelled 'Bail out!' on his radio.

"Now, my back-seater, [USAF Captain] Gary Hughes, who had just gone through simulator training that day (and bailing out was part of it), heard the Lead yell 'Bail out,' and, man, he was gone! We hadn't even cleared the airdrome. He landed inside the perimeter fence.

"Fortunately, we had individual canopies, so I'm sitting there thinking, it's flamed out, so I've got to relight this bugger. I went through a relight procedure, but it didn't light. All I could think of was, damn it, I'm doing something wrong, because it always lights in the simulator if you do it right. Now that's stupid; that's almost over-trained. I can remember reaching and touching the relight switch, moving the throttle back up again; and all of a sudden the airplane just stalled in the air.

"At that point, I tried to aim toward a place with no houses, but thought I'd better go. So I pulled the [ejection release] handles and I went.

"I remember thinking, God, that hurt, and then I guess I was unconscious. The next thing I knew I was sitting in a few inches of dirty water in the deep end of a nearly drained swimming pool near downtown Tucson."

Jack Hamilton sat there in the water, almost too dazed to move, trying to piece together the sequence of events that had just occurred. In the gloom, he noticed that half his parachute was ripped away, and indeed it was draped over the fence at an adjoining house. Some time later the seat from the jet turned up in the back yard of a house a block away. By coincidence, people named Hamilton lived there.

In the meantime, several blocks away, the falling Phantom became a lethal projectile. The doomed aircraft hit the ground about a mile north-west of the runway, destroyed a house, and tore into the rear of a supermarket. The plane exploded on impact and 1,700 gallons of burning jet fuel, shredded hunks of metal, plastic, and rubber spilled over everything in its path. At the time, more than fifty people had been inside the Food Giant supermarket, and three of them lost their lives as a result of the crash. Five shoppers were injured and as many firefighters received treatment later for smoke inhalation suffered from battling the roaring flames. Within minutes, the first bulletins about the crash were aired on radio stations across the city.

"I don't know how long I was in the swimming pool," says Hamilton, "but I finally shrugged out of my chute, and climbed out of the water up to the shallow end. A young fellow came running from the house and asked if I was all right, and then he helped me inside.

"It's funny the things you remember. They had a beautiful

white velvet chesterfield and they wanted me to lie down on it, even though I was soaking wet and my flight suit was covered with muck from the bottom of the pool.

"I asked them if they could get me a straight-backed chair instead and let me sit in the kitchen, someplace where I wasn't going to slop so much dirty water around. They got me into a chair and asked if I would have a drink of brandy. I could have used one all right, but I didn't think it would look good if I had booze in my system. They called the Air Force for me.

"Then I waited, and waited, and waited, and finally, about forty minutes passed and a service policeman came to the house. In the meantime, I was in a lot of pain because, as I learned later, four of the vertebrae in my back had been crushed. Anyway, the policeman charged in and asked, 'Were you in that airplane?' I told him I was, and he said, 'Don't go away.' Then he left. I certainly hadn't intended going anywhere.

"I continued to sit there in the kitchen, by myself, for *another* forty minutes till finally an ambulance showed up. The attendants laid me down, tied me on a stretcher, and put me in the back. I could see people standing around and looking in at me and I imagined they were saying 'That's the guy that did it,' because the news had spread about the tragedy at the supermarket. I felt pretty bad and wanted to get out of there.

"But the ambulance wouldn't start.

"We were there for another twenty minutes, until finally they went for jumper cables, got it going, and we left."

While all this was happening to Hamilton, Captain Gary Hughes, who had also bailed out of the plane, had floated down in the dark and landed on a small island, surrounded by flooded drainage ditches on the air base property. He lay on the ground with minor injuries while his parachute settled into the water behind him.

"The poor guy was terrified of water," explains Jack Hamilton, describing his unfortunate navigator, "so he sat up on this little island and didn't move. In the time after he landed there, *three* different searchers went past with flashlights. Each time he yelled to them, 'Did you find the pilot?' 'No,' they answered, 'but we're still looking.' Then they left. He never said a word, and the searchers wandered off each time. Finally, the third time

they came around, he said, 'Did you find the pilot?' 'No,' one
guy yelled. It was not until then that Hughes told them who he
was. 'I was in that plane too, you know.'

"At last, they came for him, but the whole thing was a crazy
charade. Later that night both of us were together in the base
hospital."

During the period of his recovery, Hamilton recalls filling out
questionnaires for the service about the accident. "When you do
an after-ejection report for the United States Air Force, the thing
is about sixty pages long, there are about thirty questions on each
page, and boy, is it complete. But because I had been knocked
out during the bail-out, I couldn't answer a lot of them.

"They wanted to know how high I was when I jumped, and I
told them seven or eight hundred feet. They wanted to know how
long I was in the chute and I said a minute and a half or so. Then
there were a lot of other questions I had to guess at. As it turned
out, from Control Tower tapes, the elapsed time from brake
release to everything back on the ground was only thirty-seven
seconds. The whole thing happened that fast."

Hamilton's back gradually healed in the three months he was
hospitalized, but when he was released he had to wear a back
brace and was restricted to a desk job. After seven months he
resumed flying. Today, as a major in the Canadian Forces, he
still treasures the letters and expressions of sympathy he received
from Americans in the days following the accident. His letters at
the time were screened, and the United States Air Force withheld
the much more hurtful and voluminous hate mail. He is grateful
to them for doing so.

Another young Canadian pilot owes his life to luck, the ability to
hold his breath, and the instant action taken by his colleagues.
Like Hamilton, Jack Flannagan later became a major in the Canadian Forces, but at the time of the accident he was in the Royal
Canadian Navy, on the deck of a ship in the Caribbean, several
miles north-west of the Puerto Rican city of San Juan.

"The accident happened on the 16th of February, 1969," Flannagan told me. "I was flying Trackers off the deck of our aircraft
carrier, the HMCS *Bonaventure*. It was a beautiful day for flying.
There wasn't a cloud in the sky, and the water down there was

warm, of course, and clear. I had been in the navy for some time.''

At about 6:00 p.m. that Sunday, Flannagan, his co-pilot, and two observers climbed into the grey twin-engine Tracker aircraft, a de Havilland-built Grumman anti-submarine patrol plane. They fastened their seatbelts, did all the checks, wound the engines up to full power, and signalled the catapult officer that they were ready to go. As they made their preparations, the hatches were open on the roof of the airplane, the engines were roaring an arm's length away, and the massive machine that would shoot the plane down the deck and into the sky had already built up enough pressure that the nose wheel of the aircraft was in the air. The Tracker looked like a tiger ready to pounce.

Then the flight deck officer dropped a green flag, and the catapult fired.

"We went roaring toward the edge of the deck, down what was called the catapult track," says Flannagan, "and suddenly I realized something was terribly wrong. The sense of acceleration just disappeared. The aircraft is rapidly approaching the end of the ship; it's going too fast to stop, but not fast enough to get airborne.

"I hollered into the intercom that we were going to ditch," says Flannagan, "for the guys to get the hell out of there. All this took up a couple of seconds at most, and the fellows in the back reacted first. I'm not sure to this day if the co-pilot realized at that moment what had happened. Anyway, the two men in the back jettisoned their hatch covers and they were out, one of them before we hit the water.

"The aircraft rolled off the bow of the ship, while I'm telling myself to keep the nose of the plane up if I can, so that we can pancake into the water. If we had dived in, the acceleration likely would have flipped us over on our back. As it was, we were doing about fifty knots when we hit. The co-pilot went up through the hatch and escaped serious injury.

"Because the wheels were down when the aircraft impacted, a column of water shot up from the nosewheel well, passed between my legs, and shot out the hatch in the roof. All the while, I'm sitting there frantically trying to get my harness undone, and the cockpit is filling with water. As soon as I got unbuckled, I climbed up on the seat and started to pull myself through the hatch to get out. That was when the ship ran into the plane.''

The 720-foot-long aircraft carrier slammed into the Tracker, and the escape-hatch cover hit Flannagan on the back and knocked the wind out of him. Then the bow of the big vessel ran up on the plane, sucked it beneath the surface of the ocean, and took the pilot with it. Just as he went under, Flannagan fumbled for the inflation valve on the right side of his Mae West. The life preserver did not inflate. A couple of seconds later, he popped out through the top of the sinking plane, only to find himself dragged down under the hull of the still-steaming, 20,000-ton ship.

"In no time I was right under the ship," recalls Flannagan today. "There was a great deal of turbulence, and I was being tossed around like a cork. Fortunately, I still had my helmet on, because first my head banged against the hull, then my back and shoulders and so on. I rolled over and over, end over end, with my arms flailing around and my eyes open, fully conscious.

"Then I ran out of air.

"I had held my breath as long as I could, until my chest hurt so much I could no longer stand it. Then I knew; I came to a definite conclusion: I wasn't going to survive. With that decision out of the way, I sucked in sea water and the pain in my chest went away. However, I now had another problem: Just before we left for our flight, I had eaten two bacon, tomato, and lettuce sandwiches. All the upheaval, plus the salt water I had swallowed, made me sick. I was throwing up, then ingesting some of the vomit, along with sea water, all the while being tossed every which way.

"Finally, when I thought things could not get much worse, I looked up and saw the damned propellers. I remember clearly saying to myself, 'God, not this too.' I saw the white water which was the cavitation of the propellers, and a fraction of a second after I saw them I realized I was about to go through them."

The two huge, churning, screws on the *Bonaventure* each weighed about eight tons. And although emergency bells were already ringing up on the deck, and the order to stop the engines had been given, the screws were still turning – fast. Flannagan was pulled into the vortex created by the deadly rotation, all the while conscious and only a second from his fate. He was ready to die.

"Then one of the propeller blades hit my right leg and cut it off below the knee. The shock and the pain caused me to double over, and I remember seeing the next blade just miss my head. The jolt of the whole affair made my adrenalin pump faster, I guess, and I thought to myself, 'There's nothing *left* to hit, I just might get away with this.' I pulled the toggle on the other side of my life jacket, and it inflated! Then the screws tossed me up the twenty-six feet to the surface, where I found myself bobbing around in the wake of the ship.

"I'll never forget the sunshine when my head came out of the water, but I was not in very good shape. I was only twenty-six at the time, but I'd been through a lot in those last few minutes. I guess it was instant aging, but I was alive."

While Jack Flannagan was surviving his personal hell deep under the surface of the Caribbean, a rescue helicopter was hovering above the *Bonaventure*. This was always the case when planes were being launched. As soon as the screws spat the mangled pilot to the surface, a red cloud of blood welled up around him. The chopper crew saw Flannagan's helmet, then the circle of red, and they made for him.

"A couple of guys from the helicopter must have jumped thirty or forty feet down to me. They put a horse collar around me and started to winch me up. That was when I passed out. I knew then it was all up to someone else now."

Flannagan was on board the chopper in no time, then he was flown directly to the deck of the carrier, lifted onto a stretcher, and whisked to sick bay, where he regained consciousness, all in the space of six or seven minutes.

"Once they had me there, I knew I'd make it," says Flannagan today. "They pumped a lot of blood into me, worked to get the sea water out and to stop the bleeding of my leg, and flew me to a U.S. army hospital in San Juan. From then on, it was just recovery time."

Jack Flannagan recovered completely, learned to walk on his artificial leg, and a year after his accident was back flying planes – this time, helicopters. He now jokes about his adventure, and walks without a trace of a limp.

On the morning of August 27, 1980, Rob Porter was flying one of the fastest jets ever used by the Canadian Forces. The CF-104

Starfighter was little more than a rocket with wings, but it was loved by those who drove it. Capable of speeds up to 1,200 miles per hour, the controversial fighter was dubbed "The Widow-Maker" by the media, because so many pilots had been killed in it. Porter was a single second away from being one of them.

The hazy sun over Holland that warm August morning was both welcome and pleasant. It was ideal weather for bombing practice at Trescheling, a range being used by Canadian pilots on a small island in the North Sea. Although based at CFB Baden, West Germany, Porter and the three men with him had taken off from Soesterberg and had flown, fully armed, to the range some twenty minutes' flying time to the north-east. The group was led by Lieutenant Colonel Larry Crabb; Captain Luc Trepanier flew in the number two position; Major Rob Porter was number three, and Captain Gary Lacroix was number four. All were part of 441 Squadron at Baden.

The practice proceeded without incident for a while, and Porter and the others made several passes over the target. They were guided by a man at Range Control, who was not only close enough to see the jets forming up, but was also able to observe the accuracy of the bombing. Radio transmission referred to him simply as "Range." The lead aircraft flown by Crabb was called "Whiskey Lead." Others were designated by the sequential numbers Whiskey Two, Three, and Four.

"I was approaching the range, at about 300 feet, and at a speed of about 600 miles an hour, when my troubles started," explains Rob Porter. "The aircraft began to roll to the left, for no reason. I immediately attempted to put in opposite aileron, but to no avail. The aircraft continued to roll to the left, until I approached 120 degrees of roll, and I realized this was going to be a nasty situation. All my efforts to right the aircraft were unproductive."

As his bomb-loaded jet screamed down out of the sky toward the island target, Porter very quickly found himself almost upside down in a plane beginning to self-destruct. Range Control had just given him permission to make his bombing run when they called back to say: "You're losing quite a lot of things, Number Three." At that point, the Starfighter was falling apart and rapidly taking Porter to almost certain death. On the Range Tower tape of the transmission, there is an ominous silence at this point.

Meanwhile, Porter was frantically trying to get his plane

upright. By now, at perhaps 200 feet above the North Sea approach to the range, he knew that to eject from the plane would be fatal. Because he was virtually upside down, a bail-out would only drive him downward and there would be no hope of his parachute ever opening. In a last-second, desperate move, he deliberately introduced aileron in the direction of the roll.

The gamble paid off.

The jet rolled farther and became completely inverted; parts ripped off; it turned more and was now a roaring missile ripping apart as it dived. Then, during the last possible second in which he could save his life, Porter got the plane righted enough to eject, sidewise, into a brick wall of a slipstream, no more than 100 feet above the water. His oxygen mask and helmet were torn from his head, and he tumbled wildly through the air as his seatpack fell away.

Up above, Colonel Crabb heard the report concerning the breaking up of Porter's plane. The following is a partial transcription of his radio transmissions with Range Control. In this transcription, Crabb is designated as "Lead."

LEAD	– What happened, Range?
RANGE	– Stand by. Your Number Three has just bailed out. He is in the water. He is at the moment in the water.
RANGE	– He is in the water about a mile out.
LEAD	– Okay, I have contact. Numbers Two and Four, climb above the range and orbit. [Trepanier and Lacroix went to 8,000 feet.]
LEAD	– Request permission to do a low pass over the area.
RANGE	– Permission granted.
WHISKEY TWO	– Lead, do you wish me to contact the Base?
LEAD	– Go ahead. Contact the Base.
LEAD	– Range, did you see a chute?
RANGE	– Yes. We did see a parachute. It was very short but he was hanging in a parachute.
LEAD	– Thank you.

RANGE	– Quite a lot of parts fell off.
LEAD	– I was not able to observe anything. Request permission to make another pass.
RANGE	– You are cleared for another. He is exactly in line with the bombing run.
LEAD	– Thank you.
LEAD	– Range, did he hit the ground, or what happened there?
RANGE	– Negative. He just dropped a bomb at about three or four hundred feet and quite a lot of parts came off.
LEAD	– I'll make one pass down the run-in line.
RANGE	– Exactly the run-in line, about a mile from the coast.
LEAD	– Thank you.
RANGE	– We did observe a parachute. It was only for a few seconds but it might have broken his fall. Let's hope and pray. [A minute and a half pass.]
RANGE	– Whiskey, stay at 500. The chopper is going to the scene.
LEAD	– Roger.

Rob Porter came down in the water at almost the same time his broken plane cartwheeled into the sea, where it exploded in an orange-and-black fireball. In no time, the machine was scattered in an oil-slick circle, while billows of greasy smoke rose into the hazy sky.

"I was never unconscious," Porter says. "Everything happened too fast. By the time I was out of the plane, I was in the ocean, and my chute never fully deployed. I had no feeling of fear that I recall. Nor did I have nightmares about the thing later.

"The chopper was over me in six minutes, and the water was not cold.

"When the canopy went, I remember the shriek of air over the cockpit, and I wondered if the seat was ever going to fire. At that point, everything moved in slow motion, until I hit the air. If you can imagine putting your arm out of a car window at 80 miles an hour – I hit the slipsteam at 600.

"When they pulled me into the chopper, I had cuts on my face and behind my ears, my right shoulder was separated, my back hurt, but I felt damned lucky to be alive. There was plenty of pain but I'd survived. I was able to walk into the hospital at Leewarden, where they took me. By this time someone had contacted my wife, Jan, to tell her she still had a living husband."

After his recuperation, Rob Porter returned to ride the Widow-Maker. "I always loved that plane," he admits.

Another individual who loved the Starfighter, and also survived a crash in one, is today a highly respected and popular general in the Canadian Forces. When he went down in the 104 in 1967, he was a young flight lieutenant on an exchange tour with the Royal Danish Air Force flying out of Karup, Denmark. In a way, his story begins four years earlier and thousands of miles away on the Canadian prairies at Penhold, Alberta.

After his graduation from the Royal Military College at Kingston, Ontario, in 1963, Garry "Sky" King was posted to Penhold to learn to fly the Harvard. At the time, several Scandinavians were training at Penhold, and some of them were on the same course as King. One of them, nineteen-year-old Ova Stolle, became twenty-one-year-old Sky King's closest friend. "We hit it off right away," says King today, "and we soon began competing for just about everything. This went to the point that, on graduation day, I won the trophy as the top pilot, and Ova came second. However, he got the top academic award and I came second there. When graduation was over, we said we would keep in touch. Then we shook hands and said goodbye. However, as time passed, we went our separate ways. He left Canada, and I started on the Sabre in Chatham, Ontario."

Following a period of time flying Sabres, King trained on the CF-104 and was posted to Europe as part of Canada's NATO commitment there. By July 1967, however, he and his squadron were on the exchange in Denmark. Part of their job involved reconnaissance patrols.

"On July 21, I was on a routine patrol mission over the Baltic

Sea looking for East bloc shipping coming out of the Baltic Straits and into the Kattegat,'' says King. ''It was a warm, sunny day, with a brisk wind. My cruising speed was 420 knots. Below me, 300 feet down, the sea was rolling and beautiful, and I was having a great time, flying along, enjoying myself.

''Then, about two miles off the Danish coast, I suddenly saw a bird, right in front of me, flapping its wings wildly. The next thing I knew, this seagull bounced off the windscreen and then went straight into the left engine intake. It happened so quickly, all I did was duck. I had no time to react in any other way.

''The seagull's impact broke off a couple of compressor blades, and the engine began to break up inside. The noise was godawful, very, very, scary, beyond anything I could have imagined. It was a classic compressor stall that we learned about in simulators, but this one had all the sound effects.

''I turned the engine off, then attempted to use my airspeed to climb and to relight, but the engine would not start. I went through the procedure again, but to no avail. By this time I was losing both speed and altitude, and the plane had become a glider. It was now very quiet, and I knew I was going into the water.

''At that point, I reached down between my legs and pulled the ejection handle and waited for what seemed twenty years before anything happened. It was all slow motion, with no surprises.

''Then I felt myself tumbling forward, felt the butt-snapper push my seat away, and then, after about three forward somersaults, the parachute opened. The next thing I knew, I hit the water. All this involved three seconds at most.''

No sooner had King touched the sea than his wind-filled parachute started to blow farther from shore, dragging him on a wild, frightening ride across and through the waves. Salt water filled his mouth, stung his eyes, and generally made his efforts to stop the ride more difficult. Finally, he was able to release the chute, but still could not locate the handle to inflate his Mae West. When the parachute released, King sank below the surface.

''I swam to the surface,'' he continues, ''treaded water and attempted to inflate my Mae West. However, I couldn't find the toggle for activating the carbon dioxide cartridge on the Mae West. The more I looked, the more elusive the damned thing seemed to be. I sank below the surface again, fumbled around trying to find the thing, and then swam back to the top. My clothes seemed to weigh a ton. I had taken my helmet off and got rid of it, but my flight boots were heavy, and several maps in my pockets were soaked, so even they were heavy.

"This whole sequence of coming to the top, looking for the toggle, and then sinking was repeated several times, until I began to get a bit panicky. I was also getting very tired. Swimming in a flight suit and jacket and boots is not much fun. Finally I decided I *had* to get the problem solved or I wasn't going to survive.

"I decided to let myself sink and concentrate on finding the toggle, so I took a deep breath, relaxed, and sank below the surface. Then I opened my eyes under water, grabbed the bottom of the Mae West, folded it up toward me so I could have a good look, opened a flap on it, and there, under the carbon dioxide activator, was the red toggle handle. I gave it a yank. The Mae West inflated, and I floated to the surface. My God, was I relieved!

"For some reason, and I can't explain why, I punched my stopwatch at that point.

"The whole experience so far had been pretty depressing. I vividly remember knowing that I could still die if I didn't keep my head and keep my cool. I was relying now on my survival instincts alone, because I had nothing else in me. However, it was great to at least know I wasn't going to sink."

This feeling was premature. Shortly after King got to the surface, he looked down and saw a ring of bubbles around the oral inflation valve of his life jacket. The Mae West was deflating!

"You know," he continues, "we had been taught how to depress the valve and blow it up more, but I was afraid to touch it, I guess because I had such a difficult time getting the thing inflated in the first place. I was afraid that if I touched it, I might make it worse. Some air in it was a lot better than no air at all.

"After about ten minutes in the water, I began to get quite cold, but I was still floating around there. I had already taken off my boots and spurs and removed any extra stuff from my flying jacket and the leg pockets of my flying suit, because I wanted the Mae West to hold out as long as possible. I figured the lighter I was, the better my chances were.

"I kept treading water for the time being, and just when I started feeling that I was absolutely alone, I noticed a sea gull circling over my head. The bird stayed with me all the time I was there, just flying around and around. I even began to feel bad for it, because I had obviously killed its mate.''

The water, though not freezing, was far from warm, and the longer he stayed in it, the colder King became. Finally, he decided to attempt to swim to shore, because, occasionally, when he came to the top of one of the ocean swells, he could see a faint strip of land on the horizon. He knew this had to be the Danish coast. However, almost as soon as he caught a glimpse of the distant shore, the rolling sea would drop him into a long trough between two waves. When that happened, the walls of water were far above him and all he could see was water.

''As I floated around there, trying to dog-paddle to Denmark, I started to wonder if there was any hope,'' admits King. ''I had been so low when I parachuted out, I assumed no one could have seen me. I tried to blank out that feeling, but I did think of it from time to time. However, on the whole, I told myself I *would* be rescued, somehow.

''And,'' laughs King today, ''I thought about what I should be thinking about. I thought to myself: 'Here I am in this life-threatening situation, and I should be thinking about something profound – like my mother or my girlfriend or something.' But all I could *really* think about was, 'I'm damned cold. I want to get out of here.' ''

While Sky King was struggling to stay alive in the sea, a fourteen-year-old Danish boy named Preben Malgaard was racing along a coastal road that ran by the edge of the ocean. When King's low-flying Starfighter had appeared in the sky, Malgaard had watched it, fascinated. But, as he watched, the plane suddenly disappeared.

Malgaard stood transfixed, staring out to sea, vainly trying to comprehend what he thought he had seen. Then, when he was convinced his eyes were not fooling him, and that the jet had crashed, he raced down the beach, then up through the rocks and reeds to the coastal road, where he climbed on his bicycle and pedalled furiously to the nearest telephone. Instead of calling his mother, or even the police, he called Danish Search and Rescue and told them the plane he had been watching had blown up. No, he had not seen a parachute. There was an explosion. The pilot must be dead.

Meanwhile, at the Danish Air Base at Karup, worried members

of the Canadian squadron and the scores of Danes who knew King waited anxiously for news about him. He had not returned from patrol on time, and this was not like him. When news spread that his plane had suddenly disappeared from radar screens, Flight Lieutenant King, the dashing young Canadian in the 104, was listed as missing and presumed dead.

But Preben Malgaard's action had not been in vain. Impressed by the youngster's insistence and apparent sincerity, an alert switchboard operator had transferred the fourteen-year-old's call to the rescue control centre. From there, the sighting report was radioed to a Sea King helicopter which was training off the Danish east coast. The chopper was diverted to look for the downed pilot.

"I didn't see the helicopter until it was right over me," explains Garry King. "Actually, I felt it first. The water became very choppy and I thought I heard something. Then I looked up and there was this helicopter. It was the most fantastic thing I'd ever seen in my life!

"The back door was open, and they came lower and lower. I waved at them and they waved back. Then the next thing I knew, a paramedic was beside me in the water and I grabbed his arm. He put a harness around me and we were hoisted up to the chopper. My God, I was glad to see those guys."

The helicopter carried four men: two pilots and two para-rescue specialists. The men in the back hauled King inside, slid the door closed, and lowered the trembling Canadian onto a stretcher. As soon as he was secure, the chopper pilot swung his machine around and headed for land. King glanced at his stopwatch. He had been in the water for twenty-five minutes.

"By this time, I was thankful I was alive," Sky King told me, "but I was damned cold. I had dog-paddled to keep warm, and I thought I was getting somewhere, but the guys who picked me up said I was right in the middle of a huge oil slick. I had made zero progress toward land, so I know I would have died if it hadn't been for the boy who saw me."

But the story does not end here.

"I was lying there, my teeth chattering, in the back of the chopper," continues King, "and I could hear the fellows talking as they worked around me. After a few minutes, the pilot shouted something in Danish to one of the men in the back. The guy glanced at my shoulder patches, saw 'Canada,' and yelled up to the front: 'Canadian.' I later learned that the chopper had been sent to a crash, but the Search and Rescue guys did not know the nationality of the man who was down.

"Anyway, the pilot then shouted something else from the front. The guy beside me looked at my name on my flight suit and called back 'King.'

"At first there was no response up front, then I heard one great commotion, and the pilot jumped up from his seat and more or less bounded into the back. The guy was yelling, swearing, and laughing all at once. At first I wondered what in hell was happening, but then I turned my head and looked up to see Ova Stolle looking at me. Ova! My old buddy from our days at Penhold, Alberta!

"Well, I'll tell you. Excited! Ova was so excited he hardly knew what to do. *He* was more excited to find me than *I* was to have him find me. He kept punching me, and laughing, telling his crew about me, and so on. We had a great reunion. I'll never forget it."

King was flown to a military hospital at Ålborg, Denmark, for observation and treatment for the effects of hypothermia. Shortly afterwards, he was returned to Karup and an emotional reunion with his squadron and other friends. Later he sent Preben Malgaard his personal thanks, an engraved plaque, and a model of a CF-104 Starfighter. General King and the boy who saved his life have never met.

While the instinct to fight for survival in the face of tremendous odds is undoubtedly part of the makeup of every human being, some individuals seem to have within themselves a will to live that is almost beyond comprehension. One person who fits this description is a retired automobile dealer and pilot from Whitehorse in the Yukon Territory. His name is Moe Grant.

On February 22, 1950, twenty-year-old Grant was flying from Atlin, British Columbia, to his home in Whitehorse when a fuel line broke on his black-and-yellow Tiger Moth. Immediately, Grant, who was flying alone, started to look for some kind of a level spot to land. He found none. The little plane hit a mountainside, slammed Grant into the instrument panel, and came to rest on the icy, windswept snow.

Grant sat there, dazed but conscious, blood pouring from his forehead, his hands gripping the control column, his left foot throbbing uncomfortably. Outside the winter wind buffetted the plane and blew swirling snow among the large, black boulders that were on every side. When he managed to get his bearings, the pilot considered himself fortunate to be alive.

"I never blacked out," he told me, "but I was in a lot of pain. I managed to stop the bleeding on my face, but by that time I had come to the conclusion that my real problem was not going to be my face at all.

"My left foot was broken, and, as it turned out, the ankle of the same leg was dislocated. The pain was pretty bad, so I knew I would have to be careful of it or I would pass out, and then I'd be worse off."

Grant eventually succeeded in dragging himself from the wreckage, just in time to see another aircraft pass overhead. Despite waving frantically, and even shouting at the plane above, the man on the ground saw the machine disappear.

"I knew who it was," he explains, "but he never saw me, and at that point he did not know I was down."

Moe Grant waited, assessed his surroundings, and tried to judge the chances of his being spotted soon. He had no radio in the Moth, so he couldn't call for help. Emergency beacons were unavailable in those days.

"I could not move much because of my broken foot," he explains, "so there wasn't much I could do. The skis had been torn off the plane, but the fuselage was reasonably intact, so I hoped someone would see me. This was up at the 5,000-foot level, above the timberline, and there was really no protection against the wind. As it turned out, the few matches I had with me were wet, so I couldn't even light a signal fire. It was pretty cold, though, so I finally got back in the cockpit, wrapped the engine tent around me, and waited for morning. I knew when I didn't show up there would be a search."

There was a search – but none of the searchers saw the downed aircraft on the mountain top. The planes flew on.

"The next morning I was still there," Grant continued, "but I felt better. I had a sandwich with me and a couple of apples, but no other food. The only other thing I had" – and the pilot chuckles as he remembers – "was a bottle of Scotch. I was bringing it to my Dad as a birthday present.

"For a while I could not figure out why my foot did not hurt, but then I realized that the circulation had been cut off in it and now it was frozen solid. The freezing worked just like an anaesthetic, and the pain was gone. My God, that was a great relief. When I realized that, I decided to go down the mountain."

Grant climbed out of the aircraft cockpit, gingerly placed some weight on his broken foot, and found that there was no pain. Just then, a search aircraft passed overhead, but it flew on, oblivious to the drama being enacted on the ground.

"I took the engine tent, the last of my food, and the Scotch, and away I went," Grant continues. "It was windy up there, but at least I could walk on my broken foot, so I got down to the trees. When I got there, there was shelter from the wind, so I dug a hole in the snow, lay down, and wrapped the engine tent around me. Then I just waited for help."

Moe Grant's own description of his walk down the mountainside belies the hardship of the agonizing trek. He floundered through the snow, at times sinking to his waist in drifts, all the while forcing himself to ignore his injuries. As each search plane flew away, his hopes were dashed, yet he never gave up. The mountain wind tore at his clothing, made his eyes water, made him turn his back to catch his breath. When he finally got to the tree line, he was wet with sweat, but soon he was shivering in the snow. All around him the wind moaned through the trees, and then the stars came out, dazzling in their brilliance but icy cold and far away. Grant opened the whiskey.

"I only drank an ounce or so," he recalls, "particularly when I couldn't stop shivering. I wanted to make it last as long as I could, and then, if the time came that I knew I would die, I would finish the bottle and at least I could pass away in some comfort. But I kept my hopes up as best I could. The temperature was around − 15° F at night, and I knew it could have been worse."

But although Moe Grant did not know it at the time, the situation was to get worse. After three days the search for him was called off.

"They told me afterwards that they figured I had gone down and burned up," he says today. "As well, most of the searching had been in the valleys, and you'd never find anyone there. There is so much area to cover; it was like looking for spit in the ocean.

I don't blame the others for quitting, although my Dad never gave up.''

Young Grant's father was a man of faith, an Anglican cleric whose request for ''one more look'' was heard by a family friend and pilot, Herman Peterson. When the official searchers went on to other things, Hugh Grant and Peterson rented a plane and searched on their own.

''They were the ones who found me,'' explains Moe. ''They flew over the right mountain, saw the wreckage, and noticed my tracks leading down to the trees. Then I saw them wag their wings. The next morning an Air Force DC-3 showed up.

''Three Search and Rescue guys parachuted down to me, and they also dropped a toboggan. I really didn't see them until they were right beside me; I looked up out of my hole in the snow and they were there. I was so happy I could have cried. I wanted to have a good slug of the Scotch to celebrate, but they wouldn't let me. I had a third of the bottle left. They gave me a milkshake instead, and it was the best milkshake I've ever had.

''Then they wrapped me up and put me on the toboggan, and we started down the mountain – I had to have a couple of shots of morphine because when I started to get warm, my legs started to hurt. That's when I found out both feet were frozen. They dragged me to a lake, a small plane landed, and I was flown to hospital in Whitehorse. Later the same day I was transferred to University Hospital in Edmonton. In all, I was on the mountain for five nights.''

But Moe Grant's troubles were far from over.

''For six weeks they worked to get the circulation going in my frozen feet,'' he tells you, almost conspiratorially. ''The gangrene had spread, though, and then I got *really* sick. My temperature shot up and they were afraid I would die, so one night they wheeled me into the operating room and cut my feet off.

''That kind of thing is a bit hard to take,'' chuckles Grant today, knowing his listener is having trouble handling the explanation. ''But then, a while later, they amputated both my legs just below the knees. This was because artificial legs would be more satisfactory there. There is almost no fat at your ankles, so they knew my lower legs would always be cold if the prostheses were attached lower down.''

Today, Moe Grant looks back on the crash with a sigh of
relief that he lived to tell about it. When asked if he misses
flying, he bellows: "Why would I miss flying? I *still* fly – and
I've had three crashes since the one in 1950. You have to expect
that after forty years in the air. No, I don't miss flying. I do it
all the time, and I still own a couple of planes. I'm having too
much fun to quit."

When Air Canada Captain Bob Pearson arrived for work at Montreal's Dorval Airport on the afternoon of July 23, 1983, he had
no idea that this day's flight was one he would never forget.
Always the professional, the affable, gravel-voiced, veteran pilot
prepared meticulously for the flight he would make that day to
Ottawa and then on to Edmonton.

The aircraft he would fly was a Boeing 767, one of four new
planes of that type that the company had recently acquired. The
767 is a state-of-the-art carrier, a sleek, twin-engine machine with
a cruising speed of 580 miles per hour and a range of just over
3,200 miles. Its operation is also highly computerized. "In a
way," says Pearson of his job on the plane, "we became computer
managers as much as pilots."

During his preparations for the flight he was about to make,
Pearson talked to another pilot who had just flown the same jet
to Dorval. It was from him that Pearson learned that the plane's
primary fuel quantity indicators were unserviceable. If the 767
had been a car, this would mean that the gas gauge was not
working. Pearson took note of the problem and directed that a
number of carefully monitored fuel drips be made once fuel had
been taken aboard. In other words, he wanted to ensure that the
plane had sufficient jet fuel for the journey west.

The fuel was added, the levels were checked, then more fuel
was added. In all, three separate checks were made at Montreal,
and Pearson was assured that he had all the jet fuel he would
need. Maintenance Control cleared the aircraft for dispatch, and
in due course servicing was completed, the paying passengers
boarded, and the plane roared into the sky.

"It's only an eighteen-minute flight up to Ottawa," Pearson
told me later, "so we were pretty busy. As well, we noted a
mechanical problem with the right engine, so I had the first

officer, Maurice Quintal, radio ahead to have the mechanics check it out. We also requested another fuel drip in Ottawa.''

In Ottawa, the mechanical matter was rectified, the fuel levels were checked and found to be satisfactory, and the big red-and-white Boeing 767 departed for Edmonton. On board were sixty-one passengers and a crew of eight. The Saturday night weather had been pleasant in the nation's capital, and the forecast for the journey was just as good. To Bob Pearson, with some twenty-six years of flying behind him, the prospects for the trip were routine.

''Our planned cruising altitude for the flight was 39,000 feet,'' says Pearson, ''but we asked to go to 41,000 where the head-winds would be lighter and we would be able to conserve fuel. Air Traffic Control okayed the request and we climbed.

''So here we are, cruising along, fat, dumb, and happy, sitting there in the sunshine, with everything running well. I had just finished dinner, just past Red Lake, Ontario, when one of six low-pressure fuel warning lights comes on.

''We got out our quick reference handbook, the on-board manual that covers mechanical problems and in-flight emergency situations. All that was required, according to the manual, was to shut off the pump. We shut it down, and assumed at this point that it was simply a pump failure. However, a few minutes later, a second warning light came on.

''At that stage, we started to feel uncomfortable, but I did not think we were short of fuel. I thought we had computer problems. After all, this was a new airplane and some of the bugs still had to be worked out.

''By this time, we were about one hundred miles north of Winnipeg, so I elected to divert there and find out what the problem was. We called Winnipeg, requested descent clearance, and started down. Then, one by one, the other four warning lights came on, and this cast a bit of an eerie spell in the cockpit.

''But when the left engine failed, we knew it was not a computer problem.

''So we did the engine shutdown drill and then went over the single-engine landing checklist. My intention was to land straight in on Runway 18 at Winnipeg. It was the longest runway, and also the quickest to get to. At this stage of our descent, we were still going to be quite high for Winnipeg, but we had speed brakes, so we thought there would be no problem.

"However, just as we finished doing the engine shutdown drill and completed the single-engine landing checklist, the cockpit went black.

"That's the only way to describe it," Pearson continues. "This sophisticated glass control console that is very pretty to look at and very easy on the eyes and is a marvel – went black. When that happens, it's a bit of a shock. I know that on the cockpit voice-tape my initial reaction was: 'What the hell is that?' " Pearson is able to laugh now at his reaction, but at the time, the situation was far from funny.

The right engine had failed.

"When the second engine went, our last electric generator went along with it," says Pearson, "along with all our hydraulic pumps. So now we had no electrics, other than the battery which powered a few stand-by instruments.

"We notified Air Traffic Control that we were without power, and that both our engines had quit. At this point we were about 100 miles from Winnipeg and we were going down. However, I still thought we could glide to Winnipeg. In this I was wrong. I thought the aircraft would glide better than it did."

At this stage in the 767's ill-fated flight, the situation had indeed become critical. The plane was falling fast, now without speed brakes or flaps, a crippled man-made bird that, without power, without jet fuel, could not stay aloft.

Passengers had been asked to fasten their seatbelts and prepare for an emergency landing. Fortunately, there was little panic – largely due, according to Pearson, to the efforts of "a fantastic cabin crew." The flight attendants knew that both engines had failed, but they did not know the aircraft's glide capabilities. "In a way, they were preparing to die," explains Bob Pearson today. "Maurice [Quintal, the co-pilot] and I knew we would be able to glide for a while, but the cabin crew did not realize this. They continued their work, even as they were sure they would be dead right away. I have the utmost respect for them, and I can't praise them enough.

"As we went along, Maurice was calculating our descent rate," continues Pearson, "based on the distances provided by Air Traffic Control and our altitude. At some point, it became apparent to him that we might not make Winnipeg. At thirty-five miles out, we were at 9,000 feet, so we considered other airports. We decided a couple we knew about were not suitable for us, and it was Maurice who came up with what would be our best chance.

"He had been in the Air Force, and he knew about an airport at Gimli, some fourteen miles behind us. We turned and headed for it.

"In a glide," explains Pearson, himself a glider pilot, "you have an air-speed indicator to tell you how fast you are moving forward, a vertical-speed indicator to tell you how fast you are going down, and speed brakes, of course. We had neither the vertical speed indicator nor speed brakes with which we could control our vertical speed. Nor did we have the hydraulics to put the gear down.

"Maurice hit the alternate gear switch, which, using battery power of course, pulled the pins for the undercarriage gear so that gravity caused them to fall out. The gear which was sitting on them came down the same way. We could hear the wheels come down.

"As I turned final I made a left-hand slipping turn and reduced our speed from 220 to 180 knots. The plane was in a fairly steep side-slip but it handled quite well."

Unfortunately, there were two runways at Gimli, only one of which was now used for flying. The active one was Number 32 Right, a narrow asphalt strip that blended into the landscape. Runway 32 Left, the main runway when the place had been an Air Force base, was cement. It was 200 feet wide, had all the old approach poles still in place, and looked from the air to be the one to use. Both were 6,800 feet long. Pearson did not see the strip on the right because in those last heart-stopping seconds to touchdown he was doing everything in his power to reach that piece of cement ahead of him. Local time was 8:38 p.m.

The critical moment was at hand.

"We touched down at about 170 knots," says Pearson, "at about 800 feet down the runway. I jumped on the brakes and the nose hit with a hell of a thud because the nose gear had not extended. It had been sitting at about a forty-five-degree angle. When the nose hit the cement, the sound was like a shotgun going off.

"We screeched along that way, and I was riding the brakes. But the worst moment came when I looked up and saw people running on the runway, and some vehicles farther on.

"I still have a very vivid image of a young boy on a bicycle, wide-eyed with terror, heading for the edge of the runway.

"Fortunately, we were decelerating at a great rate, and we stopped at under 3,000 feet. By that time the cockpit was full of smoke from burning insulation, wiring, and so on. When we finished the checks to be sure everything was off, we couldn't breathe; the place was full of black, oily smoke, and we couldn't see."

The two pilots stumbled from the cockpit as the last of the passengers were sliding down the escape chutes. The evacuation had been orderly and gone well, and as soon as the in-charge flight attendant appeared, he and Pearson took flashlights, covered their mouths, and searched the plane for possible stragglers. When they found none, they got out themselves.

All passengers and crew survived the ordeal, and the fire in the aircraft nosewheel was extinguished. The plane was repaired and is still in use. A long, detailed inquiry was held into the matter, and Air Canada was blamed for the fact that that 767 ran out of gas.

"Air Canada first blamed the two pilots and three ground technicians," wrote Fred Cleverley, one of the country's most respected aviation reporters, in the *Winnipeg Free Press* (July 9, 1985). "The airline disciplined the five men, and then backed off." In direct contrast with Air Canada's actions, Mr. Justice George Lockwood, who headed the inquiry, praised the crew of the ill-fated jet. Lockwood said, in part: "Thanks to the professionalism and skill of the flight crew and the flight attendants, the corporate [Air Canada] and equipment deficiencies were overcome and a major disaster averted."

The report of the Board of Inquiry continued:

> The consequence [of the incident] would have been disastrous had it not been for the flying ability of Captain (Robert) Pearson, with valuable assistance from First Officer (Maurice) Quintal. Ironically, the avoidance of disaster was, to a considerable extent, due to Capt. Pearson's knowledge of gliding. He applied such knowledge to the successful flying and landing of one of the most sophisticated commercial aircraft yet built. (*Winnipeg Free Press*, July 10, 1985)

Yes, Bob Pearson had become a hero, although his corporate bosses were reluctant to admit it. Shortly after they tried to blame him for the crash, Pearson was honoured by the United States Air Force. Later he was given several awards, among them one from the Fédération Aéronautique Internationale. The organization made the presentation in Spain. Finally, on July 1, 1986, Pearson and his entire crew were guests in a celebration in the town where the 767 had landed. By this time, everyone knew the plane as the Gimli Glider. It was a "happy ending" crash, and now they could joke about it.

16

Canadians in Vietnam and Korea

The last two wars that involved Canadians were fought in Korea and in Vietnam. In the Korean war, some 25,000 men and women from this country participated in the so-called United Nations Police Action between 1950 and 1953. Only a few years later, upwards of 10,000 young Canadians flocked to the United States and fought with American forces in the jungles of Vietnam. While neither involvement resulted from a formal declaration of war, both meant frustration, hardship, danger, and, sometimes, sudden and violent death.

Joe Liston remembers Korea.

"I was in the army," he explains, "and we needed pilots who could observe artillery fire. Normally, the fire is controlled by an officer who stays with the infantry, often several miles ahead of the big guns. That person can watch where artillery shells are landing and give directions by radio to those in control behind the lines.

"In World War I balloons were employed for aerial observation. Then observer aircraft came along, and these were used in both World Wars and in Korea. It was not until the later stages of World War II, however, that Canadians did this. Up until then, the British handled the job for us. By the end of the war, we had several trained observers." Liston was one of them.

"I had been a pilot before this," he continues, "but it was in Europe that I became an observer. Actually, I had learned to fly in Canada with the RCAF, but at the time I started the observer training I was with the army. We all had to do the same flying training, because several of the fellows had been in the army in Italy and had not flown before. The standards were high.

"They trained us to fly low, and sometimes in Holland you could go for miles and never have to go higher than about fifty feet. That was a lot of fun. However, there was danger to it as well. I remember that one of our own guys was killed by a shell from one of our own guns. He was directing the fire and a mistake was made. He just disappeared when he was hit.

"Years later in Korea, I was afraid the same thing might happen to me, so I stayed well out of the line of fire from our guns. Unfortunately, I was thinking of our guns too much, I guess, and I got shot down by the enemy. It wasn't my day.

"Anyway, they trained us to fly as close to the deck, or the ground, as we could. We took off from near the guns, flew to the area where the shell should land, had a look at the explosion, assessed its effects, and came right back down again. In Korea, however, we had to fly high because of all the hills in that country.

"One Canadian army pilot, Peter Tees, won the Distinguished Flying Cross in Korea. He was there from about September 1952 until near the end of the war, and he was the first army pilot to win the DFC since World War I. None were awarded to the Canadian Army in World War II.

"Pete got the decoration for continuous observation and reporting, but one action stood out. Because of his flying he was able to warn our people of a Chinese attack, and in doing so saved a number of lives. He deserved the award."

Liston had only been in Korea for a short time when he was shot down. He survived several months of hell as a prisoner of war and was released when hostilities ended.[1] Another Canadian, Andy MacKenzie, was also shot down during the campaign there. He, along with twenty-one other RCAF fighter pilots, flew with the United States Air Force. The bulk of the Canadian pilots with experience in Korea were involved with air transport.

426 Squadron flew North Star transport planes to the Canadian West Coast, and subsequently to McChord Air Force Base in Washington State. From there, they travelled to and from Tokyo, hauling personnel, supplies, and equipment for Korea. In all, 599 round-trip flights were made in the course of the war. The plane-loads were later trans-shipped to Pusan, Taegu, and Seoul.

Our fighter pilots who went to Korea flew there on a rotation basis with the United States Air Force. The Canadian who scored the highest was Flight Lieutenant Ernie Glover, who shot down three enemy planes and damaged three more, while the most experienced in terms of air time in the theatre was Flying Officer S. B. Fleming, who flew more than eighty missions.

"There should have been an entire Canadian squadron in Korea," Andy MacKenzie told me. "None of us had any operational experience flying jets in a war." Nevertheless, the few Canadians who flew in this forgotten war did their job. In all, they shot down nine enemy aircraft.

Steve Monroe was born and raised in Toronto, and after a year at college was living with his grandmother and working full-time at Toronto International Airport. But the job did not involve flying, and flying was what he had always wanted to do. When he attempted to join the Canadian Forces and then the Royal Air Force he was told he needed more education to become a pilot.

"Then one day a man I worked for suggested I should go down to the States and see if I could get into their Air Force," Monroe recalls. "Well, I took him up on it, drove down to Niagara Falls, New York, and presented myself at an Air Force recruiting office. I had just started filling out forms when the guy said, 'How much education have you?' I told him, and he said I would need a degree. I asked about flying for the navy. Still a degree.

"I was at the door of the guy's office when he called me back – just like one of the Hollywood scenes. 'You know,' he said, 'the army has some kind of a program. All I know about it is that they fly helicopters. Why don't you talk to them?' This was just what I needed, although I had not even *dreamed* of choppers. At any rate, I went right to the army and they accepted me with open arms. The background checks, medicals, and so on took a few months, but I was finally sworn in on December 27, 1968. I was twenty years old. Basic training started the next week, and from the very first day it felt as though the world was collapsing. The drill sergeants yelled and screamed all the time. They slammed us into walls, threw us down, threw us through windows, tore our clothes, ripped our shirts off – over and over again. I survived, though." Monroe grins as he says it.

"Then there was the flight school, so altogether the training lasted eleven months.

"I had one weekend pass in all that time," Monroe would later write in the December 1985 issue of *Saturday Night*. "I had survived physical abuse, and a number of terrifying helicopter manoeuvres. There were crashes and there were fatalities. We had a lot of midair collisions in training. Five hundred helicopters would take off in sequence and then come back at one time. The sky was full of helicopters. Collisions were inevitable. But none of the training in any way prepared me for Vietnam."

When Monroe finished his training, he returned to Toronto to visit his family and friends, then packed his bags and went back to the United States in order to get ready to go to the Far East. His last base had been Fort Rucker, Alabama, but he left from Oakland, California, on January 4, 1970, to go to war. There were stops along the way, but finally he looked from the window of the civilian-chartered DC-8 and saw the lush green hillsides of South Vietnam. The view from the air was one of beauty and peace. The view on the ground was quite different.

"I remember, as the plane's door opened, the terrible stench, the heat, the humidity, the dust, and the noise," he says today. "There were masses of people everywhere, and everything happened so fast, I was in total confusion, and awfully scared. When the movie *Platoon* came out, I went to see it. My wife wouldn't go, and it had taken me a long time to get up enough courage to see anything about Vietnam. The theatre was packed, but that film was like home movies with sound. I was right back there, and when the thing was over, I just sat there in silence. The whole thing was so realistic. That's what it was like.

"We had landed at Tan Son Nhut Air Base. This was in the suburbs of Saigon. Then they shipped us to a place called 90th Replacement Centre where we waited for our assignments. We filled out all kinds of forms there, you wouldn't believe the number, and all pilots were issued new flight suits.

"There was a tremendous cross-breed of people at the Replacement Centre. All the new people like myself were there. Then all the guys who had finished their tour and were going home. And you sure could tell the two groups apart. Those of us who had just arrived were in our new flight suits, trying to be as inconspicuous as we could. The fellows who were going home had on worn, faded, and torn suits, some with holes in them. All these guys were drunk out of their minds, and they didn't give a goddamn for anything or anybody. After I'd been in the country for a while I understood. A lot of them were trying to count how many of their buddies were still alive. No one seemed to know.''

Monroe was assigned temporarily to two locations before being sent to the 135th Assault Helicopter Company, at Bear Cat, ten miles south of Saigon. The 135th was made up of U.S. Army personnel and the Royal Australian Navy, and now Steve Monroe, the kid from Canada, was to get his baptism of fire as a combat pilot with them. ''I was there for a year,'' he explains, ''and I was scared all the time.''

Monroe's first real contact with the horror of Vietnam came as he waited to hitch a ride in a search-and-rescue helicopter that had gone to look for a second machine that was missing. The search craft returned, and Monroe climbed aboard. He did not have to ask for many details. Lying on the floor at his feet was a bloody helmet with a name on it – the only thing located from the missing aircraft. The name was that of a good friend who had just arrived. ''I can still see that helmet lying there,'' says Monroe, his eyes tracing an imaginary line on a desk in front of him. ''We were together at flight school.''

''The 135th was chronically short of pilots,''[2] wrote Monroe, ''and I was soon promoted to aircraft commander. The company check pilot told me to forget everything I'd learned in flight school because I was going to learn to fly right there. All the check pilots were senior warrant officers – career soldiers who had been in the army for a zillion years. They were like gods to us. At the last minute, they rescheduled my first check flight and the guy who flew in my place was shot down. They crashed and I helped cut their bodies out. They were burned beyond recognition. The second time they scheduled me for a check ride, we had mechanical problems. . . .'' But this time the check was successful, and Monroe became aircraft commander. The promotion bothered him. ''Suddenly I had the responsibility of three other guys,'' he explains, ''and we were flying into some terrible places. In the next few months I was shot up, shot down, had two tail rotor failures, a fire on board, and a crash. I didn't drink when I arrived in Vietnam, but I sure drank there. We were either flying, sleep-

Punch Dickins, ninety years old, holds a portrait of himself from his early bush-flying days. In 1928 Dickins was the first to fly the uncharted Barren Lands, a historic achievement that won him the McKee trophy. Later Dickins was an executive with Canadian Pacific Airlines (now Canadian Airlines International) and de Havilland Aircraft of Canada. Today he is regarded as Canada's greatest living bush pilot. (The Toronto Star/W912-16A)

In 1946, the young Max Ward started the one-plane Polaris Charter Company in Yellowknife. (Courtesy Max Ward) Seven years later he established Wardair Limited, with a fleet of four (below). (Canada's Aviation Hall of Fame)

Max Ward in the executive offices of Wardair Inc., Canada's third-largest scheduled air operation. (John Melady)

Grant McConachie was not only one of the most successful characters in Canadian aviation history, but also one of the most colourful. Like Ward and Dickins, he made the move from the bush to the boardroom, becoming president of CP Air in 1947. (National Archives of Canada/C61894)

Above, Jack Flannagan is rushed to sick bay aboard the aircraft carrier *Bonaventure.* Just minutes before, in a bizarre accident during launch, he had been sucked beneath the surface of the ocean and dragged under the hull of the 20,000-ton ship, where he lost a leg to the ship's propellors. (Canadian Forces) Today, *right,* he walks without a limp, and is back in the cockpit. (Courtesy Jack Flannagan)

Air Canada Captain Bob Pearson. In 1983 his steady courage and knowledge of gliding brought a crippled Boeing 767 safely to landing at an abandoned airstrip in Gimli, Manitoba. (Courtesy Bob Pearson)

On April 10, 1978, at age twenty-three, Judy Cameron became Air Canada's first female pilot. One of Cameron's first jobs was at Slave Lake, Alberta, where she survived an engine failure on a DC-3 during the first scheduled flight she flew. (Courtesy Air Canada)

From left, Lewis Leigh, Mrs. Leigh, and Field Marshall Montgomery, Rockcliffe, Ontario, 1946. Leigh was the first pilot hired by Trans-Canada Airlines (now Air Canada). He joined the fledgling operation on August 20, 1937, ten days after its incorporation, at captain's pay of $400 a month. (National Archives of Canada/C-58060)

Captain Peter Cutsey and crew of Air Canada flight 109. (John Melady)

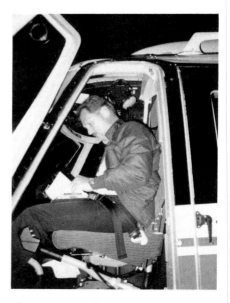

Captain Joan Gordon, pilot with 424 Squadron, CFB Trenton, in the cockpit of a Labrador search-and-rescue helicopter. (John Melady)

Vietnam veteran Steve Monroe, now an air ambulance pilot, seconds before takeoff for an accident site. (John Melady)

Air and ground ambulances meet to rush the injured to medical care. (Ministry of Health Ontario 82-430)

In 1967, while on an exchange tour with the U.S. Air Force, Jack Hamilton ejected from his stalled F-4D Phantom into a Tucson, Arizona, swimming pool. The falling plane went on to crash into a supermarket. Seven months after the accident Hamilton was flying again. Today he is a major in the Canadian Forces. (Canadian Forces)

Now a general in the Canadian Forces, in 1967 Garry "Sky" King was a flight lieutenant on exchange with the Royal Danish Air Force. When a seagull flew into the left engine intake of his Starfighter, the young pilot crashed off the coast of Denmark. He was rescued thanks to the quick response of a fourteen-year-old boy, who sped on his bicycle to phone Search and Rescue when he saw the plane fall from the sky. (Courtesy Garry King)

Test-pilot Jan Zurakowski (centre), jubilant after the first flight of A. V. Roe's Avro Arrow CF-105 fighter, March 25, 1958. Just eleven months later, amid great controversy, the Arrow project was scrapped. (National Archives of Canada/C-61731)

Lt.-Colonel Rob Porter with the CF-104 Starfighter. While on bombing practice over Holland, just months after this photo was taken, Porter was to survive a spectacular crash in the "Widow-Maker." (Canadian Forces)

Major Pierre Rochefort in the Ops room at CFB Baden-Soellingen, minutes before take-off with the author in Canada's F-18 jet. (John Melady)

ing, or drunk. We saw so much horror every day we had to get drunk every night just to cope. Then we'd get up in the morning, at four or so, and still be in bad shape when we had to fly. It was just a matter of trying to hold on and stay alive. But even then, it got to the point that we just expected to be killed, so we took chances. We just didn't give a damn.''

Steve Monroe took part in the massive invasion of Cambodia (Washington preferred to call it an incursion). The purpose was to wipe out communists who were holed up there. To Monroe, the operation was an invasion, regardless of what President Richard Nixon might have claimed at the time. Monroe describes what took place.

''We started the whole thing with a briefing at two in the morning,'' he recalls, ''and that in itself was earlier than usual. The Company Commander conducted the briefing, and by the time he was finished we started to get some idea of what this thing was all about. He said we were going into Cambodia, and that we would be part of the largest airborne operation the world had ever seen.'' Monroe later wrote about his experiences.

Because we were sent directly to the front line, we didn't have a lot of time to think. That was good. In fact, what we were about to do really didn't hit us until we were ordered to surrender all wallets, photos, and ID before taking off. We were not to wear or take anything that would identify us as Americans. We even had to turn out our pockets to prove we weren't carrying anything. I don't know why; I sure as hell wasn't going to pass for a Vietnamese or a Cambodian. [Monroe is a tall man, blond and muscular.]

We flew to our assembly points that night, landing in Vietnam but right next to Cambodia. All night long, you could hear the choppers coming in. We slept in our aircraft, waiting for daylight, and when the sun finally rose all you could see were aircraft. I have never in my life seen so many at one time, and we were only one part of the invasion force. There were more gunships and troop-carrying slicks [helicopters] than I could count, all in neat rows.

The invasion was a relentless wave of helicopters. Because there were so many, I was still on the ground hours after the first company lifted off.[3]

Monroe remembers being extremely nervous when his slick finally got ready to go. He would find the experience the most terrifying of his life. In Vietnam he was used to dropping men almost anywhere in jungle territory, but the drop in Cambodia was in an open field that seemed to be completely deserted. The terrain on either side was flat, with few trees and even fewer hiding places.

"Really all there were were some shrubs," Monroe continues, "and some bundles of what looked like hay here and there. The area was as large as several football fields, and I thought it would be a piece of cake to drop the troops off here and leave. The gunships had gone in earlier, had a look, and left. I can still remember wondering why we were coming here. There was nothing around.

"Well, I was wrong.

"The first guys had gone in and dropped a red smoke bomb where we were to land. The place was well marked and quiet. There was very little chatter on the radio. It was *so* quiet.

"Then, just as soon as we landed, the whole goddamned earth opened up. The North Vietnamese had concealed themselves in holes in the ground, under the haystacks, all over the place. The haystacks opened up and there they were. There was shooting everywhere, in every direction. Guys were yelling, screaming, swearing. The radios are going wild. Helicopters are trying to lift off, then they're being hit and crashing and burning, and a lot of good people are dying right on the spot. There's fire and smoke everywhere.

"One aircraft didn't even unload the men. It exploded, just blew all to hell and chunks of human beings are flying all over the place. Later I went back to get some of our guys out of there. When I landed there was a burning helicopter almost right beside me and the flames were so bad I couldn't tell who was in it. It was a nightmare."

Flying ground troops in to specific locations was always nerve-racking, and Monroe did more than his share of this job. The chopper flew in and hovered a couple of feet from the ground, and the soldiers in the back jumped out. The helicopter did not land because of the danger of putting down on a hidden mine. However, the aircraft could still be blown to smithereens if one of the men hopping out came down on a mine.

Often the choppers were ordered in to pick up ground personnel who had been mauled by the Viet Cong. Monroe says that the worst job involved bringing South Vietnamese soldiers from the field, particularly when they had casualties among them. "I was more interested in trying to get the ones who were alive out," he explains, "but the Vietnamese wanted to bring their dead at all costs. They would put corpses in green garbage bags and toss these in the chopper first. Then the wounded would be pushed on top of the dead, and finally the survivors got in. At times like these, we would hold the aircraft just above the ground and hope like hell they'd get loaded *fast*. My God, I hated those pick-ups. Later, we would hose the blood out of the plane."

In the *Saturday Night* article, Monroe described another of his horrific experiences in Vietnam:

I remember the time the aircraft in front of me just disappeared: it exploded in midair. There was no ground fire, no rockets, *nothing*. Someone – a V.C. [Viet Cong] agent – had slipped a grenade into the fuel tank, wrapped in an elastic band. The fuel had gradually eroded the elastic and the grenade exploded. There's no defence against that. You have to remember, there were South Vietnamese civilians who worked at our base. They carried the sewage from the latrine. They would pace off the distances between strategic targets; when the Viet Cong mortared our base, they were always on target. They were my only contact with native civilians aside from days off in Saigon or nearby villages. I always felt they didn't want us there.[4]

And the time came when Steve Monroe did not want to be there either. He was ready to get out long before he was able to do so, but finally his tour in this most barbaric of wars was over and he was on his way home. In the years since Vietnam, he has had nightmares about what he saw, about what he had to do there as a man in uniform, and about what happened to him as a stranger in a strange land, a human being who shared the hopes and fears of the people in whose country he fought. Given the chance, he would never go back, yet he does not regret going in the first place. Monroe still flies choppers; today he is an air ambulance pilot in Ontario. But that is another story.

17

Help on the Wing

Air ambulance work, search-and-rescue operations, forestry patrolling, and law enforcement flying: All are essential public services sometimes taken for granted, and all have their share of drama and danger. Anyone who has stood helplessly as a loved one lay beside a road, waiting for an air ambulance, knows how essential that service is in time of greatest need. Anyone who has ever been lost in a northern wilderness understands the relief when search-and-rescue aircraft appear overhead. And anyone whose home town has been threatened by a forest fire will long remember the water bombers, the supply aircraft, and the evacuation planes.

The types of machines used for public service work vary as much as the service itself. A small police traffic patrol plane and a large search-and-rescue Buffalo aircraft are as different as night and day. The modern, fast, and expensive medivac helicopters are nothing like the fixed-wing Otters used for fire-spotting over wilderness bushland. Yet while each kind of service has its own characteristics, air ambulance is unique.

Robert Blakely flies air ambulance helicopters in southern Ontario and routinely transports emergency cases from outlying districts to hospitals in major cities. In downtown Toronto, for example, he often lands high above the streets on the helipad at the Hospital for Sick Children on University Avenue. Landing here is as routine a part of his day as a weather check at his base at Buttonville Airport, north-east of the city. Blakely loves his work, but admits he got into it by chance.

"I had my licence to fly fixed-wing aircraft," he told me, "and one day I just happened to watch a helicopter working a short distance away. I went over to have a look and got talked into going for a familiarization ride. That experience blew me away. I signed up for lessons and I've never looked back. Today I have over 5,000 hours in choppers."

Blakely began working at the same airport where he took that first flight, and later on he gave dozens of introductory flips himself. He describes the sales pitch with unabashed candour.

"The idea," he recalls, "was to offer some guy – and it was generally a male – a flight for a ridiculously low price. Then after you got going, you would let him fly the chopper straight and level. Then you would compliment him on how well he was doing, regardless of how he was really doing.

"At the time we had a couple of confined areas where we could land. Both were fairly tight spots to get into – one was on a river bank – but both would impress the pants off someone who had never been in a helicopter before. After that was over we would fly to a little restaurant and go in for a coffee. When we walked in, the lady behind the counter would pretend to be amazed at the helicopter landing in her back yard – even though we did it two or three times a week. She would always say: 'Hello. Which one of you is the pilot?' And you would always point to the guy with you and say: 'He is.' The guy's head would swell up, and when you got back he would sign up for the $10,000 lessons."

I asked Blakely about his work flying ambulances. "Well," he began, after some consideration, "the job is interesting, and it makes use of pretty well all of your flying skills. For example, a while ago we had a call to an automobile accident on Highway 69, north of Sudbury. Well, even though the weather was not much better than marginal, the pilot made the decision to go because he felt he could do so safely. And he was right.

"Anyway, he located the accident scene, and that is sometimes not as easy as it sounds. However, after he landed on the highway – and that takes some skill – he had to wait for quite a while before the occupant of the car could be extricated. In the meantime, the weather closed in and he had to get permission from air traffic control to fly IFR – that means using Instrument Flight Rules. He had flown to the scene using VFR – Visual Flight

Rules. When he got to the area near the hospital in Sudbury he had to descend, but before doing so he again had to get permission to use a special VFR clearance to proceed. The patient was delivered. Now, to the general public, who sometimes think all we do is swoop and scoop, there may not seem to be much involved in the scenario I've just described. However, there is. There was the weather check, the decision to go, the flight plan, the landing at an unfamiliar site, and the three types of flight rules. There is the flying itself, the radio work, the attention to the vehicle – and, most important, the care, comfort, and life of the patient.

"But we are not heroes," says Blakely, "nor do we pretend to be. Our track record is good because we don't take foolish risks, nor do we let ourselves be influenced by the type of call we get. Often we don't know who is being transported, and that's the way it should be. For example, if we knew we were to pick up a little girl whose legs had been amputated in an automobile crash, that information would really not make a difference to us. Now, this may sound callous, but if we became emotionally influenced by such a situation and we took off in below-minimum weather and crashed the aircraft, then everyone is worse off than if we'd stayed where we were. On the other hand, when a life is saved, it is the medical people in the back who are the heroes, not us. We just fly the plane. No, we don't need to know the patient."

Despite the fact that four men were killed in an air ambulance crash in northern Ontario on November 29, 1988, the service in the province is probably as safe as similar operations anywhere. This one tragedy was the worst in Canada since the service began twelve years ago. In only two years, thirty-four people died in similar crashes in the United States, where the competition to collect the injured and the dying is entirely different from the working methods here. In Canada, safety is the primary consideration. Profit is not a factor.

Vietnam veteran Steve Monroe takes his share of the flying at Toronto's Buttonville Air Ambulance offices. When I interviewed him recently, Monroe explained that "if the phone goes, I'm gone," then went on to describe his work carrying accident victims and other critically ill patients in Ontario. In one instance, he had to fly to the town of Port Perry to pick up a teenager who had been in a car crash. The boy had been in the back seat of a friend's car when it went out of control and slammed into a ditch, then through a fence. Somehow, a chunk of a wooden fence post went through the rear window of the car and into the boy's neck, impaling him. In order to get the youth from the car, a bystander cut both ends of the wood off with a chainsaw. The boy was alive but unconscious by the time he reached the Port Perry airport. Steve Monroe was already there, and the paramedics on the air ambulance turned their attention to the patient.

"I couldn't believe it," recalls Monroe. "There was only a small piece of skin at the front and back holding everything together. Everything else had been pushed out of the way."

The chopper was airborne in no time, and the boy was soon on an operating table at Sunnybrook Medical Centre in Toronto. His arteries, his windpipe, and even his spine had somehow escaped serious injury because they were, in effect, pushed aside. The patient sustained some nerve paralysis in his face, along with a badly bruised larynx, but he survived. Monroe has no hesitation in saying the boy was "very, very lucky."

Lots of others were not so lucky. Paramedic Steve Deuchars told *The Toronto Star* in a December 10, 1988, interview that in the two and a half years he had worked on air ambulances, three examples of "incredibly bad luck" came immediately to mind. One concerned a motorcyclist who landed relatively unscathed on the road after catapulting over a car, but was then run over by another vehicle. Another involved a man left quadriplegic after he fell on a patch of ice while gassing up his car at a self-serve station. A third was about a man who conscientiously left his car behind at a party because he had been drinking, only to be struck and killed by a drunk driver from the same party.

The air ambulances are virtually flying intensive care units, and the critical care attendants who work in them are trained to be ready for almost anything. The response time, as long as the weather is safe for flying, is swift. During an interview with Steve Monroe, an emergency call came in to the base at Buttonville airport. When the dispatcher phoned Monroe, I shut off the tape recorder and glanced at my watch. "Gotta go," he told me as he replaced the receiver. Exactly three minutes later we shook hands beside the helicopter. Two minutes and twenty seconds after that, the air ambulance was out of sight, en route to a hospital in Barrie. Apparently, there had been an accident . . .

The Search and Rescue organization of the Canadian Armed Forces is another operation concerned with the saving of lives. Here, the "search" part of the name means what it says. When a call comes to any of the Search and Rescue bases across the nation, the specialists who respond often do not know where to locate whomever is in trouble. For that reason, the search aspect of their duties is often far more time-consuming and frustrating than the actual rescue. Sometimes, the missing plane or boat or individual is never located, and then the heartache for the loved ones at home, and for those searching, is acute. And when searchers locate a wrecked plane but find no survivors, the depression can last for days. But when the searchers are able to save lives, the relief and satisfaction make the risks involved eminently worthwhile.

"These are the happy ones," explains Captain Joan Gordon, a 424 Squadron helicopter pilot at Canadian Forces Base Trenton. "When we find a person alive after a crash, or when we are able to rescue the crew of a sinking sailboat or something, we all feel terrific. It's just the greatest feeling in the world. That's why this job is so satisfying.

"I remember one incident that made everyone involved feel pretty happy.

"During the night of June 13, 1988, we got a call about a plane that apparently was down in the bush, about forty miles west of Sudbury. An ELT [Emergency Locator Transmitter] had been picked up by satellite, and a high flyer [commercial airliner] had also heard somebody call a mayday on the radio. A Buffalo aircraft was launched first because it moves faster than we do in helicopters. There are SAR Techs [Search and Rescue Technicians] on board, and they are trained to parachute to a crash and render first aid if required. When we come along, we can hover overhead, land, pick up people, whatever."

Joan Gordon was the aircraft commander on the Labrador helicopter that departed Trenton immediately after the Buffalo had cleared the runway. With Gordon that night were three others in addition to her co-pilot Stephen Demers. "Sluggo" Demers was an army pilot who had served with Search and Rescue for more than a year. Gordon herself is from Vancouver originally, and has a degree in microbiology from the University of British Columbia. Both were well qualified for the task at hand.

"The flight north went without incident," says Gordon. "By the time we arrived on site, the Buffalo had located the crash and had determined that there was no medical emergency.

"A man had gone fishing for a few days in a little float plane, without filing a flight plan, and when he crashed he was not even overdue. He had landed on a small lake in the middle of nowhere, and had fished there all day. When he wanted to leave, it was quite windy, and he decided he had better wait for the winds to calm down.

"In the early evening, things looked better, apparently, and he thought he would be able to fly to another lake nearby. But, because there was still quite a cross-breeze, he got off the water but could not clear the trees along the shore. He was barely airborne when he lost power and mushed into the bush.

"At first, the plane wasn't too badly damaged, and it settled into the trees, fairly high up. It hung there long enough for the man to get his bearings. He scampered out, held onto a tree, and the plane crashed to the ground. The pilot climbed down afterwards."

The unfortunate fisherman did everything right from then on.

"He checked to make sure there was no fire, then pulled out all his gear, set up a little camp, with tent, fire, lantern, and so on. He then cut down the trees around the plane so that when we got there we spotted the lantern in the clearing and the plane sitting on the ground.

"There was absolutely no other light around, and with no moon I couldn't see to come low enough to pick him up. We radioed the Buffalo, which was circling overhead, and they dropped a couple of flares. Then, using those and our own lights, I was able to come down and hover just above the ground. The ELT was turned off, the man collected his things, and we hoisted him on board. The guy was okay, and he was so apologetic because he had brought us out in the middle of the night.

"The ELT had actually not gone off by itself. The man had turned it on after the crash, and he knew that once it was on, he should not turn it off. He said he was sorry he had not waited until morning because he had kept *us* up all night. We took him in to Sudbury airport and said goodbye. That was a pleasant one."

Other operations have not ended on such a happy note. One of those was the largest-ever combined ground and air search in

Canadian history. It began in the late summer of 1951, and would involve thousands of hours' flying time, scores of aircraft, and hundreds of searchers. The code name for the whole thing was Operation Hudson, after the surname of the pilot. There was one other person aboard.

Henry Hudson was a dentist in Timmins, Ontario, and the man flying with him was William Barilko, a star defenceman for the Toronto Maple Leafs hockey team. In April of that year, Bill Barilko had scored the winning goal in overtime to win the Stanley Cup for Toronto, in a hard-fought playoff against the Montreal Canadiens. The goal made the twenty-four-year-old a national hero. Little wonder, then, that when the Fairchild 24 he and Hudson were flying the following August disappeared the search became widely known. However, despite extensive civilian and military efforts, the small aircraft with the missing men could not be found.

Eleven years later, a bush pilot named Gary Fields sighted the wreckage, half-obliterated by underbrush, some sixty miles north of Cochrane, Ontario. The skeletons of the missing men were still strapped in the plane. The hockey player, especially, has not been forgotten. His picture is in the lobby of Maple Leaf Gardens, and the skates and sweater he wore in his last game are on display in the Hockey Hall of Fame in Toronto.

Occasionally, a SAR Operation has left those who took part in it with very real misgivings about the purpose served. Joan Gordon recalls such an incident, far out in the Atlantic, almost due east of Sable Island. The call came in to Canadian Forces Base Summerside, Prince Edward Island. The date was June 18, 1986.

"From what we could gather," Captain Gordon explains, "a man was critically ill on a naval research vessel at sea, and he required immediate hospitalization. We were asked to go for him."

Two aircraft left Summerside, one a Buffalo and the other a Labrador helicopter. The flight was long – four hours to reach the ship, with a twenty-minute refuelling stop for the helicopter on an oil rig en route. The flight out to the rig was fairly routine, but the fuel stop presented certain dangers.

"They prefer you to hot refuel on the rigs," explains Gordon, who was the Labrador co-pilot. "This means you don't shut down, and it would be much the same as putting gas in your car with the motor running. There is a danger involved for the choppers, though, because the turning of the rotors can set up static electricity and result in a spark, and, of course, there are gasoline fumes present. Fortunately, all the while you are refuelling on an oil rig, they have fire-fighting equipment pointed right at you.

"As soon as we had refuelled, we left for the ship, but it was still 150 miles away, and the weather started deteriorating. There was a lot of low cloud, fog, and rain, and we had to fly about 200 feet above the water. It was not a pleasant trip."

The Labrador helicopter used by the Canadian Forces is somewhat under-powered, meaning that if, for instance, the aircraft was to hover in an area, and then lost an engine, the pilot would be forced to ditch. In a near-shore incident, there would probably be less danger, but far out, over a heaving ocean, in fog and rain, with night coming on, the risks are undoubtedly acute. When I asked Joan if she was afraid at such times, she responded: "No. You cannot afford to be. If you are scared, you can't do your job the way it should be done."

Gordon continues: "The Buffalo was up top by the time we got to the ship, and they were in radio contact with someone on board, and with us. There was a nurse on the ship, and from her the SAR Techs in the back learned that the man we were to pick up was a diabetic, so they asked if the nurse could start intravenous. If she did so, it would save our people time, and we could get our critically ill patient to a hospital quicker.

"The report back from the ship was 'not required.' The SAR Techs questioned this, but got the same answer. By the time we were over the ship, we were not sure what was going on. But then we saw the patient.

"The guy was standing there, on the deck, waving at us. We hoisted him up to the chopper, closed the door and left. On the way back, the man sat on one of the SAR Tech seats, and seemed to enjoy himself. We hot refuelled again, picked up supper from the oil rig, and flew to Halifax. The man ate his supper, walked into the hospital when we arrived, and was discharged twenty minutes later. Whether he was really sick or just wanted a night on the town, I don't know. We were annoyed, of course, but there was nothing we could do about it.

"The whole escapade cost the Canadian taxpayers a lot of money, though. Even if you don't count the salaries of the five people in the Buffalo, and the five of us in the helicopter, the recovery was expensive. Each aircraft flew for about ten hours in total, and the cost of each is about $3,500 an hour. There was also the risk involved. We had pushed weather and fairly rough seas to do the whole thing, and for what? When such a call comes in, we're expected to respond. We have no other choice."

Colonel Gord Diamond recalls another type of flying involving Search and Rescue aircraft. His story takes place on the West Coast of this country.

"During my first year at 442 Search and Rescue Squadron at Comox, I was introduced to the frenzy of the herring roe fishery. The Japanese, having depleted their local herring stocks, had discovered herring sources on the North American West Coast, which soon created a 'Klondike Gold Rush' atmosphere in the fishing industry in pursuit of this cherished Japanese delicacy, herring roe. Fish that used to fetch only a few dollars a ton for fertilizer and bait were now bringing several hundred thousand dollars for one catch.

"Everybody who could get a boat in the water was out to make his or her fortune during the month of March, a terrible period for rough weather, storms, and loss of life on the West Coast. That was why there were always Search and Rescue people around," says Diamond.

"As the herring roe fishermen moved up and down the coast and through the Straits in search of a fortune in fish, we often counted up to 300 boats in some of the little bays. From our Buffalo and helicopter patrols, I saw light aircraft landing among the boats and bringing payment from the banks in Vancouver and Victoria, up to two and three million dollars at a time, *in cash*.

"It was not uncommon," remembers Diamond, "to see people in downtown Comox or Courtenay with paper bags full of fifty-dollar bills.

"The frenzy reached such a peak that safety and caution were sometimes thrown to the wind. There were several times when we circled overhead watching trawlers that were so full they finally sank with fish coming out the wheelhouse. Lots of other boats stood by offering to assist (and of course split the catch and profit) but the owners refused to budge or give up even one fish in return for help. As a result, they lost both the catch and the boats themselves.

"Lots of 442 crew members joined these fishing exploits on their days off. We also often wondered aloud on the intercom why we were flying overhead, at public service wages, when we could be making far more down below! To add insult to injury, we even got feedback that a few fishermen were not happy with our presence because they suspected we were spying on them for Revenue Canada.

"Even though we often heard that the Japanese were paying $200 an ounce for pickled herring roe in Japan, I would not have traded a fisherman's life for the fun of flying any day."

Every so often, Canadian military pilots serving as exchange officers in the United States are commended for meritorious service. Several have received letters of thanks, wall plaques, oil paintings, and the like, but few are decorated. However, within the last four years one man has been the recipient of two United States Air Medals. He is a tall, easy-going Search and Rescue pilot with a thousand stories. He is a native of Alberton, Prince Edward Island, and his name is Rick Hardy.

In June 1985, Hardy was flying with the United States Coast Guard on Cape Cod, Massachusetts. While there, he and his crew rescued two men from a lobster boat just before the vessel capsized. For this he won the first medal. Two years later, in June 1987, he flew a Sikorsky Pelican helicopter through a violent storm to save the lives of sixteen crew members from a sinking Russian freighter.

The cargo on the Russian ship had shifted in the storm, and a hole was torn open in the hull. The winds at the time were strong, upwards of fifty knots, and the waves were as high as twenty feet. Nevertheless, Hardy held his chopper above the ship, and painstakingly loaded the terrified sailors aboard. "We just kept picking them up until we reached the maximum the aircraft could hold," he says. "Two other crews rescued the rest."

Forty-eight hours after his heroics, Hardy found himself standing before President Ronald Reagan at the White House in Washington. There, along with thirteen United States Coast Guard personnel, he was given his second decoration. After the presentation, Reagan addressed those before him:

> Here we have a case where . . . pilots from Mission Fiejo, California, Cincinnati, Ohio, and Prince Edward Island, Canada, reached out to sailors from Leningrad, Novgorod, and Yaroslavl. I hope and pray that no matter how stormy international affairs, the leaders of the world can look at what happened between these fliers and sailors and be duly inspired. We must reach out to each other in good will. For we have no other alternative.[1]

18

A Love Song to the Sky

For most pilots, flying is the essence of dreams. It is an escape, an adventure, a love song to the sky. It is a chance to defy gravity, to leave the world behind, to break the bonds of every day. No matter whether they are civilian or military, male or female, have flown for years, weeks, or merely a few days: those who fly love to fly. First World War veterans swap stories with jumbo jet pilots, and each understands and appreciates what the other is saying. The flying fraternity has few limits, but lots of bonds. The bonds are within the pilot cadre itself, and one flyer is accepted as much as another. The delicious terror of the first solo, the joy of the first flight, the blissful exaltation of flirting with the clouds on a summer afternoon; all these are interwoven into the fabric that is flying.

I once spent time with Jack Wells on the flight deck of what was then a Canadian Pacific 747 as he followed the Kuril Islands chain southward toward Japan. It was early in the morning, and in the distance the morning sun was making the mountains of the U.S.S.R.'s most eastern fringes glow with gold. I was enthralled by the magnificent scenery that stretched to the horizon; Captain Wells was more interested in the marvels of the jumbo jet he flew.

Ed Yakachuk used to be a Mountie, but he no longer tells you about police work. Instead, he wants to talk about flying, whether it's jockeying a fighter jet over the prairies in the middle of winter or moving a DC-8 full of holiday travellers out to the main runway at London's Gatwick airport.

Ruth Dwyer does not want to dwell on her work as a professor of Cinema Studies at Hamilton's McMaster University; she would much prefer to tell you about flying her own plane from a dirt strip through a corn field near her home.

Gord Diamond may be the Commanding Officer of Canada's biggest airbase at Trenton, but he loves to describe how he got his first airplane ride, at age four, in Ottawa, on the knee of a Flight Sergeant friend of his father's.

Art Spooner sits on the rung of a stepladder in his workshop at Cooking Lake, Alberta, and when he isn't telling you about what he thinks of ex-Premier Peter Lougheed, he is describing the way men such as Bing Crosby, Bob Hope, and U.S. General George C. Marshall were flown in to his float-plane base in years past. "They all loved to fly," he tells you, "but George knew more about it than the others." (Never in awe of rank or position, Spooner tells you he liked George Marshall, the same man who once told the President of the United States to call him "General" at all times, and to never use his first name.)

Doug Redford stands on the fringes of a crowd watching an air show, but the resident of Pakenham, Ontario, is doing more than just watching. He is dreaming of, perhaps even longing for, the past, for the days when he used to fly Starfighters far beyond the speed of sound.

Con Platz drives you along an autobahn in Germany, but does not want to tell you much about his job as the Canadian Military Attaché in Ankara, Turkey; he prefers to tell you of driving a 104 across the skies over the Rhineland.

Beverly Grenville, an X-ray technician and ex-motorcycle racer, is far more enthralled with flying than she was with moto-cross. Now an instructor who has taught scores of people to fly, she says she will never lose the joy of what she does. She does, however, stress that the days of flying as a male-dominated profes-sion are coming to an end. "They may not be accepting women in the airlines the way they should," she points out, "but that is changing. Perhaps not in this generation, but certainly in the next. Their party is over in the cockpit, and we are moving in."

All of these people have had adventures in flying; all have done things and have been to places the rest of us may never see. And all will tell you about them, with little prompting.

Pilot Ruth Dwyer enjoys describing her flying club.

"Even though I live here in Ontario," she says, "the flying club that I belong to is based in Fort Wayne, Indiana, at an uncontrolled airstrip there. There is no control tower; most of the members have no radios in their planes. We fly for fun.

"We call ourselves 'The Seventy Knotters' because the average airspeed of the members' planes would be about seventy knots. We fly across country for the adventure of doing so; we are not interested in speed. As a matter of fact, we often see cars on freeways travelling faster than we are. It is a romantic concept of flying. It's relaxed and easy and I love it.

"We go on a week's trip every year, and we take tents and sleeping bags, or if the weather is really nice, a lot of people just sleep under the wing. We fly into uncontrolled airstrips and we go where we wish, with no sense of rushing here and there.

"I have never lost the sense of awe of being up in the air. I take my little boy. We take off and land on grass strips for picnics. He loves being in the air as much as I do, and he flew for the first time when he was two weeks old.

"I love long-distance flying very much, and I've had many a wonderful adventure flying to Nova Scotia, to New Orleans, through the American West, Iowa, Wisconsin, and so on. But I'm happiest when my son Michael is with me. By the age of two, he had spent over a hundred hours in the air, and I had a baby seat permanently strapped in my airplane. Occasionally we take my husband," laughs Ruth Dwyer, at my unspoken question, "and he is a good passenger. He never feels threatened because his wife is flying.

"Most of my flying experiences are very happy and delightful memories," Dwyer continues, "but there have been a few trying times. Once I got lost over the wilds of New Brunswick, where, even from 8,000 feet, the bush stretches to every horizon, without any sign of a road, or any civilization. New Brunswick is an amazing place.

"I had a passenger with me, but my passenger was a very bad navigator," she explains with a laugh, "but we finally got ourselves organized. I simply followed a compass heading and we came across an L-shaped lake with a bridge across it. My aeronautical charts showed an L-shaped lake with a bridge, and from that we deduced where we were. That may not be the way to fly, but we got out without trouble.

"Luckily, the weather was good and the experience was pleasant in hindsight.

"Another time, I flew all the way home from New Orleans without a radio. A dear friend was with me, a doctor from Toronto, and my radio gave out shortly after we started the trip home. My friend was a great navigator, though, and she plotted the route without a hitch. We stopped at uncontrolled airports for fuel, stopped in Nashville to hear some wonderful bluegrass music, cleared customs in Sarnia, and arrived home in good shape."

Private pilots are not the only flyers who sometimes are not certain exactly where they are. Some years ago, Gord Diamond was flying with 412 Squadron out of Ottawa. One of the important tasks of 412 was to carry VIPs here and there. These included the prime minister, various cabinet ministers, visiting heads of state, and high-ranking military people. Diamond's favourite passenger was Roland Michener, the popular Governor General of the day. Colonel Diamond recalls that flight.

"One day we were up in Labrador, looking at the electrical power installations there. We had just taken off from Churchill Falls when Mr. Michener sent a note up to the cockpit. In it he asked if we would take him up to one of the other new dams that he had been unable to see before.

"Roger Landry, my co-pilot, read the note to me, then grabbed the only tourist brochure that we had – one that had been given to us about the construction in the area. We had no other maps pinpointing the dams.

"Anyway, we studied the brochure for a while, trying to figure out where this dam was. After a time, Roger gave up in disgust and said to me, 'I don't know where the hell the stupid dam is.' Unfortunately, the PA switch was on and the whole plane heard the comment. A steward came running up to the front and told us what had happened. We heard later that Mr. Michener loved the remark."

A similar situation livened up a trip that Worldways pilot Gil Atwood was making to the south, during the winter of 1984.

"We were en route to the Dominican Republic in a DC-8," he recalls. "Somewhere around Grand Turk Island, we were listening to the usual Air Traffic Control chatter between Miami Center and numerous aircraft. Then loud and clear came the voice of the captain of a flight of one of the major American airlines briefing his passengers on the scenic wonders of the Bahamas. He had used the wrong mike and was transmitting over VHF and being heard by every ground station and aircraft within 200 miles. Just before the completion of his briefing, he obviously realized his error and stopped talking in mid-sentence.

"For the next few minutes the air was filled with the sarcastic comments of dozens of pilots, 'I wish *I* had said that.' 'Now say it again to your passengers.' 'I just *love* your voice,' and, 'I didn't realize the Bahamas were so *beautiful*.' The poor guy was probably mortified. All airline pilots live in fear of making the same mistake."

A couple of years ago, Atwood made an in-flight announcement that had surprising results.

"During a flight from the United Kingdom to Toronto, we were making landfall just off the coast of Cape Breton Island. The day was clear, so during my briefing to the passengers on the progress of our flight I pointed out that the eastern shore of Nova Scotia and Cape Breton was clearly visible, and if one looked closely a major historical site could be seen: the restored fort at Louisbourg, next to the existing town of Louisbourg.

"Seconds later the cockpit door opened. A flight attendant came in and asked if she could bring a visitor. I agreed, and in came the mayor of Louisbourg! He thanked me for the announcement I'd just made, and said I had just given his town the type of publicity money could not buy. He then passed out several tourist brochures of his home town to the crew."

The love of flying sometimes keeps men and women in the air, even though outsiders might wonder at their persistence. Marg and Ed Sykes both fly, but following a trip to the southern United States a few years ago, one might wonder why. Both were relatively novice pilots at the time, but their instructor organized a cross-country trip to Florida, and suggested they become part of it.

"So we did," Marg says today. "In all, there were fourteen people in four airplanes, but my husband and I were not flying together. That was probably just as well.

"The first leg of the trip was across Lake Ontario to a town

called Sandusky, Ohio, where we planned to meet and have lunch.
Now, don't forget, this was March, and we ran into a series of
snow squalls over the lake. The planes bounced around a lot, and
in general the trip was horrible. However, most of us found an
airstrip at Sandusky and landed safely – except for my husband
in his little Cherokee.

"At first we thought he would be along soon, so we found a
place to eat and began to have lunch. The time dragged on and
he wasn't arriving, so we started phoning other airports to see if
a Cherokee 140 had arrived. It hadn't.

"In the meantime, we struck up a conversation with an American pilot-in-training, who, after his lunch, was planning on flying
to his home elsewhere in the state. When we finished eating, we
said goodbye to him and continued watching for my husband.
The longer we waited, the more worried we became. Then we
received a terrible shock.

"Word came in that a blue-and-white Cherokee 140 had
crashed in Sandusky Bay. The pilot had not survived.

"By this time I was in shock. My husband's plane was blue
and white, and we all knew he was to come to Sandusky. In the
meantime, the weather was getting worse, and because all of us
were too upset to try to do anything else, we booked rooms in a
nearby motel and waited, hoping for any news, praying that the
dead pilot was not my husband."

Then the phone rang.

Marg Sykes picked up the receiver and almost cried with joy.
The voice on the other end was her husband's. He had flown into
the same weather she had encountered, but had turned back and
then flown around it. He was now safe and secure at another
airport some distance away. The man who died in the Cherokee
crash was the young pilot-in-training who had lunched with the
Canadian group.

The next morning, the travellers decided to continue. This time
Marg Sykes rode in the rear seat while two novice pilots sat in
front. The first part of the journey was uneventful.

"But while we were flying over the Smoky Mountains, enjoying the sunshine and the scenery, the engine quit. We were not
far above some of the highest peaks, and I was sure we were
headed for a crash. There was absolute silence in the cockpit,
and the pilot broke out in a cold sweat – as did the other guy and

myself. In the meantime, we're going lower and lower.'' Mrs. Sykes shudders at the memory.

"I was ready to die, when the guy flying suddenly remembered that he had not switched gasoline tanks. When he did so, the engine came to life again and so did we. By now I had decided *never, ever* to fly with this guy again. But at least we had enough gas to get to our next stop: Waycross, Georgia.''

It was at Waycross that the three almost did meet their Maker.

"The pilot was getting landing instructions from the Waycross tower,'' continues Mrs. Sykes, "but because he was so inexperienced, he could not follow what the tower was saying. Instead, he simply guessed at the instructions. Unfortunately, his guess was wrong, and he started to go the wrong way in the landing circuit.

"Suddenly a huge 747 jumbo jet crossed right in front of us. As it did, the tower screamed, 'Get out of there! Climb up out of there!' We had come *this close* to a mid-air collision.

"We started climbing to come around to another runway. When I looked at the gas gauge, it read 'empty,' and I wasn't sure if we would get around. We all knew the other one was dry because we had proved that over the Smoky Mountains. Well, the Good Lord was with us, I guess, because the gas held out and we landed safely. I even walked on my rubber legs to the airport lounge.''

Gord Diamond recalls a flight that was as fun-filled – in hindsight – as it was unique. It began one day in May 1971, when he and co-pilot Jerry Elias flew a small Falcon jet from Ottawa to Fort Smith in the Northwest Territories. They were to stay at Fort Smith overnight, and the following morning they would pick up some special passengers. Diamond explains:

"We were to fly Audubon Society personnel, Canadian and American wildlife ornithologists, and six whooping crane eggs from their nesting area near Fort Smith to Andrews Air Force Base in Maryland for relocation to a protected sanctuary. The military executive jet flight was part of the joint government effort to save the whooping crane population, which eventually, through such efforts, proved successful.

"We arrived in Fort Smith in the late afternoon,'' says Diamond, "and after checking into the hotel and changing, went over to the Wildlife office to have a look at their project.

"It was a good thing that we didn't stop for a cold beer on the way, because when we arrived, the first chick had already picked his way through the shell and was sitting in a cardboard box kept warm by a light bulb on an extension cord, and a second was threatening to do the same. The scientists were concerned, to say the least, and they made an impassioned plea for us to fly immediately and take the whole lot to Andrews Air Force Base before they all hatched.

"So we ran back to the hotel, checked out, rounded up all the equipment and personnel, and launched off for an overnight flight via Winnipeg to Washington, D.C.

"Naturally, it was one of the worst trips I can recall in the Falcon. We experienced some of the most challenging weather I had yet encountered in flying, and the whole route was cluttered with heavy thunderstorms. All the unhatched eggs were individually placed in moulded foam sections in two modified executive briefcases with large thermometers inserted through holes drilled in the tops. For the duration of the six-hour flight, the briefcases remained on the laps of the scientists, more attentively guarded than the crown jewels.

"The one hatched VIP travelled extremely well in his cardboard box, which was held secure by a seatbelt, with an extension cord for the lamp plugged into the electric razor outlet in the washroom.

"For our quick fuel stop in Winnipeg in the early morning we called ahead to have food delivered because we didn't have time to get any supper at Fort Smith. As fate would have it, the only place Base Ops could get to deliver at that hour was the Colonel's Fried Chicken, which brought a few laughs from the unfeathered passengers.

"The hardest landing I ever made in a Falcon was on our 6:00 a.m. arrival in Washington, at the end of a twenty-three-hour day. I breathed a sigh of relief when it was reported from the back that all our fragile flyers were okay, and there were no further breakages."

Another pilot who recalls flying unusual cargo is a man whom we will call Edwin Yanovar. Several years ago, Yanovar was flying C-130 Hercules aircraft on Canada's West Coast. One morning, just before Yanovar was ready to take off at Comox, the base padre came running out to the plane. "He handed me an ornate-looking box," recalls the pilot, "and he said it contained the ashes of George Somebody-or-Other, who had just been cremated. The ashes were to be sprinkled over the Strait of Georgia.

"I thought we'd be able to fly out over the Strait and chuck the box overboard, but no such luck. The family wanted the box back.

"Anyway, we got everybody on board and took off. When I figured we were out far enough, I told the loadmaster to do his thing. He went to the back door to sprinkle the ashes once the door was open.

"I dropped down to just over the water and held the plane there until they told me the ashes had been dumped. The door was closed and I started to climb. After I was up to 5,000 feet or so, I felt a tap on the shoulder.

"When I turned around, I damned near fell out of the seat.

"The loadmaster stood there, and for a second I hardly knew who it was. He had a greyish powder all over his face, in his eyes, in his mouth, and in his hair. I said, 'What the hell happened to you?' All he said was, 'George didn't want to leave.' Then he turned around and left the cockpit.

"I didn't know whether to laugh or cry. The ashes of poor old George were in that Herc for weeks, flying all over the place. An updraft had blown them back into the plane. I guess George liked flying."

Sioux Lookout native Arnold Wallace would agree with poor George. As a flight engineer on a Canso with the Hudson's Bay Company, he loved flying and flew with several excellent pilots, one of whom was Joe Coombes.

"Joe was originally a Saskatchewan farm boy from near Prince Albert," says Wallace. "He flew for years with the Air Force in the West, and spent time in the air during the building of the Alaska Highway. After the war he came to the Bay as a captain on a Canso.

"One day we were sent on an emergency flight from Winnipeg to Cape Dorset on Baffin Island to get the HBC post manager. Apparently he was quite ill and needed hospitalization immediately. His name was Jim Bell.

"We took on a maximum fuel load and set out. Now, this was in June, and the Hudson Straits were mostly ice-bound, but there were odd leads, or stretches of open water, where the plane could land.

"When we arrived over Dorset, we cut back on power in order to preserve as much fuel as we could, while the Inuit men pulled a boat and the sick manager at least five miles to where they could reach an open lead. On every side, the ice was broken into huge pieces and tumbled into a chaotic mess due to the high tides. Just getting the boat out to the lead was a tremendous task, and those men deserve an awful lot of credit for their work.

"However, just as they were about to launch the boat in an open lead where we could land, the fog rolled in and we couldn't see a thing. We postponed the rescue attempt until the next day, and flew to an old American landing field on Southampton Island. By this point, we had been airborne for fourteen hours and thirty-five minutes. I knew Joe was dead tired, as we all were, because he had been at the controls for so long.

"Anyway, we were able to get fuel on Southampton, so we filled up, had a good rest, and headed back to the Straits. The second attempt to pick up Jim Bell was successful, and the Inuit helped us load him into the aircraft.

"We flew back to Winnipeg to get Jim to a hospital. After I helped him off the plane, he removed his new duffle parka and handed it to me with the words: 'Here, Arnold, I want you to have this. I won't need it any more.' The poor guy was dead from cancer in a very short time, and we learned later that he had been terribly sick all that winter, but had not wanted to inconvenience anyone, or have them risk a long rescue flight until the safer summer flying season came around. I'll never forget him, nor will I forget the great flying that Joe Coombes did in getting him out of the North."

Arnold Wallace pays tribute to his fellow flyers, the men who flew for the Hudson's Bay Company: "They were a breed unto their own," he explains. "So often bush pilots operate in a given area for their entire career, but the HBC pilots had to cover the entire country, and this included the high Arctic as well. This was at a time when there were few aircraft, and the maps of the Arctic were often totally blank because the area was unexplored.

"It was just an ordinary flight to leave our home base in Winnipeg," continues Wallace, "then work our way east, stopping at Bay posts en route for inspection tours, then end up in Labrador. We often crossed the entire Arctic from Baffin Island to the

Yukon. It was work, even if it was both exciting and dangerous at times.''

Judy Cameron was born in Montreal and raised in Vancouver, has flown out of Inuvik and elsewhere, and resides today in the southern Ontario city of Oakville with her husband and family. On April 10, 1978, at age twenty-three, Cameron became Air Canada's first female pilot. She has never regarded herself as a trail blazer and will tell you about flying in the far North before she even mentions her current job. From her story it's clear that she loves what she's doing, and has never backed down from a challenge.

"I had no intention of becoming a pilot," she says today, "nor had I any immediate family who flew. I was in an arts program at the University of British Columbia, and one summer I got a job doing a general aviation survey for the Department of Transport. This took me to a lot of airports, and it also resulted in invitations to go flying. Flying intrigued me, so I left U.B.C., got into a college aviation course, and took it from there."

One of Cameron's first jobs was at Slave Lake, Alberta, where she survived an engine failure on a DC-3 during the first scheduled flight she flew. "Maintenance was not a big thing with that company," she laughs, "and they operated on a shoestring budget and eventually went bankrupt. However, I was endorsed on the DC-3, so I was hired by Gateway Aviation up in Inuvik. As it turned out, the chief pilot there really did not want to hire me. 'At least,' he told me, 'the airlines will never hire you, so we won't have to worry about losing you.'

"At Inuvik, I was co-pilot on a DC-3, and as there was only one crew, we were on call most of the time. The fellow I flew with was Inuit, and he had a reputation of being pretty hard on co-pilots. The man I replaced looked like a stricken beast when I arrived, and he kept his eyes on me all the time we were in the terminal building. He wanted to make sure I didn't get away before he got on the Pacific Western mainliner back to Edmonton. He looked as if he was getting out of a cage. I should have taken a hint from that.

"I was there for about nine months, and it was a difficult period.

The fellow I was with was hard on all co-pilots, but I suppose he had a special reason to resent me. Most of our work was hauling freight, and it involved a lot of loading and unloading. We did the work by hand, 6,000 pounds a load, much of it being oil drums. Unfortunately, I was not strong enough to tip the drums over gently when we were taking them off the plane, so he had to do that and roll them to the back. I would stand outside the door and roll the drums to wherever they were being left, generally on a gravel strip just beside the runway. A lot of times he was not too choosy about when he rolled them out the door, whether I was standing there or not. I wore a one-piece jumpsuit and steel-toed boots and I was quite a sight. The work was hard but I stuck it out until I was laid off later on.''

Judy Cameron remembers some of the cargo carried on the various flights throughout the North.

"One day, a replacement pilot arrived, and he and I flew half a dozen men and several spools of wire from Inuvik to Tuktoyaktuk. Someone else loaded the plane, and put far more on than they should have, probably thinking the replacement would not catch on in time. Well, he didn't, and we barely got into the air. I had a great deal of trouble retracting the gear, because, instead of carrying 6,000 pounds, we had 9,000 or so on board. Both engines were roaring away, but we could barely maintain altitude. We got to Tuk, but the trip was pretty exciting.

"Another time, I was flying several natives to the Northern Summer Games, and I'll always remember that trip for a different reason. It was a very hot day in July and we were on our way to Coppermine. Many of the supplies for the contests at the Games were on board, and this included whale blubber in big vats. The stuff was called muktuk and it was chewed in one of the competitions. By the time we landed, those on the ground could probably smell us coming.''

In due course, Cameron left the North and began jumping through the various hoops that led her to the flight deck of a Boeing 727 with Air Canada. She remembers the day she graduated, and the media reaction to her at the time.

"While I was on course, the public relations people with the company were good about shielding me from the media, but of course, once I graduated, I was on my own,'' she says. "One afternoon in Montreal, it was agreed that I would meet the press, and this was rather new for me. Most of the afternoon went well, but it was a rude awakening for someone who had never had dealings with the press.

"I'll never forget one of the television reporters. She was very polite to me, and she gave me an outline of what she would be asking me. Everything was smiles and chuckles and she was *so* friendly – until the camera came on. Then she looked at me and said: 'So, how do you manage to fly despite pre-menstrual tension?' Needless to say, I was somewhat taken aback.''

Cameron has experience on several types of planes, and has done a great deal of North American flying, as well as a stint travelling to Europe and back, since she started with Air Canada. The pioneering role she has played has had its humorous moments, and these have made the job a joy.

"One day, just after I'd made the in-flight announcements, a flight attendant came up to the front giggling. Apparently two guys on board heard me on the PA, and at precisely the same moment they leaned into the aisle and looked toward the front. As they did so they bumped heads, and this caused some embarrassment, I guess. The cabin crew broke up. A lot of times the passengers just assume a flight attendant is doing the talking.

"Another day, on a flight to Quebec City, I made the announcements and federal cabinet minister Barbara McDougall was on board. When I had finished, she sent a card up to the front, congratulating me. She said she had never heard a woman do the announcements before. That pleased me.

"From time to time, male passengers make smart remarks, but in those situations, the flight attendants generally set the guys straight or come to my defence. The attendants are often far more bothered by that kind of thing than I am. As a group, they have been especially supportive.

"Back when I was learning to fly the DC-9, I was with a training captain, taking off from Toronto International. On the first takeoff, I had taxied out to the end of the runway and was doing some checks prior to departure. There were a few seconds of radio silence, then a voice from the tower said: 'What's the matter? Still trying to get your nerve up?'

"Another day, the passengers were boarding and one man

looked into the cockpit. He saw me sitting there and muttered to his friend, 'Well, at least it keeps them off the roads.' I thought that was clever, and it showed some imagination.

"Quite often, older women who come on board will be really supportive. They tell me how much they like seeing me in the front end, and how secure it makes them feel. I remember one little old lady, though, who came up, looked me up and down, then looked over the cockpit, and finally said she was terrified of flying. She did say that she was happy to see me there, and would now feel so much better. Before she went back to her seat, she leaned closer to me and pointed at the captain: 'But you keep *him* under control!' "

Shortly before interviewing Judy Cameron, I talked to a Canadian Forces captain who was one of the scores of pilots leaving the military to fly commercially. After Mike Skubicky finished talking about his career in the air, I asked if he would want his daughter to become a pilot. He paused for several seconds, then stated: "I don't know. I am not sure if I want any of my children to be pilots. I'd rather they got a real job."

Skubicky's offhand remark is as expressive as any about a pilot's love of flying – few flyers, if any, face a Monday morning in the cockpit with aversion. However, if all flyers enjoy their work, some seem to thrive on it. One of these is Peter Cutsey.

19

Flying the Flight Deck

I first met Captain Peter Cutsey one hot summer morning in the Maple Leaf Lounge at Toronto's Pearson International Airport. Air Canada publicist Maureen Curow introduced him as one of the company's senior pilots, and said that he would show me the ropes during a quick return flight to Vancouver. Cutsey had been chosen to shepherd me because, according to Curow, "he knows his job, he's safety-conscious, and he can communicate what he's doing to anyone." (Presumably she also meant that the poor guy was stuck with me and would cheerfully answer the dumbest questions imaginable.) If he'd been cajoled into taking me under his wing, Cutsey never showed it; he went out of his way to be helpful and was always both enthusiastic and congenial. The guy is a press agent's dream! He's also a damned good pilot.

I had asked to fly with our national airline, on the flight deck of a Boeing 767, in order to try to appreciate – and then describe – just what it is that commercial pilots do when they're not breezing through customs while the rest of us are explaining the unclaimed hootch in our luggage. We know pilots fly planes and get to wear smart uniforms, but do we know how hard they work to earn a better-than-average salary, lots of time off, and a lifestyle that most of us drool over with envy?

After flying with Cutsey, I can assure you that, yes, pilots earn their pay, and indeed are worth every cent any employer would wish to pay them. The job requires long hours of training, an unflappable personality, and the flexibility to cope with time differences, plastic food, strange hotel rooms, and the vagaries of weather. Then there are the layovers, dead-heads, bag drags, unserviceable aircraft, and customs officers who have had bad days. On top of everything else, there is the ever-present need to be alert and safety-conscious.

After thirty-two years as a pilot, Peter Cutsey knows the ropes. He has flown everything Air Canada flies, has gone virtually everywhere its planes go, and has never lost a passenger. "But I have been lucky," he admits. "There have been times when the job took everything I had to give, but that's what it's all about. I'm sure every pilot who ever flew would tell you the same thing. We have just as much of a vested interest in arriving alive as those who fly with us. Perhaps even more so; we often have to fly again the next day."

Cutsey was born in North Bay, Ontario, and says he became interested in flying at the age of five. He did a six-year stint in the RCAF and was based at such places as Penhold, Alberta, and Gimli, Manitoba. He professes to be excited about every flight he ever made. "The day I dread going to work is the day I quit," he says.

After answering most of my questions about safety, about himself, and about what I should expect from the forthcoming trip, Cutsey suggested we go to "flight planning." On the way, he told me about the 767, one of the most sophisticated carriers that flies today's skies. His description of the aircraft was far more extensive than I required, but it told me the man certainly knew his stuff.

"The 767," according to Cutsey, "is made by Boeing, one of the best outfits in the business. We got the first four 767s toward the end of 1982, and each of them cost over sixty million dollars U.S. at that time. It has a range of over 3,000 miles and flies almost 600 miles per hour. There are two engines made by Pratt and Whitney. We can carry 179 people, and today we will be almost full. It's a great airplane."

Cutsey introduced me to the co-pilot for our journey to the coast, a young man named Dan Servos who, like Cutsey, loves flying and shows it. "The best part of it," says Servos, "is that you can escape gloomy weather no matter where you are.

"If I am someplace for a few days, Toronto, Vancouver, Halifax, or wherever, and there have been grey skies for a week, all I have to do is get up in the sunshine above the clouds, and things look a lot better." A handsome, gentle individual with 6,000 hours of air time, Dan Servos complimented Cutsey as a co-worker and as first officer on the flight. "Peter is one of the best," said Servos, "and I have flown with several. But Air Canada is a good outfit too, or probably neither of us would stay with it."

Before any of us went near the airplane, the two pilots reviewed the weather – in Toronto, in Vancouver, and en route as well. A series of thunderstorms on the prairies came in for special attention, not because we would be flying through them, but because the disturbances sometimes boiled far above the surface of the earth, and winds there were sure to be affected. Runway closings, on-ramp construction problems, navigational irregularities: all were noted and accounted for.

Once on board the aircraft, the two pilots went through an extensive series of checks, one calling off the items for the other. At one point, mechanics in Toronto came on board and discussed with Cutsey and Servos some minor problems that had been examined and corrected. To an outsider, the professional rapport between the mechanics and the pilots was impressive. The teamwork was essential, since the responsibility for the plane's smooth operation on this flight was shared by many people. After the conference with the mechanics, the pilots programmed the on-board navigational system for the day's trip. Air Canada Flight 109 was to depart from Gate 83 at precisely 12:00 noon. And, despite the overcrowded airport in Toronto, the takeoff was delayed by only six minutes. If one considers the volume of air traffic in and out of our largest city every day, such a prompt departure time is remarkable. Often, pilots, flight attendants, and passengers find they actually encounter far more problems driving to the airport than they do flying away from it.

Once Peter Cutsey had completed the pre-flight routine for our journey, he told me about the on-board computers, some of the most advanced and sophisticated in existence. With these machines at his fingertips, Cutsey could determine, in an instant, the best possible altitude at which to fly, the plane's speed, the rate of fuel consumption, and dozens of other vital elements pertinent to this trip. The on-board computers could, and would, give him up-to-the-second information on our progress and performance in a way that had been impossible a decade earlier.

"But no computer is perfect," he explained. "The pilot still has to feed in the proper information. And even though our autopilot can fly and land the plane, without the pilot monitoring it the computer is still just a machine. We work harder than ever before,'' he insists, ''because we have to monitor the information constantly.''

As we talked on the flight deck prior to departure, an Air Canada employee named Bob Knight was making a videotape of the departure preparations. The tape would ultimately serve as an in-house training tool for the scores of new personnel a company the size of Air Canada brings on stream each year. Cutsey answered Knight's questions with the same kind of gracious attention he showed to me.

Several minutes before the 767 began receiving passengers, the flight attendants for the trip boarded and did the necessary chores in the cabin, in order to make Flight 109 pleasant and safe. Then Captain Cutsey met with them as a group and told them what they could expect in the hours ahead. He mentioned the prairie thunderstorms, which were not expected to be a problem, ''but I'd give you plenty of warning,'' he said. The warning would be necessary because the meal service and passenger comfort and safety could be affected by turbulence.

Cutsey also asked the cabin personnel to tell him exactly where each fire extinguisher was located. ''We do this,'' he told me, ''because our flight attendants are flying on different planes, and the locations of the extinguishers are not all the same. In case of a fire, lives could be lost if someone hesitates, even for a second or two, to act.'' His briefing complete, Cutsey introduces me, and tells the men and women before him why I am there. But by now, the paying customers are starting to arrive.

The boarding routine is a familiar one: those flying first class, those requiring assistance, and those with small children board first. After that, people at the rear of the plane enter, then those farther up, and finally the passengers whose seats are at the front. The cabin crew directs passengers to the correct seats, does other last-minute checks, and secures the doors. Then the crew members demonstrate the proper fastening of seat belts, the use of oxygen masks in the event of a cabin pressurization failure, and, on flights over water, the donning and inflation of life jackets. Up on the flight deck, Cutsey and Servos are ready to go. I am buckled into a jump seat just behind and slightly to the left of Cutsey, on the left-hand side of the cockpit. He turns to me.

"Here's a headset," he says. "Put it on and you'll be able to hear the air controller. I don't want you to get bored on us." There was little danger of that.

He also says something else: "One rule that I want you to obey to the letter," he tells me, "is to avoid any chit-chat until we get to 10,000 feet. Both Dan and I will be pretty busy for the first while, and we want to have a safe departure. You are important, but together, all of us in this aircraft are more important. If there are things I think you should know I will tell you when I get the chance. Okay?" I agree.

Now, outside the plane and down to the side, a member of the ground crew, wearing a headset, supervises the departure of the aircraft. Cutsey talks by radio to him, and the leaving reminds me of backing a car out of a garage. Just prior to taxiing away from the terminal, Cutsey thanks the man on the tarmac. The man nods and gives a thumbs-up sign, and away we go.

As we trundle out to Runway 24, I cannot help but marvel at this magnificent machine and the statistics that are part and parcel of this trip today. The distance to Vancouver by air is 3,342 kilometres or 2,077 miles. The flight will last about four hours and fifty minutes, and there are 173 passengers and a crew of 9 on board. There are 64,700 pounds of fuel in the tanks. (In contrast, Richard Rutan and Jeana Yeager flew their little plane *Voyager* non-stop around the world in December 1986 on less than 9,000 pounds of gasoline.) We will get permission to fly at 41,000 feet, and it will take twenty-three minutes to get up there.

There are other aircraft ahead of us, so we play follow-the-leader, down the taxiway to the end of the runway. When the traffic ahead has departed, Cutsey gets clearance from the tower, eases onto Runway 24, and opens the throttles, and we roar down the strip of cement and into the sky. The wheels are retracted, and the climb to altitude continues. Back in the cabin, the NO SMOKING and seatbelt signs are still lit.

Both Cutsey and Servos have been busy flying the plane and checking the myriad of dials, video display screens, and other instruments in front of them. To the uninitiated, the confusing array of knobs, indicators, and lights is something from science fiction. Then there are the colours: magenta, blue, yellow, purple, green – each significant and each important. I think of Punch Dickins and the advances in flying since his day.

Once we reach our cruising altitude, Servos does the flying while Cutsey punches some buttons in front of him and one of the on-board printers begins chattering. He tears off a strip of paper, glances at it, and hands it across to Dan. Then Cutsey turns to me and says: "Ordinarily we would be at 39,000 feet, but because of the weather ahead, we will make better time and save gas at 41,000. We will also have a smoother ride."

The in-flight service manager taps on the door and comes into the cockpit. She glances outside and then asks Cutsey and me what we want for lunch. Servos will eat later. We place our orders and Cutsey turns back to me, pointing as he does. "See that."

Down below, silhouetted against the dazzling white of low clouds and some distance to our left is another plane. It moves like a dart in the direction we have come, and in no time has disappeared. I am thankful there are air corridors up here where the fast-flying planes of today are kept well apart. Suddenly, all the stories of "near-misses" have new meaning. I see how quickly two oncoming jets could come together.

As our flight continues, the prairie thunderstorms become a reality. Masses of cloud billow up ahead, and in one or two places they even tower above us. "When they are at that altitude," explains Cutsey, "we would be fools to try to fly through them." A slight course change is made, and the danger is averted. There is some turbulence but nothing of import. Air Canada 109 continues.

In no time, we are over the Rockies, but I have to take Cutsey's word for it. The cloud carpet below is unbroken. By now, meal service is over, Cutsey has made his second and final in-flight announcement to the passengers, and preparations are in place for our approach to Vancouver. The weather there will be rather gloomy, 18° C and overcast, with showers predicted soon after we arrive. To many of us on board, the respite from the humidity will be welcome.

Our descent begins. Probably only the passengers who fly often would have noticed the change. The gentle tipping down of the nose of the plane, the slight variation in engine noise, and the change in pressure on the human eardrum are about the only indicators. Cutsey turns to me.

"Providing there are no surprises here," he says, "the automatic pilot will land the plane. I want you to see how this is done. If there is the slightest danger, I will take over, of course, but things are looking good. As we come in on final, watch my hands. I won't touch the controls.''

The automatic pilot on the 767, as on other planes, can fly the aircraft, but it is only an extension of the men and women on the flight deck. They feed the information to the on-board computers, and the machines can do the rest – from just after takeoff to the landing and after. The device is good, safe – but only as good as the human beings in the cockpit.

We break through cloud, and Canada's most beautiful city is spread out before us, embraced by the mountains and the sea. The towers downtown, the green of Stanley Park, the white circular roof of B.C. Place, and the handsome homes below Grouse Mountain: all are there, enchanting, inviting, and, from my vantage point in the sky, serene.

The runway is just ahead.

I look over Peter Cutsey's left shoulder. His hands are in front of him, but neither is touching the control column.

Lower.

Finally there is a slight jar, and I know we're down. The engine thrust-reversers slow the plane, the brakes come on, and the flight terminates. The machine-landing has been as good as any I've ever experienced. Cutsey and Servos exchange glances and both smile. Back in the cabin, the passengers are asked to remain seated until the plane has come to a full stop.

A few minutes later, Cutsey unfastens his seat belt and climbs from his seat. "Excuse me for a moment," he says, "I want to say goodbye to the folks." He steps out of the cockpit and stands just at the door, talking to the passengers as they leave. Several thank him, almost all of them smile, and one or two ask to see the flight deck. Later, I asked Servos if Captain Cutsey always says goodbye to the paying passengers. "Almost always," he replies, "except when somebody gets up here before he has a chance to get out. He loves meeting people and talking to them."

We collect our luggage, and Cutsey, Servos, and I share a cab downtown. Outside, it is raining.

Over dinner that night, I ask Cutsey to tell me more about himself and about his job. "Well, I love doing what I do," he says. "Although you have probably realized that by now. Flying is fun, and I hate to see people afraid of it. It's far safer than driving, but that is sometimes hard to get across.

"For some time now, I have been involved in a program to help people overcome their fear of flying. A therapist works with me, and we take our clients, if you want to call them that, into one of the company flight-simulators in Toronto. After they are there for a while, after they understand and experience what it is to fly, they really do get over most of their apprehension. Without the simulator, however, that would be more difficult.

"I also love challenges," continues Cutsey, "and it's the unexpected that makes my job appealing. For example, a couple of winters ago the reservations people got telephone bomb threats concerning the 767 flight I was doing to Vancouver. The guy calling sounded pretty convincing, so we returned to Toronto immediately. We turned back at 23,000 feet, but we were on the tarmac in thirteen minutes. Fifty-five seconds later, everyone was down the chutes and on the ground – in the fog and rain and darkness. Some slid right into water puddles on the cement.

"Naturally, most people were upset, some angry, a lot scared. In order to try to reassure them, my first officer and I went through the crowd and talked to *every* passenger. Doing this type of thing was against company policy at the time, but I felt we owed our customers some explanation. Later we were commended for what we had done, but it was just our gut reaction when we did it. By the way, no bomb was found."

I asked about alternate arrangements at such a time.

"Yes," Cutsey replied, "if we felt we could have gotten into another airport quicker, we would have gone there. The same things hold true no matter where we are flying. We always take enough fuel to enable us to land at, say, Edmonton, if Calgary is closed due to weather or some other factor."

Could the alternate be in the United States?

"Oh, yes," said Cutsey, "but if a problem cropped up during a domestic flight here, it is better for everyone concerned to land at a Canadian airport. That way, there are no customs problems and so on. You don't go looking for more hassles than you have."

The next morning we checked out of our hotel at 5:00 a.m. and arrived at Vancouver International thirty minutes later. The trip back to Toronto was uneventful until just before touchdown.

Then, crosswinds, unexpected and severe, buffetted the plane and threatened to pull it away from the glide path. Fortunately, we were close enough to the ground that all on board were buckled in. First one wing tilted upwards, then dipped as the other came up. The 767 shuddered and skewed to one side. Then the nose came around, only to swing back as quickly.

Cutsey gripped the controls and fought to keep our approach correct, the knuckles of his hands white as he held the course. No automatic pilot could do this.

Then we were down, off the runway, then at the gate. A flight attendant told me later that she had never heard so much applause as when the plane landed. As they filed off the aircraft, I heard several passengers commend Cutsey. He had earned his pay, and more, in those two minutes before touchdown. We were back – safely – and all of us were glad.

Now I know what pilots like Peter Cutsey do.

20

The Jet Jocks

Fighter pilots are special. They work hard, play hard, love what they do, and hope the fun lasts forever. Some of them have inflated egos, and this they readily admit. Most of them would rather fly than eat, and this they also admit. And almost all of them look upon their time as fighter pilots as the most exciting of their careers.

All pilots talk shop, but fighter pilots revel in doing so. Whether they flew Sopwiths, Hurricanes, or Hornets, the afterglow is the same. It is the afterglow brought about by the ecstasy of being alone in the sky, against the elements, the enemy, and the constraints of the craft. In the Ops room, in the mess, or in living rooms later in life, they talk shop: how fast they flew, how high, how low, and how bravely. As they talk, their eyes dance, they gesture, and they drift into a jargon the outsider can barely follow. But they are happy, happy beyond words, and they *show* it.

Long after he chased his German counterparts across the European skies of World War I, George Howsam, who has passed away since being interviewed for this book, was able to recall, in vivid and colourful detail, the way he felt, what he thought, and what he did while in the air. Presumably his German counterparts could do the same. In World War II, men like Jan Zurakowski and Bob Norris fought the Battle of Britain and, despite the fact that Winston Churchill cited them and others for special praise, did what they did without looking upon themselves as superhuman, or even particularly talented. They loved flying, in spite of the danger and the risks they had to take.

J.D. "Red" Somerville, now living in retirement in Victoria, looks upon his years as a fighter pilot as years he hoped would never end. Somerville soloed back in 1929, but he never let his age stand in the way of his flying. He did a lot of barnstorming prior to 1939, but when war came he flew Mosquitos, because he was told that Spitfires were too fast for the "old man" to fly. Undaunted, when the hostilities ceased, Somerville decided he would not take a back seat to anyone. The jet age had arrived, and he intended to be part of it.

"I loved the jets," he told me. "I don't think you've flown until you've flown a jet. Jets have their faults. For instance, in the earlier ones you didn't get the response you got in a propeller-driven airplane, but jets are the way of the world today."

One of the first jet fighters purchased by the RCAF was the de Havilland Vampire in 1948. Four of the new planes were destined for 442 Squadron in Vancouver, and Somerville decided he should be the man to deliver the first. He talked his way into the Vampire conversion course in Trenton, and, shortly after completing it, arrived at the de Havilland plant in Toronto to pick up the first new plane.

"The day could hardly have been better," he recalls. "I took off in a brand new Vampire, on one of the most enjoyable flights I can remember. At 25,000 feet, without a cloud in sight, Ontario and the Great Lakes were mine."

The first leg of the journey was uneventful. Somerville landed at Kapuskasing, waited out some poor weather, and then took off for Armstrong, a small town on the Canadian National line in northwestern Ontario. The April sky was cloudy, but visibility at his destination was acceptable for landing, and, indeed, Somerville could see Armstrong once he descended below the 1,200-foot cloud bank.

"Levelling off below the cloud, I pulled in the dive brakes and eased the throttle open again," he wrote later on.

Nothing happened. The engine had flamed out.

All that training back at Trenton had not been wasted: I quickly went through the emergency relight procedure. Nothing. I was listening to the sound of the wind blowing around the canopy and looking at 'scenic' northern Ontario bushland from about 1,000 feet altitude. The airspeed needle fell back to 'optimum glide' and I was forced to push the stick ahead to keep it there. 800 feet and descending.

Although it was your basic pilot's nightmare – three miles-on-approach-I-just-lost-my-engine – I did not think of that. Instead, I went through another relight sequence. No joy.

My flight path was parallel to the CNR main line and I thought briefly of dropping the wheels and landing on the railway track. Then, and better, I spotted a clear area beside the flag station at Wagaming. It had been cleared as a temporary siding during the construction of the railway 60 or more years earlier. I could see the carpet of tree stumps on my tiny landing field but they looked old and grey and . . . Hell! . . . I'd run out of options.

The glide ratio of a Vampire is not good. From 800 feet I think it took maybe 30 seconds until I was skimming the tree tops. My planning was impeccable. That is, I reached the desired touchdown point deadstick, at an appropriate landing speed. It was roundout time in the Vampire.

As I eased back on the stick I saw that immediately ahead and at right angles to my direction of glide, was a dried-out watercourse. The embankment was only three or four feet high but smacking into it at 100 mph was an unwelcome thought. Pull!

The Vampire staggered into the air, cleared the ditch, stalled and flopped. CRUMP! Thump, bump, slither and slide . . . most of the way across the clearing. Incredibly, when I climbed out to take a look at it, the sturdy little Vampire appeared intact.

Three Indian track workers came pumping along on their handcar about this time, on their way to Armstrong. I asked them for a ride as far as the airport. The only space available on the car was that of the missing fourth pumper. I pumped my way the final three miles to Armstrong.[1]

Later, a replacement aircraft was flown to Winnipeg, and Somerville continued his flight in it. This Vampire was safely delivered to Vancouver.

The arrival of the plane became a major news story for the

media of the day. In its coverage of the event, the Vancouver *Sun* pulled out all the stops and put the item on the front page of its May 4, 1948, edition. Under a headline that said: "Jet Plane Streaks in from the East," the paper reported:

> The RCAF's Vampire came to town today, a blazing streak of speed and power that frightened housewives and had veteran fliers bug-eyed with excitement.
>
> The roar of the plane frightened residents of Burnaby and the Fraser Valley. A dozen persons telephoned *The Vancouver Sun* to report a 'mysterious, lightning-fast missile.' Many said the roar of the craft rattled dishes in their homes.

And the Vampire that Somerville put down in the bush? It was destroyed by those who came to retrieve it for shipment back to Toronto. Because they couldn't figure out what to do with the protruding wings when they had the aircraft on a flatcar, they simply hacked them off and sent the plane in pieces. It never flew again.

Somerville fared better – in the long run.

After his historic flight was over, he reported to a doctor, complaining of back pain. After several X-rays and assorted medical examinations, it was determined that he had broken a vertebra in his back. When it healed, the man who was supposedly too old to fly Spitfires during the war began driving the newest fighter the RCAF had, the Canadair F-86 Sabre.

There were Sabres in Canada and Europe, and there were CF-100s and others through the years, but the Sabre, to those who flew it, was a special plane. Canadians flew it in battle over Korea and on patrols over France, and they loved it.

Chick Childerhose, perhaps the most literate fighter jock we've ever had, wrote several books about his love affair with the plane. "The Sabres were the best fighter planes in the world and Canadians were the best fighter pilots. Our Air Division was the best in all NATO,"[2] he has written. Some years later, in a conversation with me, Childerhose stood by his beliefs. "Yes, we were the best, if being cocky makes you the best," he laughs. "We thought we were damned good, and maybe we were. But we must have bored everyone who had to listen to us. I learned much later in

life that all other pilots resent fighter pilots – and I guess we often
gave them reason to do so. Still, I wouldn't have missed fighter
flying for anything.''

Nor would many of his kind. Gil Atwood almost shot himself
down but he still loved the fighters. ''In March 1955, I was
involved in shooting practice in one of four T-33 trainers at a
range west of Lake Manitoba. We flew to the range and delivered
bombs and rockets,'' he recalls. ''Then the final part of the
practice involved shooting our .50 calibre machine-guns against
a ten-foot by ten-foot canvas ground target.

''Each pilot's bullets were dipped in coloured wax so that the
holes in the target could be identified and the scores allocated.
When our rounds were fired off, we formed up and returned to
RCAF Station MacDonald, where we were based at the time. During taxi-in, I was informed by the Tower Controller that fuel was
pouring from the right tip tank of my plane. After stopping the
aircraft, it was inspected by a groundcrewman who discovered a
hole in the front bottom of the tank.

''We could shake the tank and hear a rattle inside,'' continues
Atwood, ''so we opened it up. Then we found a spent .50 calibre
bullet with my identifying colour on it. Obviously, I had flown
through my own ricochet. Fortunately, the bullet hit the tank and
not the engine or I would have shot myself down. Things like
that made that kind of flying interesting, to say the least.''

During the late 1950s, Jan Zurakowski became the first man
to fly the most exciting airplane ever built in Canada. His flights
in the ill-fated Avro Arrow were more than just interesting; they
were unique.

The Arrow was a twin-engined, all-weather, fighter-interceptor
capable of supersonic speeds, built by A.V. Roe of Canada. It
was first flown on March 25, 1958, and was ordered destroyed
by the government of John Diefenbaker eleven months later. And,
though more than three decades have passed since the Arrows
were destroyed (there were five that flew), those who had anything to do with the plane have never forgiven the Prime Minister
for his decision. Zurakowski is still angry about it.

''It was a magnificent aircraft,'' he says today. ''It was far
ahead of its time, and it showed that this country was in the
forefront in aircraft technology – world-wide. There will never

be another Arrow. When we were told that the plane was to be scrapped, I was totally dumbfounded, and so shocked I could have cried.''

Recently, in a foreword to Greig Stewart's book on the Arrow, Zurakowski writes:

The story of A.V. Roe's Avro Arrow has a sad ending: the cancellation of an aircraft that, for many Canadians, had become the national dream. On February 20, 1959, it was with disbelief that we heard of the announcement, in Parliament, by Prime Minister John George Diefenbaker that the Arrow program would be terminated.

I can still see the faces of the people, the thousands of men and women who had contributed to the design, development, and production of the Arrow. Their dream of providing Canada's defence with the best fighter plane in the world, and the jobs they had been so proud of, had suddenly disappeared.

. . . The outstanding performance of the Arrow can best be appreciated through speed comparisons with other aircraft. . . . Thirty years ago the Arrow was flying faster than today's most advanced fighter, the CF-18, which we purchase from the United States.[3]

The former test pilot reminisces about what it was like to fly the Arrow.

"It was the experience of a lifetime. It lived up to everything a pilot could ever want in a fighter plane. I used to take the job very seriously, though," he added. "So much was riding on that plane, so many jobs and so on, that I didn't want to jeopardize anything. But then, in the end, I guess it didn't matter.''

Zurakowski is circumspect, but he nonetheless leaves no misunderstanding as to his feelings about the entire fiasco. "There isn't even a single plane in a museum," he points out, "and that is such a loss to those of us who worked on it, to the company, and to the country.''

"Did you ever meet Mr. Diefenbaker?" I asked.

"No," replied the test pilot.

"What would you have said to him if you had met him?"

Zurakowski tenses at the question, pauses for several seconds, and then muses: "I don't think such a meeting would have been pleasant."

Ken Harvey is now a 747 pilot, but from 1956 to 1959 he was instructing on T-33s at Portage la Prairie, Manitoba. He loved the flying, the adventure, and the life of the fighter pilot, but one Friday he almost didn't come home.

"I had the afternoon off," he recalls, "but I dropped into the flight office for something or other, and Bill Christiansen, a fellow instructor, was there. He asked me if I would help him in a two-plane formation exercise because he had two students who were behind in their schedule. I agreed."

Harvey and a young student pilot named Papworth took off and had barely climbed into cloud when they noticed smoke seeping into the cockpit of their aircraft. Harvey immediately called Christiansen, then dropped below cloud to see if the source of the smoke could be found. Unfortunately, it could not, and instead became worse and worse, to the point that Harvey could not see the controls. At any moment, he feared the T-33 would burst into flames.

"I finally had to tell the student I would blow the canopy and return to the base and land. He agreed."

No sooner had the canopy gone than Papworth's helmet, earphones, and radio microphone were torn away as well. In the meantime, Harvey was in the back seat, in $-25°C$ weather, travelling at almost 300 miles per hour. Because he had no windshield, he became so cold that his eyes began to tear and freeze until he couldn't see. Papworth ducked behind the windscreen in the front seat and held on for dear life.

"I simply could not see," continues Harvey, "and I could not talk to the student because his radio equipment was gone. I wiggled the control column all over the place, hoping he would take control, but he didn't realize what was happening to me. I could talk to the Tower, but there was such a roar from the wind and the engines I couldn't hear what the Tower was saying.

"A couple of times I thought I could make out the artificial horizon, but that was about all. All I could see outside was black and white, black for forest and white for snow, and I couldn't find the airport at all. I somehow knew I was heading north, so I headed for what I thought might be Lake Manitoba because in one area everything was white. I thought I might be able to do a wheels-up landing on the ice, but I couldn't find the damned lake either.

"I finally found that if I looked behind me my tears would melt and I could make out trees. All the while I was getting lower and lower, with my speed brakes on, but I didn't want to stall if I could help it. In the end, I simply pulled back on the stick and pointed the plane down.

"When we hit the ground, the aircraft bounced into the air, then hit again and finally came to a screeching stop on top of a road. All the while, trees had been flying past on one side and hydro poles on the other.

"After we finally stopped, Papworth stood up in the cockpit and turned toward me. His face was covered with blood, and a barbed wire fence we had crashed through was all wrapped up over the cockpit. We were both alive, but we were lucky we had not been decapitated.

"There was a farmhouse about half a mile away, so we climbed out of the plane and started walking. The farmer was outside, near his house, so I yelled to him. No response. Finally we got up close, and it was only when we were right in front of him that he saw us. The man was deaf.

"He got us into the house, and his wife began to patch us up. One of the student's eyelids was badly torn and his scalp was ripped back. I was so cold I didn't realize my throat had been cut, but the farmer's wife did some great emergency first aid on us. We both were able to talk to the board of inquiry."

Airplane crashes are an inherent part of flying, and, every so often, accidents occur, even to such outfits as the internationally renowned Air Force aerobatic team, the Snowbirds.

Late in the afternoon on June 10, 1972, I stood in a crowd and watched a Snowbird named Lloyd Waterer die. I will never forget it. I didn't know him; I had never met him and had not even heard of him before. He was just twenty-three, in the prime of life, highly trained, physically fit, a true professional. But after two decades of growing, years of schooling, and months of training, he was given only three seconds to die. And he died – as we all shall – alone, though thousands of us stood and watched.

We had been watching all afternoon. That year's Armed Forces Day at Canadian Forces Base Trenton was larger than any held previously. At 1:30 p.m., the Red Arrows of the Royal Air Force screamed across the field to open the show. At 4:15, the Snow-birds were scheduled to close it. Between these events, the Otters, the 707s, the CF-5 and the rest did their stuff. Even the fire department got into the act. We all saw their trucks race down the runway, foam a "burning" jet plane, and pull the trapped dummy from the cockpit. The kids cheered. It was all just part of an act.

By 4:00 p.m., most of us had seen enough. If it wasn't for the imminent Snowbird performance, some would have left. A few minutes later, most of us were wishing we had. Instead, we crowded toward the runways and stood, watching, leaning into the gusty wind, listening for the public address system to announce the grand finale.

And then, almost as soon as the announcement began, it was lost in the blast of jet engines. The nine single-engine Canadair Tutors roared upwards, spread out, and were lost in the clouds. A few seconds later they reappeared, swift, sleek, mildly terri-fying, in formation. Then two sped away to opposite ends of the field, turned, and, as the PA described the manoeuvre, hurtled toward each other at close to the speed of sound.

Then it came. The bypass. The torn metal. The debris in the air as wing tips touched. The disbelief on the ground. One of the two performers gained altitude and disappeared over the airfield and the crowd toward the west. The other, broken and doomed, rolled and plummeted unchecked to the tarmac on our right. My God, he's going in, I recall thinking at the time. Almost instantly, amid the sparks and dust, the explosion came. A massive, sickly, red-orange, movie-like fireball. Dense black smoke billowed upwards as a siren screamed.

For a few seconds no one moved. You read of temporary paral-ysis. Now I know it is real. Even the PA commentator fell silent. His first words, when he found them, were sluggish, strained, full of the shock we all felt. "Would everyone hold their places," I think he said.

Across the field, fire trucks raced away – this time to pump foam over real flames that engulfed a dead man. No one cheered this time. But many prayed. Some got sick; others fainted. An old man sat down, buried his face in his hands, and cried. I saw a young woman clutching a handrail leading up to the cabin of a 707. Her face and knuckles were white in the wind. Finally, when it seemed she could not stop shaking, she lowered herself to the steps and sobbed.

Five minutes later, the other damaged jet limped home. Its wing tip gaped open and the crowd stopped breathing. The landing was successful.

"It is always sobering when some fail to return," Yogi Huyghebaert, a former commanding officer of the Snowbirds, told me not so long ago. "When you're on the team, you become very close, and then when something happens everyone is saddened. Generally, the way pilots cope is to go to the bar and drink to the one who is no longer there. That is accepted. As a matter of fact, many pilots stipulate in their will that a certain amount of money is to be set aside to buy drinks for the house. I'm one of them. The job is dangerous, but there also has to be a tomorrow. We fly the next day."

I interviewed Major Huyghebaert in a car as we drove in south-central France, heading for the Royal Canadian Air Force cemetery at a place called Choloy. There, in the shade of dozens of trees on a peaceful hillside, are the earthly reminders of scores of Canadians who died while serving their country in peacetime Europe. As I walked with Huyghebaert between the well-kept rows of white crosses, he stopped every few paces to remember old friends whose names he recognized. The experience was difficult for him, but it helped me understand that a peacetime stint far from home carries its dangers. A lot of young men who left to fly in Europe as part of our NATO commitment never came home.

"There have been a few Snowbird deaths," says Huyghebaert, "but fortunately, the numbers are still small. The way the team is selected and the types of men chosen cut down on the chance of accidents."

Former Snowbird Mike Skubicky recalls the way the team was put together when he was part of it. "You are with the outfit for two years," he says, "and I don't believe that has changed. The members are chosen from the entire Canadian Forces, and any pilot can apply. All are volunteers, and half the team changes each year. The pilots on the team who have been there for a year choose the best of the applicants. You're chosen based on how well you fly, how compatible you are, and so on. Political pressure is no help. The year I got on, thirty-some applied and I was one of the lucky ones picked.''

Carl Shaver, another ex-Snowbird who today is in Europe flying one of the Boeing 707 Airborne Warning and Control System (AWACS) aircraft, says being a Snowbird is like being married to an organization. ''You are together from spring until fall,'' he says, ''living out of a suitcase, always on the road. It can be tough on family life, and, if you are married, your wife has to be as committed as you are. She has to cope with a lot. We had three small children when I was with the team, so I have to give an awful lot of credit to my wife. Even when you get home, it's really just in the door and out again. There are shows every weekend, weather permitting.

''The years I was on the team were exciting, though. We did shows for fifty people in the Northwest Territories, and a million at Coney Island in New York City. Then there were all the others in every province and in several states in the United States.''

Paul Giles talked to me just before a show in Ontario. ''Flying with these guys is fun,'' says the jovial, ever-smiling Giles. ''We do everything together when we're on the road, and we are not special in any way. Some of us are overweight, one or two are losing their hair, none of us has movie-star looks, but we are reasonably good at what we do or we wouldn't be here.

''There is not much time for family, but when we are on the road, the team is the family. We have to look after ourselves, though. Before the show, there is a briefing, covering what we intend to do, the local weather, the terrain around the show area, and so on. Then, as soon as the show is over, we try to meet some of the people in the crowd and sign autographs. Then there is a de-briefing, often a reception, and then, the next day, it's on to the next show. In between, there are practices, media flights, and so on. We also get a lot of letters, and these are divided up and we all help to answer them.''

The interview over, Giles changed from sneakers and jeans into the red spandex Snowbird suit. We shook hands, and then he and the rest of the team trooped out to their planes. People who saw them walk to the flight line cheered. Five minutes later they were gone, down the runway, into the sky, ready to start another show. Ready to thrill the thousands who waited below.

But after the tour with the Snowbirds is over, team members go on to other types of postings, perhaps on the ground or outside of Canada. One of the most popular locations is Baden-Soellingen, a Canadian Forces base on the banks of the Rhine in the Black Forest area of Germany. Here, in the midst of some of the most beautiful scenery in Europe, young Canadians fly the F-18 Hornet, one of the most sophisticated airplanes in the world today. Here, as at Cold Lake, Alberta, and Bagotville, Quebec, the Hornet rules the skies.

The plane is a pilot's dream.

"It's a wonderful aircraft," says Bill Motriuk, a young major who got the bug to fly after he watched planes passing over a golf course he was playing in Winnipeg. "I've flown the trainers, the 101s and the F-5s," he continues, "but the F-18 we're using here is something special. Sometimes flying fighters over here is looked upon as the leading edge of Canada's defence system, and that may be so. When you are at 10,000 feet, in an air combat, it's an exhilarating, free-wheeling, wonderful experience that is hard to describe. I wouldn't trade it for the world."

Motriuk's colleague, Ottawa-born glider pilot Dave Smith, agrees. "Being here on 421 Squadron, in this part of Europe, is great," he tells me. "But flying the F-18 is flying a dream-machine. It's everything I ever wanted."

I asked Smith what, in his opinion, made a good pilot. "Perhaps the degree of professionalism," he replied. "Being a pilot is a vocation. My father is a Mountie and he's a professional in what he does. It's the same with flying. Good pilots know the plane, the weather, the terrain, and the job. But most of all, they know themselves.

"And even though we are often called cocky, and brash and so on, the good pilot should have a bit of humility. When you screw up, when you over-correct, when you scare those around you in the sky, you have to be humble enough to admit it, to admit your mistake. On the other hand, when you strap on that airplane, you have to leave all your other cares and worries behind. The F-18 is forgiving, but you shouldn't be up there making mistakes either."

I asked Smith about his tactical call-sign, the nickname used by his buddies on the ground and above it.

"Well, it goes back to the time a group of us were involved in 419 Squadron training on the F-5. One night there was a party at one guy's place, and the steaks were good and the drinks were flowing – lots of them. For the grand finale of the evening, one guy made some flaming drinks with somebody's home-made rye whiskey.

"Unfortunately, when I went to drink the stuff, the flame wasn't out and my nose caught fire. The guy sitting next to me put my face out with a table napkin. The burns healed, but ever since then I've been called Torch. I'm sure there are several people over here who don't even know my real name."

Stories of partying among these pilots are legendary, and most of them are true. Friday night in the mess is a special time: rowdy, rambunctious, sometimes hilarious, sometimes crude. The mess is where flyers relax after work, after doing a job that demands constant alertness. The camaraderie is important and the hi-jinks are part of the lifestyle. Sometimes they have a way of getting, well, carried away . . .

Ken Harvey recalls the mess get-together during his time in Germany when the Sabre was the plane for the time.

"One Friday night at Baden, after most of the crowd was sufficiently inebriated, a sheep herder and twelve sheep were invited into the mess for a beer. (Many sheep grazed on one side of the main runway.) The man and his charges stayed for over an hour until the Station CO came and kicked them out. There were no casualties.

"The following Friday night, another squadron invited a farmer and his cow for a beer. The next morning, the farmer was okay, but the cow was dead – apparently from a combination of old age and beer.

"Two weeks later, on a Saturday night, a dance was held at the same mess. The eight-piece German band showed up on motorcycles. During a lull in the dancing, somebody started one of the bikes, and in no time all were being ridden faster and faster through the various rooms of the place. The German bike-owners were not very happy."

The men who fly fighters work hard and play hard – and some of them die hard. In the post-war years in Europe, a lot of young men ended up at the bottom of smoking holes when the Sabre or the F-104 they were driving crashed. Yogi Huyghebaert points out that at one time "anyone who wanted a 104 had only to buy an acre of land in Germany and wait." Sooner or later, one of the widow-makers would crash on it. Fortunately, the pilot's sense of humour helps in most of the rough spots.

Huyghebaert recalls standing around the Ops room one night as a team of 104s practised formation flying. Two planes approached from opposite directions, met head-on at more than 500 miles per hour, and then pulled up overhead. As they climbed into the night sky to about 25,000 feet, one pilot reported pitch-up, that is, an uncontrolled flight when the Starfighter effectively becomes a rocket. "It's difficult to get the 104 out of uncontrolled flight," says Huyghebaert. "In most cases, it means you have to eject.

"Several of us were listening to the pilots talking, and the room became quite tense. 'Don't stay with the airplane,' one guy was saying to his wing man. 'Get out of it if you have to.' We knew there could well be a crash if the first fellow did not regain control.

"Then, just at the point that no one knew if there was an ejection or not, another voice said, 'Can I have your car?' We all roared laughing. The moment passed and everyone felt better. The guy landed okay."

Another F-18 pilot, twenty-seven-year-old James Kyle, talks of the flyer's dependence on others, and cites his father's experience. Jim Kyle's father John retired from the RCAF but now flies the Lockheed 1011 Tristar for Air Canada.

Several years ago John Kyle was alone in a T-33, doing a check of radar bases in Quebec. During the flight, which originated at St. Hubert, near Montreal, the oxygen feed to the pilot became inoperable. Gradually, Kyle received less and less oxygen, and finally passed out. Fortunately, he was at a high altitude when this happened. The jet flew on, heading nowhere, but getting there fast, its pilot slumped unconscious at the controls.

Down on the ground, the radio man at one of the radar installations realized what had happened, and frantically called and called the insensible pilot. Meanwhile the jet flew lower and lower, turning in wide, lazy circles in the sky. Two minutes passed, then three, then four, and finally almost ten.

All the while, the radio operator called Kyle, alternately shouting, then lowering his voice, then raising it, finally screaming at the man in the plane. The man on the ground knew Kyle's life was now in his hands. If the pilot did not come around soon, his life was over.

After what seemed an eternity, Kyle stirred, puzzled by the din in the headset, then raised his head and broke out in a cold sweat. He sat up straighter, looked around to regain his bearings, and slowly, sluggishly, responded to the insistent voice on the radio. Gradually, he recovered, thanked the radio operator, and flew back to base and landed. The mechanics fixed the plane, and Kyle went to locate the man who had saved his life.

"It's the same for us here in Baden," James Kyle told me. "Without all the ground crew, mechanics, radio operators, and so on, we'd be nothing. A fighter jock is only as good as those supporting him."

Marty Tate of the Baden 439 Tiger Squadron recalls having trouble in a plane, but it wasn't for lack of oxygen.

"Before I was in the Air Force, and not long after I learned to fly, I kept bugging a guy I knew in Toronto to let me take his new aircraft up for a spin. The plane was the man's pride and joy, and he was reluctant to let me take it. He was just preparing to leave Toronto, where this happened, to fly to Ottawa in a few minutes' time.

"Finally, the guy gave in," says Tate, "so I took off, climbed to 5,000 feet or so, and started doing a few aerobatics. I knew the plane would fly upside down, so I tried it, then I decided to practise knife-edge vertical, with the plane on its side. Things were going well. It was a beautiful warm morning in August, and I was having a lot of fun. I would roll to the right, the side where the door was, and keep the left wing straight up.

"I did this a few times, always on the right, and then I decided to do a roll to the left. However, just as I rolled, I heard a rush of air and I looked down toward the ground at my left.

"It wasn't until I reverted to level flight that I realized I had no door. I looked at the big open space, and I was suddenly amazed and scared. I was amazed at the fact that the door had popped open and fallen off, but scared of what would happen when I returned the guy's new airplane. Just what do you say? 'Here's your plane. Sorry about the door. It seems to be missing.'

"As I came over the field to land, I could see the fellow's car parked near the runway, and he was standing beside it. My landing was one of the worst I've ever done, but I got the plane down and taxied over to the car.

" 'Where'd my door go?' was all he could manage.

" 'I don't know,' I said. 'It's gone somewhere.'

"Later on, the door turned up, but it was wrecked. I left as quickly as I could, and things were a bit tense for a while."

Another pilot, now with 409 Squadron at Baden, remembers a time when things were tense in a Tudor trainer he flew in Moose Jaw.

"I had been instructing there for a while," recalls Doug Stroud. "The job was a good one and I enjoyed it, but every so often you had to vary the routine a bit. Now, the Tudor is the sports car of jets, and it's fun to fly, but you can get careless.

"One day I was doing a flying test with a young French-Canadian student. The guy was sharp and didn't miss a beat, and he was doing some excellent work. Because he was so good, we had extra time part-way through the test.

"This was in the summer, and the clouds were big and cumulous, about 8,000 feet above the ground. I asked the student if he'd ever chased clouds. He said he hadn't, so I told him to relax and enjoy the flight because I had control.

"Well, we dived and looped, and swung up and down, all over the place, enjoying ourselves. I was having so much fun that I completely forgot the student. When I turned to him, he was partly slumped over, completely unconscious. I'd forgotten I had been pulling four and five Gs and the guy wasn't used to it.

"So I reached over and gave him 100 percent oxygen, and he came around. Because of his mask, I couldn't see his face, but I'm sure he was smiling. 'You know, Sir,' he said in a delightful accented voice, 'I was just thinking about my wife.'

"I was feeling terrible. The guy then had to do the rest of his test, and fortunately he passed without trouble. All the while he was doing it, I had visions of appearing before a review board, listening to the student explain that he failed because Captain Stroud blacked him out. I never did that again."

Doug Stroud is a cool, laid-back, jet jock who loves his job and can talk for hours about it. Born in Clinton, Ontario, in 1956, he prides himself on being a military brat. His business card, "Have Hornet, Will Travel," lists several of his specialties, none of which are printable. The card also says: "Touch my drink and I'll level your hometown."

One of his friends, Chris Grasswick of 439 Squadron, is just as laid-back, but in a different way. Grasswick came to the military after a period as a bush pilot on the Canadian West Coast. "The civilian experience was good," he says, "because I saw flying in a different light entirely. But I always dreamed of the day I would fly jets in the Air Force. Doing what we do has to be the best job in the world, and at times I wonder at the fact I'm getting paid for it."

I asked him about the F-18.

"It's a marvelous aircraft," he says, "one of the best in the world. The designers, the guys with the coke-bottle glasses, sure came up with a winner in this one.

"My only criticism is that perhaps all the aircraft should have two seats rather than one. That way, the guy in the back could drop the bombs, or whatever, and the pilot could concentrate on flying. But then, I like nothing better than being alone in the sky. It's a great feeling. You are so free.

"Not so long ago, my father, who flew fighters, got permission to fly with me. I tell you, the plane blew him away. He was so impressed. We got a great aircraft when this one was selected."

Later on, after I had interviewed several F-18 pilots, I asked the Commanding Officer at Baden-Soellingen, Colonel Al De Quetteville, about his base, his work, and the selection of the F-18 as Canada's jet fighter for the 1990s.

"Well, as you know," De Quetteville began, "there was a short list of proposed aircraft, and this one was chosen because it seemed to have everything we were looking for, for our needs. I was on the selection team that chose the plane, with the Directorate of Air Requirements in Ottawa. I had flown the Sabres, the 101s, the F-5s, and the 104s, and I had also served a stint as a test pilot.

"When it came to the new fighter, there were seven competitors, and the competition was intense. But we were never really sure if the government was going to go the final mile and actually contract for the new fighter. We brought in a lot of experts to do evaluations for us on each proposal, and finally the Hornet was chosen. Before its selection, however, we had already test-flown it, as well as all the others, most of them about a dozen times.

"Finally, on Sunday, October 24, 1982, I had the pleasure of flying our first F-18 from St. Louis to Ottawa to deliver the aircraft. A company test pilot was with me.

"There was to be a big celebration at CFB Ottawa the next day, and three cabinet ministers were scheduled to be present, as was Prime Minister Pierre Trudeau. When we landed in Ottawa on that Sunday afternoon, we were told for the first time that not only would Mr. Trudeau be present, but he was also going to fly in the new plane. The company test pilot would be the pilot.

"The chief test pilot for McDonnell Douglas, the F-18 manufacturer, was a tremendous chap named Jack Krings. Along about that time, someone suggested that the Prime Minister might be a bit nervous about the flight. That was when it was decided that the next day, before the flight, Jack Krings and I should go out to 24 Sussex Drive and brief Mr. Trudeau on the plane, and on what he could expect on the flight in it.

"So, as it turned out, about an hour before the flight, Krings and I were stuffed in a helicopter and flown over to the lawn of the Governor General's residence. There an RCMP car whipped up and took us across the street to the Prime Minister's residence. Then the car drove off.

"Well, there we were, at the door of the most important home in Canada, ringing the doorbell. While we waited for it to be opened, we were laughing to ourselves and saying: 'What if nobody is at home?' 'What do we do now?'

"Then a young woman opened the door, told us the Prime Minister would be right with us, and ushered us out into the rose garden.

"A few minutes later Mr. Trudeau came out, and we sat there and talked about the plane and the forthcoming flight for forty minutes or so. The Prime Minister was totally engaging and we had a delightful visit.

"Then a limousine arrived and took us and Mr. Trudeau to the chopper, and we flew together to the Ottawa base for the flight and reception. The Prime Minister went flying and had a great time."

And so Canada acquired a new fighter plane. I knew, from my research, that the men and two women who are now being trained to fly it will ride in a state-of-the-art flying machine. But research and interviews could not tell me why flying it was so great. On a cool, sunny February morning at Baden-Soellingen I would find out: On that morning I would fly in the Hornet, and I would see for myself why fighter pilots sing its praises. The flight would also tell me why fighter pilots are, indeed, special.

21

Riding a Rocket: The F-18

My one-hour-and-twenty-minute flight in the F-18 had its origins in a functional, nondescript briefing room at Canadian Forces Base Trenton. There, several weeks before getting near the Hornet, I took what the military calls the HAI – the High Altitude Indoctrination course. This is a day-long endeavour: almost half a day each for lecture and decompression chamber, followed by a one-hour test and a medical examination. The medical is reasonably thorough, with particular focus on the electrocardiogram.

The lectures dealt with basic chemistry, the diffusion of gases and so on, but stressed such things as the physiological effects of positive and negative gravitational or G forces on the body, and the various signs and symptoms of hypoxia, the state of oxygen deficiency in human beings that can occur during high-performance jet-flying. An entire hour was devoted to coping with aircraft emergencies, especially ones where a crash was imminent and a bail-out necessary.

This last part scared the hell out of me.

No matter how safe the plane, no matter how sophisticated the engineering, flying in an ejection-seat aircraft is, at least potentially, a dangerous undertaking. Accidents still happen, and if something were to go wrong during the flight I was planning to take, I wanted to be able to live to write about it. For that reason, I listened very carefully to the briefing about the ejection process. And while no back-seat people have ever jumped from one of our F-18s, I was not keen on being the first. Even leaving the plane could be traumatic. The F-18 ejection seat will throw a 200-pound person 250 feet. That's when the plane is standing still! If it is travelling close to the speed of sound, the wind blast alone can break bones.

Surprisingly, the time spent in the decompression chamber was fun.

Here, eight cadets from the Royal Military College and I were fitted with oxygen masks and allocated to seats inside a long, air-tight steel tank with viewing windows down the sides. Once we were seated and an instructor had briefed us on what to expect, we were asked to perform several tasks. One of these involved drawing circles, squares, and stars on a sheet of paper, while being deprived of oxygen. The longer we went without, the worse the drawing. For those of us who were born with less than the genius of Picasso, the results were hilarious. The purpose of the exercise, however, was to show us how insidious oxygen depri-vation can be. Crashes have occurred when pilots lost conscious-ness because they did not get the oxygen they needed.

We put aside our masterpieces and prepared for another, more dramatic, exercise. The chamber was taken to the equivalent of 20,000 feet, and the hatches were suddenly opened. The crash that accompanied the opening, followed immediately by a thick fog of suspended water vapour, made the comparison to an actual ejection quite realistic. Observers watched to see how quickly each of us could locate and activate our oxygen flow for an emergency supply.

Finally, the HAI complete, I was judged ready to fly.

The young man who took me into the air that morning in Germany was Pierre Rochefort, a thirty-three-year-old major with fourteen years' flying experience behind him. When I learned that Roche-fort was married with a wife and two children I felt more secure, presuming that he would want to return to them and would not kill both of us in an attempt to impress me. Others on the squadron praised the man's flying skills and safety record in the air, telling me he was one of the best. By the end of the flight, I knew how right they were.

After being decked out in a flying suit, boots, gloves, helmet, Mae West, and G-suit, I left the Ops room with Rochefort and went to the allocated aircraft. Even walking in the paraphernalia I was wearing was strange. The high flight boots reminded me of cowboy boots; the G-suit, of chaps worn by western ranch hands. Only the helmet was out of place. Riding the F-18 is like riding a horse around the sky, so once on board I felt like a fully dressed football player on horseback. The stick, or aircraft control column, between my legs could well have been the horn of a western saddle.

The G-suit is a remarkable piece of engineering. It is essentially a pair of pants without knees or groin section, and is designed to inflate automatically when the aircraft is sustaining a higher than normal gravitational pull. The device was invented in Canada and is used in fighter planes the world over. It is both comfortable and essential, preventing the wearer from passing out when the blood rushes from the head. I didn't see much need for the Mae West, although I guess it would have kept me afloat had we crashed into the Rhine River a stone's throw away. There is no large body of water in this area of Europe.

By now it is shortly after 8:00 a.m., and the sky is filled with the roar of fighter planes, their canopies shining in the winter sun. Up ahead is the Hardened Aircraft Shelter, or HAS, in which our plane is stored. The shelter, essentially a bomb-proof, steel-and-concrete garage, looks like a silo on its side, its moss-green colour blending with the trees immediately behind it. The shelter doors are open, and the ground crew is waiting for us. While Pierre checks the plane and talks to a young corporal standing nearby, a base photographer comes over to me and announces: "We need some pictures, Sir." I presume these will be the photos for the obituaries if we don't return. By now I am not exactly brimming with confidence. Just looking at the F-18 is intimidating.

I had seen our new fighter plane several times before, both in the sky and on the ground, but my interest then always had a certain degree of detachment. I was keenly interested now. For example, it had never seemed so *big* before. While it is no jumbo jet, or even as large as a modest passenger plane, the fighter is surprisingly large, particularly when seen indoors. The machine is fifty-six feet long, forty feet wide, and more than fifteen feet high. As with virtually everything involving flying, these measurements were all in imperial specifications on the charts I checked. The plane was painted a dull grey, the colour of an overcast sky in March. A ladder led to the cockpit.

The ground crew personnel strapped Rochefort and me into the aircraft, directed me to put my helmet and face mask on, and alerted me to the closing of the hatch, something that looked for all the world like the top of a glass coffin. The cockpit of the plane is surprisingly comfortable, and more roomy than I expected, but when it is closed, man, it's *closed*. When you are in the back seat, as I was, you cannot see the pilot, nor can he see you. If you can't work the radio, or the oxygen fails, you are pretty much on your own. For that reason, having someone like Pierre Rochefort up front was vitally important. I trusted him implicitly.

Rochefort's voice crackles in my headset. "How are you doing back there?" he asks. I tell him I'm okay, hoping my voice does not betray the nervousness I feel. He goes over some last-minute instructions for me and demonstrates the inflation of the G-suit so that it will not come as a surprise to me in the air. Then he tells me how to arm my ejection seat by removing some pins, so that in case of trouble it will blast me out of the plane; suggests I lower the clear visor in my helmet (there is a darker one as well); and says we are about to leave.

The two jet engines are fired in the HAS, the sound a muted roar inside the cockpit. Finally, the brakes are released and we trundle out of doors. The photographer gives me a "thumbs up" sign.

"How's it feel so far?" Rochefort asks, his breathing and his voice both audible in my ears. "Great," I lie.

Outside, some distance from our starting point, three other Hornets are beginning to make their way down a taxiway to the runway. We will be number four in what is called a four-ship flight. In no time we reach our position. I hear, in my headset, the tower give Pierre clearance; then we move to the runway and start to roll.

The takeoff is pure ecstasy.

In a matter of seconds we are off the ground, the wheels are up, and we veer to the left in a long sweeping arc over the base. The dazzling February sun washes over the cockpit, and I lower the tinted helmet visor. The other three planes are just ahead, silver in the cloudless sky.

The beauty of the moment is indescribable.

The plane flies like a dream, a Star Wars, twenty-first-century dream. There are few bumps, little engine noise, and wrap-around visibility. This is the view from Mount Royal, the CN Tower, and Grouse Mountain rolled into one. The ride makes any roller-coaster seem about as exciting as checkers. Here, the first dip over the top of a ferris wheel never ends. The apprehension I felt in the HAS has gone and I'm wearing an ear-to-ear grin under the mask. This is a thousand times better than flat-out on an expert ski run. Here, you know the technology will get you down, even if your ability will not. I feel like cheering.

"How are you doing?" Pierre's voice cuts into my reverie, and I shout my enthusiasm.

"Want to try some things?" he asks, even though I presume he intends to enliven the ride no matter what I say. When I agree, he suggests I hang on.

Half a second later, we are upside down, streaking off to the right, the Bavarian landscape rushing past in snatches of greens, browns, and occasional blobs of white, the snow on the highest hills. Then the horizon spins, the G-suit inflates, and I don't know where in hell I am. My breath is gone, my heart is pumping, and the sound I hear in the headset is my own cheering. What a wild, wonderful, unbelievably fantastic ride!

The horizon returns, and with it Major Rochefort's voice: "Like that?" he laughs. I told him I did, and he said he would give me a taste of air combat.

He had no sooner said the words than scenes from the movie *Top Gun* became real. One of the other planes that took off with us reappeared. We chased it around the sky, up, down, over, and under, and finally the word "SHOOT" came up on one of the computer screens in front of me. A second later the plane was gone, so I knew the good guys had won. Later, when Rochefort showed me the film of the "kill," the audio had recorded my cheering.

"I'm going to go up a bit and let you fly," said Pierre.

We climb and he gives me the stick. The ease of climb and descent amaze me: A slight movement of the control column and you are somewhere else in the sky.

"Try a roll."

I take the F-18 to the left, then upside down and back. The second time I try a corkscrew to the right, a minor adjustment, and then the horizon flips back to its proper place. Because the plane can turn over in about a half second, the response in aerial dogfighting is unbelievably fast. That's one of the things this thirty-five-million-dollar marvel will do.

"Let's go up." Rochefort takes control. We climb for a few seconds, and then he tells me to watch a screen in front. "That will give you the G-force read-out," he tells me. "Let me know when you've had enough."

We dive steeply; the earth rushes toward the sky; the green digits on one of the three computer screens become larger. Two. Three. Three point five. Four. Five. My sight seems to be impaired. My peripheral vision goes grey and the blood rushes from my head toward my lower body. The G-suit is inflated and the screen shows five point three.

"Okay, Pierre, that's it," I tell him.

We level off and my vision is back to normal.

Down to our left is a beautiful castle, perched high on a hill, overlooking checkerboard fields and a nearby town. We pass over the place, turned on our side, well above the structure, but parallel with one of the tower walls. I can see down the chimneys.

"Hohenzollern Castle," says Rochefort in my headset.

The sightseeing is out of this world. Five hundred feet from the ground and five hundred miles per hour. What a way to see Europe. Stuttgart, Strasbourg, the Danube, the Rhine. Pierre is a great tour guide, but he has one more manoeuvre to show me.

"Want to do an afterburner takeoff?"

I do.

"Okay, then," Major Rochefort advises. "I'll do a couple of touch and goes, and if you are still comfortable we'll go."

He circles back over Baden, touches the runway, and lifts off. He repeats the procedure and asks if I'm still game to continue.

"Sure."

"Hang on, then."

We come in low over the runway. The wheels touch and we go, perhaps half the length of a football field.

Then, with sheets of flaming exhaust belching behind us, the F-18 leaps into the air, straight up, a mind-boggling, numbing ascent to 23,000 feet, more than four miles, all in less than sixty seconds! The wildest, most exciting, stunning ride of my life. The acceleration pasted me to the seat. I tried to lift my arm and couldn't do so. I was speechless from the thrill. Even as I write

Chapter Four

1. Ellis, p. 135.
2. *Ibid.*, pp. 152–3.
3. Ray H. Crone, in *Aviation in Canada*, Larry Milberry, p. 21.
4. Margaret Mason Shaw, *Bush Pilots*, pp. 7–8.

Chapter Five

1. Punch Dickins, in *Uncharted Skies*, ed. Walter Henry and the Canadian Bush Pilot Project, p. 60.
2. *Uncharted Skies*, p. 61.
3. Dickins, in *Uncharted Skies*, p. 61.

Chapter Six

1. Godsell, p. 101.

Chapter Seven

1. Godsell, p. 80.
2. *Edmonton Bulletin*, quoted in Godsell, p. 82.

Chapter Eight

1. Heritage House, *The Death of Albert Johnson*, pp. 57–60.
2. Earl Hersey, quoted in *The Mad Trapper of Rat River*, Dick North, p. 42.
3. *The Death of Albert Johnson*, p. 70.
4. *Ibid.*
5. North, p. 44.
6. *Up Here*, June–July 1987.

Chapter Nine

1. Alice Gibson Sutherland, *Canada's Aviation Pioneers*, p. 15.
2. Amelia Earhart, quoted in *Amelia Earhart*, Shannon Garst, p. 112.
3. Archie Hunter, *Northern Traders*, p. 74.
4. *Ibid.*, pp. 74–5.

Chapter Ten

1. J.P.A. Michel Lavigne and J.F. (Stocky) Edwards, *Kittyhawk Pilot*, p. 7.

2.   *Ibid.*, p. 10.
3.   Brian Nolan, *Hero*, p. 30.
4.   Sheila Hailey, *I Married a Best Seller*, p. 27.
5.   *Ibid.*, p. 29.

Chapter Eleven

1.   Hugh Halliday, *The CAHS Journal*, Winter 1973.
2.   Don Charlwood, *No Moon Tonight*, p. 99.
3.   *Ibid.*, pp. 110–11.
4.   Ronald A.M. Ransom, quoted in Lucas, p. 80.
5.   Jerrold Morris, *Canadian Artists and Airmen 1940–45*, p. 12.
6.   J. Douglas Harvey, *Boys, Bombs and Brussels Sprouts*, pp. 138–9.
7.   *Ibid.*, p. 18.
8.   Dave McIntosh, *Terror in the Starboard Seat*, p. 39.
9.   *Ibid.*, p. 146.
10. E.C. Cheesman, *Brief Glory: The Story of A.T.A.*, pp. 77–9.
11. *Ibid.*, pp. 178–9.
12. Douglas Harvey, *Laughter-Silvered Wings*, p. 67.

Chapter Twelve

1.   A/C Leonard Birchall, *Airforce*, March 1983.
2.   Mark Arnold-Forster, *The World at War*, p. 163.

Chapter Thirteen

1.   Milberry, *Aviation in Canada*, p. 76.
2.   Pierre Berton, *The Mysterious North*, pp. 27, 29.
3.   Sutherland, pp. 276–7.
4.   *Alberta Report*, June 26, 1981.
5.   *Ibid.*
6.   Ronald A. Keith, *Bush Pilot With a Briefcase*, pp. 8–9.

Chapter Fourteen

1.   Z. Lewis Leigh, *And I Shall Fly*, pp. 112–13.

Chapter Sixteen

1.   The full story of Joe Liston's incarceration in Korea is covered in *Korea: Canada's Forgotten War*, by John Melady, pp. 122–7.

2. Steve Monroe, *Saturday Night*, December 1985.
3. *Ibid.*
4. *Ibid.*

Chapter Seventeen

1. *Airforce*, Vol. 11, no. 2.

Chapter Twenty

1. *Airforce*, Vol. 10, no. 4.
2. Chick Childerhose, *Wild Blue*, p. 344.
3. Greig Stewart, *Shooting Down the National Dream*, pp. xi–xii.

Bibliography

ABBOTT, Kim. *Gathering of Demons*. Perth, Ontario: Inkerman House, 1986.

ARNOLD-FORSTER, Mark. *The World at War*. Glasgow: William Collins, 1973.

ARROWHEADS, The. *Avro Arrow*. Erin, Ontario: The Boston Mills Press, 1980.

BAGLOW, Bob. *Canucks Unlimited*. Ottawa: Canuck Publications, 1985.

BASHOW, David L. *Sting of the Hornet*. Ottawa: Canuck Publications, 1987.

BEAUDOIN, Ted. *Walking on Air*. Vernon, B.C.: Paramount House Publishing, 1986.

BERTON, Pierre. *The Mysterious North*. Toronto: McClelland and Stewart, 1956.

BISHOP, William Arthur. *The Courage of the Early Morning*. Toronto: McClelland and Stewart, 1965.

BOTTOMLEY, Capt. Nora. *424 Squadron History*. Belleville, Ontario: The Hangar Bookshelf, 1985.

BROOKS, Stephen. *Bomber*. London: Imperial War Museum, 1983.

CHADDERTON, H. Clifford. *Hanging a Legend*. Ottawa: The War Amputations of Canada, 1986.

CHARLWOOD, Don. *No Moon Tonight*. Ringwood, Australia: Penguin, 1956, 1987.

CHEESMAN, E.C. *Brief Glory: The Story of A.T.A.* Leicester: Harborough Publishing, 1946.

CHILDERHOSE, Chick. *Wild Blue*. Victoria: Hoot Productions, 1978.

CHILDERHOSE, R.J. *Splash One Tiger*. Toronto: McClelland and Stewart, 1961.

COLLINS, Robert. *The Long and the Short and the Tall*. Saskatoon: Western Producer Prairie Books, 1986.

DODDS, Ronald. *The Brave Young Wings*. Stittsville, Ontario: Canada's Wings, 1980.

DOUGLAS, W.A.B. *The Creation of a National Air Force*. Toronto: University of Toronto Press, 1986.

ELLIS, Frank H. *Canada's Flying Heritage*. Toronto: University of Toronto Press, 1954.

FORRESTER, Larry. *Fly For Your Life*. Toronto: Bantam, 1956.

FOSTER, J.A. *Sea Wings*. Toronto: Methuen, 1986.

GARST, Shannon. *Amelia Earhart*. New York: Julian Messner, 1947.

GELB, Norman. *Scramble*. London: Pan Books, 1986.

GODEFROY, Hugh. *Lucky 13*. Toronto: Stoddart, 1983.

GODSELL, Philip H. *Pilots of the Purple Twilight*. Toronto: Ryerson, 1955.

GREEN, H. Gordon. *The Silver Dart*. Fredericton: Brunswick Press, 1959.

HAILEY, Sheila. *I Married a Best Seller*. New York: Doubleday, 1978.

HARVEY, J. Douglas. *Boys, Bombs and Brussels Sprouts*. Toronto: McClelland and Stewart, 1981.

HARVEY, J. Douglas. *Laughter-Silvered Wings*. Toronto: McClelland and Stewart, 1984.

HARVEY, J. Douglas. *The Tumbling Mirth*. Toronto: McClelland and Stewart, 1983.

HENRY, Walter, and the Canadian Bush Pilot Project, eds. *Uncharted Skies*. Edmonton: Reidmore, 1987.

HERITAGE HOUSE. *The Death of Albert Johnson*. Surrey, B.C.: Heritage House Publishing, 1986.

HUNTER, Archie. *Northern Traders*. Victoria: Sono Nis Press, 1983.

JACKSON, Robert. *Fighter! The Story of Air Combat 1936–1945*. New York: St. Martin's Press, 1979.

JOHNSON, Major E.A., ed. *Trenton: 50 Years of Air Force*. Trenton: CFB Trenton 50th Anniversary Committee, 1981.

JOHNSON, Air Vice Marshall J. E. *Full Circle*. London: Chatto and Windus, 1964.

JOHNSON, Leonard V. *A General For Peace*. Toronto: Lorimer, 1987.

JOHNSON, Rick, et al. *434 Squadron History*. Belleville, Ontario: The Hangar Bookshelf, 1984.

JOHNSON, Rick, et al. *437 Squadron History*. Belleville, Ontario: The Hangar Bookshelf, 1985.

KEITH, Ronald A. *Bush Pilot With a Briefcase: The Happy-Go-Lucky Story of Grant McConachie*. Don Mills: Paperjacks, 1972.

KELLEY, Thomas P. *Rat River Trapper*. Don Mills: Paperjacks, 1972.

KOSTENUK, Samuel, and John GRIFFIN. RCAF *Squadrons and Aircraft*. Toronto: Samuel Stevens Hakkert, 1977.

LAVIGNE, J.P.A. Michel, and J.F. (Stocky) EDWARDS. *Kittyhawk Pilot*. Battleford, Saskatchewan: Turner-Warwick Publications, 1983.

LEIGH, Z. Lewis. *And I Shall Fly*. Toronto: Canav Books, 1985.

LEIGH, Z. Lewis. *My Lady of Courage*. Beamsville, Ontario: Rannie Publications, 1987.

LUCAS, Laddie, ed. *Out of the Blue*. London: Grafton Books, 1985.

MASON, Herbert Molloy, Jr. *The Rise of the Luftwaffe*. New York: Ballantyne, 1973.

McINTOSH, Dave. *Terror in the Starboard Seat*. Toronto: Paperjacks, 1981.

MELADY, John. *Korea: Canada's Forgotten War*. Toronto: Macmillan of Canada, 1983.

MELNYK, T.W. *Canadian Flying Operations in South East Asia 1941–1945*. Hull, Quebec: Canadian Government Publishing Centre, 1976.

MILBERRY, Larry. *Austin Airways*. Toronto: Canav Books, 1985.

MILBERRY, Larry. *Aviation in Canada*. Toronto: McGraw-Hill Ryerson, 1979.

MILBERRY, Larry. *The Canadair Sabre*. Toronto: Canav Books, 1986.

MILBERRY, Larry. *Canada's Air Force Today*. Toronto: Canav Books, 1987.

MILBERRY, Larry. *Sixty Years: The* RCAF *and* CF *Air Command 1924–1984*. Toronto: Canav Books, 1984.

MOLSON, K.M. *Canada's National Aviation Museum*. Ottawa: National Aviation Museum, 1988.

MONAGHAN, Lieut. Hugh B., R.F.C. *The Big Bombers of World War I*. Knightstown, Indiana: Jarre Publishing, 1985.

MORRIS, Jerrold. *Canadian Artists and Airmen 1940–45*. Toronto: The Morris Gallery, 1945, 1962.

MUMMERY, Robert. *Snowbirds*. Edmonton, Reidmore, 1985.

MUNRO, Raymond Z. *The Sky's No Limit*. Toronto: Totem, 1986.

NOLAN, Brian. *Hero*. Markham, Ontario: Penguin, 1982.

NORTH, Dick. *The Mad Trapper of Rat River*. Toronto: Macmillan of Canada, 1972.

PEDEN, Murray. *Fall of an Arrow*. Stittsville, Ontario: Canada's Wings, 1978.

PEDEN, Murray. *A Thousand Shall Fall*. Toronto: Stoddart, 1979, 1988.

ROBERTSON, Heather. *The Flying Bandit*. Toronto: James Lorimer, 1981.

ROBERTSON, Heather, ed. *A Gentleman Adventurer*. Toronto: Lester and Orpen Dennys, 1984.

RYAN, Richard W. *From Boxkite to Boardroom*. Moose Jaw: Grand Valley Press, 1987.

RYCQUART, Barbara. *The Snowbirds Story*. London, Ontario: Third Eye, 1987.

SARGENT, J. William. *Sgt. Sargent's Trenton*. Belleville, Ontario: Hangar Books, 1985.

SCOTT, Robert Lee, Jr. *The Day I Owned the Sky*. New York: Bantam, 1988.

SHAW, Margaret Mason. *Bush Pilots*. Toronto: Clarke, Irwin, 1962.

SHORES, Christopher. *History of the Royal Canadian Air Force*. Toronto: Royce Publications, 1984.

SIMKINS, Peter. *Air Fighting 1914–18*. London: Imperial War Museum, 1978.

SMITH, Philip. *It Seems Like Only Yesterday*. Toronto: McClelland and Stewart, 1986.

STEWART, Greig. *Shutting Down the National Dream: A.V. Roe and the Tragedy of the Avro Arrow*. Toronto: McGraw-Hill Ryerson, 1988.

STROCEL, Lt. Terry, and Carl VINCENT. *440 Squadron History*. Stittsville, Ontario: Canada's Wings, 1983.

SUMMERS, Harry G., Jr. *Vietnam War Almanac*. New York: Facts on File Publications, 1985.

SUTHERLAND, Alice Gibson. *Canada's Aviation Pioneers*. Toronto: McGraw-Hill Ryerson, 1978.

SWETTENHAM, John, ed. *Valiant Men*. Toronto: Hakkert, 1973.

TAYLOR, Michael J.H. *Jet Warplanes*. Toronto: Royce Publications, 1984.

TAYLOR, Michael J.H. *Jet Warplanes of the Twenty-First Century*. London: Bison Books, 1986.

THOMPSON, Walter. *Lancaster to Berlin*. Toronto: Totem, 1987.

WHYARD, Florence. *Ernie Boffa*. Anchorage, Alaska: Alaska National Publishing Company, 1984.

WILLIAMS, James N. *The Plan*. Stittsville, Ontario: Canada's Wings, 1984.

WISE, S.F. *Canadian Airmen in the First World War*. Toronto: University of Toronto Press, 1980.

YEAGER, General Chuck and Leo JANOS. *Yeager*. New York: Bantam Books, 1985.

Index